# RETHINKING POLICY FOR AT-RISK STUDENTS

The Series on Contemporary Educational Issues
Kenneth J. Rehage, Series Editor

*The 1994 Titles*

*Radical Education Reforms*, edited by Chester E. Finn, Jr., and
   Herbert J. Walberg
*Rethinking Policy for At-Risk Students*, edited by Kenneth K.
   Wong and Margaret C. Wang

The Ninety–third Yearbook of the National Society for the
Study of Education, published in 1994, contains two volumes:

*Teacher Research and Educational Reform*, edited by
   Sandra Hollingsworth and Hugh Sockett
*Bloom's Taxonomy: A Forty-year Retrospective*, edited by
   Lorin W. Anderson and Lauren A. Sosniak

All members of the Society receive its two-volume Yearbook.
Members who take the Comprehensive Membership also
receive the two current volumes in the Series on
Contemporary Educational Issues.

Membership in the Society is open to any who desire to
receive its publications. Inquiries regarding membership,
including current dues, may be addressed to the Secretary-
Treasurer, NSSE, 5835 Kimbark Ave., Chicago, IL 60637.

# RETHINKING POLICY FOR AT-RISK STUDENTS

EDITED BY:

## Kenneth K. Wong
UNIVERSITY OF CHICAGO

## Margaret C. Wang
TEMPLE UNIVERSITY

**McCutchan Publishing Corporation**
P.O. Box 774, 2940 San Pablo Ave., Berkeley, CA 94702

ISBN 0–8211–2271–1
Library of Congress Catalog Card Number 94–75319

Copyright ©1994 by McCutchan Publishing Corporation

Printed in the United States of America

# Contents

# Contributors

**Lorin W. Anderson,** Professor of Education, University of South Carolina, Columbia

**Aquiles Iglesias,** Temple University Center for Research in Human Development and Education

**Carolyn Kelley,** Stanford University

**Michael W. Kirst,** Professor of Education, Stanford University

**Julia E. Koppich,** University of California, Berkeley

**Ralph M. Lee,** National Center for Education Statistics, U.S. Department of Education

**Martin E. Orland,** Associate Director, National Educational Goals Panel

**Leonard O. Pellicer,** College of Education, University of South Carolina, Columbia

**Samuel S. Peng,** National Center for Education Statistics, U.S. Department of Education

**Maynard C. Reynolds,** University of Minnesota

**Lisbeth B. Schorr,** Director, Harvard University Project on Effective Service

**Thomas Timar,** Graduate School of Education, University of California, Berkeley

**Herbert J. Walberg,** Research Professor of Education, University of Illinois, Chicago

**Margaret C. Wang,** Professor, Temple University, and Director of the Center for Research in Human Development and Education

**Kenneth K. Wong,** Associate Professor of Education, University of Chicago

# Preface

As the school-age population in the United States becomes increasingly culturally diverse and economically heterogeneous, public schools are confronted with issues of program specialization and social integration. These challenges are clearly visible in inner-city schools that have a high concentration of disadvantaged students. Programs designed for students with special needs often take the form of discrete instructional structures that can be isolated from the rest of the school. One consequence of targeted (or categorical) services is that, in assisting the particular academic needs of some children, they may cause organizational fragmentation in school administration and classroom instruction. Equally important is the school's capacity to promote program integration between its special-needs students and their peers. These issues of integration and fragmentation in the implementation of major categorical programs are the focus of this volume.

Chapters in this book examine the implementation of major federally funded categorical programs for special-needs students in elementary and secondary schools, including compensatory education (ECIA Chapter 1), special education (Public Law 94–142, the Education for All Handicapped Children Act), and programs for children with limited English proficiency (bilingual and migrant education). We focus on federal programs for several reasons. First, they are designed to address educational inequities in our public schools. Although all were enacted during a period of federal activism in the 1960s and the early 1970s, they have proven to be politically resilient and have gained bipartisan support. Since they have been implemented for a fairly long time, we believe that there is a reliable empirical base for a critical reassessment of these federal programs. Second, these categorical programs involve a significant amount of federal funds that serve a large segment of the nation's school population.

Finally, categorical programs require local schools to reformulate the way services are traditionally delivered. An examination of these programs would offer valuable information on the impact (both desirable and undesirable) of federal regulation on administration and instruction. Federal regulations are intended to make certain that students with special needs directly benefit from federal dollars. In compensatory education, for example, local districts are required to use federal funds in schools with the highest concentration of students in poverty, to spend as many local dollars on these schools as on any other school in the district, and to commit at least the same level of local resources as they provided in previous years. The compensatory education program requires schools to establish advisory councils composed of parents of children participating in the program. In special education, the federal provisions give service recipients an official policymaking voice within the service delivery system. The IEP (individualized education plan) provision is designed to allow as much parental participation as possible in evaluation and placement decisions regarding the services for their handicapped child.

Developed around the theme of fragmentation and integration in both administration and instruction, the collection of papers in this volume addresses several issues. First, how does the idea of targeting services to the subpopulations develop in the policymaking system? What are the intellectual roots of categorical programs? From a historical perspective, are categoricals effective in addressing educational inequities? What is the politics of allocating categorical resources?

Second, to what extent and in what specific ways do federal categorical programs contribute to problems of fragmentation both at the district and at the school/classroom levels? What are the effects of "pull-out" services on the disadvantaged pupils? Is there curricular and instructional coordination between students in the self-contained units and their peers in the regular classroom? Do the auditing provisions (e.g., "supplement not supplant") weaken the incentives for teachers to coordinate on curricular planning? Do categoricals undermine the leadership functions of the school principal in inner-city schools?

Third, what do we know about educational outcomes in categorical services? How many Chapter 1 students move on to regular classes after one year? How effective is mainstreaming in special education, particularly in light of some evidence that suggests "second-generation discrimination" in academic placement? Do these programs produce "sustaining effects" on student performance?

Fourth, can we identify circumstances where categorical programs are successfully implemented? We want to know the conditions under which students in special-needs programs are well integrated into the educational life of the school. Equally important are the instructional and curricular consequences for these students when such organizational integration occurs.

Fifth, we examine policy implications from the categorical experience. The key question is whether we can use our resources more effectively for the education of the disadvantaged. The current debate has taken on different directions. One set of reform ideas focuses on organizational improvement within the categorical framework. What new incentives for coordination can be created? How can state and federal agencies provide better technical assistance? Would "in-class" strategies bring about better outcomes? Others propose to go beyond the categorical arrangement and look for alternative strategies—parental choice in nonpublic schools, establishing service centers that are not under the control of the local district, or integrating the delivery of educational and other social services.

To approach these complex and overlapping issues, chapters in this book are organized under three sections. The first section, "The Development of Categorical Programs," consists of two chapters. Maynard C. Reynolds offers a comprehensive review of the development and expansion of federal categorical programs for at-risk students since World War II. Clearly, categorical programs have contributed to educational improvement—access for all children, greater parental participation, and schools that become adaptive to individual needs. As Reynolds observes, the biggest challenge ahead is to restructure the categorical programs so that they merge better with the regular educational programs. In "The Changing Politics of Federal Educational Policy and Resource Allocation," Kenneth Wong offers an institutional analysis of the ways in which federal resources are allocated. He distinguishes three phases in resource allocation. First, the national legislative process decides on policy objectives and appropriates funds to states and localities. Second, the implementation process occurs when states and localities adapt their own circumstances to national policy objectives. Third, at the school and classroom level, federal resources provide supplemental instruction for at-risk students. Based on a review of the literature, Wong argues that federal dollars should be used to narrow the gap between inner-city schools and their suburban counterparts. He also suggests that the federal government play a more active role in strengthening the organizational capacity of the schools in low-income neighborhoods.

Five chapters are included in the section on "Program Implementation and Classroom Effectiveness." Using the 1988 National Educational Longitudinal Study of Eighth Graders, Samuel Peng and Ralph Lee report on the educational experiences of middle-school students who are in poverty. They find no significant differences in curriculum requirements and course offerings between poor students and their nonpoor peers. However, their study reveals deficiencies in teachers' qualifications in schools attended by poor students. To improve schools in poor neighborhoods, Peng and Lee call attention to safety and discipline, student motivation and attendance, and parent involvement. Thomas Timar's chapter examines the linkage between the federal Chapter 1 program and school practices. He argues that outcome-based assessment per se is not sufficient to promote accountability. Instead, the school organization has to strengthen its delivery of instructional and curricular services to at-risk students. Timar then suggests ways in which the federal policy can be revised to improve the school's organizational capacity.

In their case study of compensatory education in South Carolina, Lorin Anderson and Leonard Pellicer examine the way in which the federal Chapter 1 program has been coordinated with state-funded compensatory programs. The state programs, started in 1984, provide services to low achievers. Anderson and Pellicer use several evaluation reports to identify fragmentation in instructional services and limited effectiveness in student performance in compensatory education. The authors conclude with twelve recommendations to better integrate compensatory education with the regular school programs. Aquiles Iglesias's chapter discusses program improvement in bilingual education, examining the ways instruction is delivered in three major types of federal programs— projects that employ the students' native language as a medium of instruction, developmental programs that help students achieve competence in both English and a second language, and the "immersion-like" alternative programs. Iglesias offers several programmatic strategies for redesigning the federal role in bilingual education.

The section on classroom effectiveness concludes with a chapter that looks at what works. In an extensive review of the learning effects of categorical programs, Margaret Wang, Maynard C. Reynolds, and Herbert J. Walberg observe a system of "disjointed incrementalism" where narrowly framed programs result in "expensive, segregative treatments that do not improve children's learning." Based on a synthesis of effective practices, Wang, Reynolds, and Walberg make two recommendations on school improvement—(1) avoid special placements and integrate nearly all children with special needs with their peers in the regular classrooms, and (2) employ educationally effective practices that focus directly on classrooms and homes to bring about learning improvement for all children.

The third section consists of three chapters that look into the future of federal categorical programs. Each of these chapters represents a key set of ideas on systemic reform. Martin Orland observes that the existing institutional separation of categorical programs from general school functions, the so-called "picket fence" model, is beginning to crumble. The new policy system, labeled "chain-link federalism," recognizes the interdependence of federal assistance and school improvement. Using research conducted by the National Education Goals Panel and other national agencies, Orland proposes a more coherent and comprehensive federal policy. The chapter by Michael Kirst, Julia Koppich, and Carolyn Kelley argues that educational services alone cannot overcome the complex problems of poverty and learning. Instead, these authors support the idea of providing integrated social services for children. In a system of "school-linked services," the school becomes the "hub" of educational and other social services. Based on the implementation of school-linked services in San Diego, the authors demonstrate the advantages of integrating the federal Chapter 1 program with other social services. The chapter by Lisbeth Schorr takes a broad approach to school improvement and neighborhood revitalization. She draws on her own extensive research on social policy to address the crucial policy question of what works. Six strategies are proposed to bring about systemic change "that promises to turn around the escalating rates of rotten outcomes we see all around us."

In short, the analysis and the kind of reform ideas represented in this book are drawn from diverse disciplines—psychology, sociology, statistics, history, and political science, among others. The chapters are methodologically diverse, employing meta-analysis, case studies, and multilevel analysis. As a whole, the chapters offer a coherent view on the future of federal educational policy and its categorical arrangement. Federal programs can enhance learning if they are less fragmented, integrated with the school's regular curriculum, embedded in a school with sound organizational capacity, and better coordinated with other social services. Clearly, the chapters in this book lay a conceptual groundwork for more effective federal policy.

The work that resulted in this book had its beginning several years ago at the inception of the National Center on Education in the Inner Cities (CEIC), with its major research and development concern for finding ways to increase the capacity for education in the nation's inner-city schools. We are grateful for the advice and editorial support of Kenneth J. Rehage, editor for the National Society for the Study of Education, without whose encouragement and assistance this volume would not have been completed. We also acknowledge the guidance of Dr. Oliver Moles, the Center Liaison for CEIC at the Office of Educational Research and Improvement of the U.S. Department of Education, which provides funding support for CEIC. The opinions expressed in this book, however, do not necessarily reflect the position of the funding agency, and no official endorsement should be inferred.

*Kenneth K. Wong*
University of Chicago

*Margaret C. Wang*
Temple University Center for
Research in Human Development
and Education

# Section I
## THE DEVELOPMENT OF CATEGORICAL PROGRAMS

# 1

# A Brief History of Categorical School Programs: 1945–1993

## *Maynard C. Reynolds*

Hedrick Smith (1988) described U.S. Navy practices in acquiring a new ship in simple terms: "Get the hull in the water"; finishing details can be considered later. Similarly, the schools of the nation have launched a large number of programmatic hulls in recent decades, heading them immediately into heavy seas, without finishing or dry-dock relief. This chapter provides a brief history—since World War II—of so-called categorical educational programs. (See Table 1-1 for key events of this history.) They have been started one by one, and apparently on the assumption that they would not interact with one another— a false assumption as we shall see. Although many categorical programs were initiated at local and state levels, the focus here is on the expanding role of the federal government of the United States in this domain.

Veterans of World War II helped to bring more open attention and new modes of service to various categories of people. Blinded veterans, for example, were unwilling to be satisfied with limited training programs in weaving or piano tuning, common curriculum offerings in "schools for the blind." They demanded broader opportunities for training and employment and improved

## Table 1-1
### Selected Key Dates and Events Relating to Categorical Education Programs Since World War II

---

1950    Formation of the National Association for Retarded Children—mainly a parents' association

1954    B*rown v. Board of Education.* Supreme Court decision declaring separate education for racial groups to be "inherently unequal"

1957    Cooperative Educational Research Program launched by the U.S. Office of Education, with priority attention to education of mentally retarded children

1958    National Defense Education Act makes limited provisions for gifted students and for improved instruction in science, mathematics, and languages

1958    Federal provision for colleges and universities to prepare educators of mentally retarded students

1961    Federal support for preparation of teachers of the deaf

1962    Social Security Act amended to define child welfare services and to specify 1975 as year for states to make services available to all children in need

1963    Broad federal provisions for preparing educators of handicapped students

1965    Elementary and Secondary Education Act (ESEA) including "Chapter I" provision for education of disadvantaged children and youth

1968    Provision for bilingual instruction added to ESEA

1970    Public Law 91–230 includes specific provisions for research, training, and model centers in the area of learning disabilities

1972    *Pennsylvania Association for Retarded Children v. Pennsylvania,* the federal court decision establishing "right to education" and "least restrictive environment" principles for education of retarded students

1973    Rehabilitation Act amendments guarantee rights of handicapped persons in employment, education, and access to public buildings and programs

1974    U.S. Supreme Court act upholding right of non-English-speaking students to bilingual education (*Law v. Nichols,* 42 L.W.4165, U.S., Jan. 22, 1974)

1975    Education of All Handicapped Children Act (PL 94–142) guaranteeing "free and appropriate public education" to all handicapped children of school age

1981    Migrant Student Record Transfer System (MSRTS) funded under Education Consolidation and Improvement Act

1986    Federal law mandating education for handicapped preschoolers

1987    Homeless Assistance Act relating to access to education for homeless children

1987    U.S. Dept. of Education launches transition programs (bridging from schools to community employment) and the "regular education initiative"

---

preparation for mobility so that they had access to all of the community. A remarkable staff at the Hines (Illinois) Veterans' Hospital responded by advancing white cane travel techniques. Soon the Hines staff was leading summer training for teachers, and, even in the 1950s, the new travel techniques were beginning to appear in school programs for blind children. Similarly, a version of the Wechsler Intelligence Scale used with adults was adapted for use with children. New departments of physical medicine in universities and hospitals were first oriented to veterans but soon developed children's units. This spread from adult veterans to school children occurred widely.

The first item in Table 1-1 shows a key event in the history of categorical programs—the formation of the National Association for Retarded Children (NARC), later known as the Association for Retarded Citizens. In 1950, the NARC, mainly a parents' group and a prototype of dozens of groups newly formed around various categories of children, had affiliated groups in nineteen states. Soon there were units of the NARC in forty-eight states. In the post-World War II period, parent groups were the main agents in bringing the needs of their children into political focus. Several of their earliest efforts were addressed to the courts to establish the rights of their children to education. Legislation then followed, reflecting gains made in the courts. These parents were organized narrowly; thus their first efforts resulted in categorical policies and programs.

To follow the example of the NARC story a bit further, it is noteworthy that the first major federal provision of funds for research in education came in 1957, a result of critical support by parents of retarded children and a few associated professionals. A large portion of the funds in the early years of the program was earmarked for studies relating to mental retardation. Just a year later, in 1958, the first program for federal support of teacher education in a categorical area—mental retardation—was established. In the early 1970s, a federal district court case, supported in several ways by NARC leaders, established for children who are mentally retarded a "right to education" under the equal protection clause of the Fourteenth Amendment to the U.S. Constitution (*Pennsylvania Association for Retarded Children (PARC) v. Pennsylvania*, 1971). The "right" of the children became the obligation of educators to provide the necessary programs. Soon after the PARC decision, an attorney in far-off southern California was heard advising his local school board that the implications of the case, legally binding only in a district of Pennsylvania, were "only slightly off shore for all of us"—and so they were. A year later, the right-to-education principle was extended to all handicapped children (*Mills v. Board of Education of the District of Columbia*, 1972). The principles established in court were then summarized in the very important Education for all Handicapped Children Act (Public Law 94–142) in 1975.

So far, this story suggests a nicely progressive, almost linear set of developments, and so it was in the main. But there were negatives. As might be expected, most active members of NARC were white and middle-class and many of their children were moderately or severely retarded. But the development of special school programs in this period occurred disproportionately in inner-city situations and for mildly handicapped children of minority families. The labeling of minority children as "retarded" resulted in much backlash. For example, in California, in the case of *Larry P. v. Riles* (1972), the classification of black children as retarded was rebuffed. In the wake of this case, the California State Board of Education banned the use of IQ tests to classify children.

Special classes for children described as educable mentally retarded, a term used for the "highest grade" of retardation in the 1950s, had their start in the work of Alfred Binet in France on intelligence testing. The Binet test, produced at about the turn of the century and adapted quickly for use in the United States, was oriented to predicting which students were likely not to perform well in regular school programs. After finding students with low IQs, it was but a small step to set them aside in special programs, not because of evidence that they could be expected to achieve better when taught in special places but only because they were expected to do relatively less well than their peers in regular education. As Lee Cronbach put it, "When ability tests became available they were used by the schools—to put it bluntly—to decide which pupils should be allowed to drop by the wayside or to vegetate in an undemanding slow classroom" (1967, p. 24). It was to such low expectations and undemanding classes that the parents of Larry P. and many others objected.

Some categories and labels, such as mental retardation, are considered to be subtractive, even demeaning, in their effects on students. Others may be regarded positively, at least by some stakeholders. There appears to be relatively positive reaction to the label "learning disabled." Other terms get mixed reactions. For example, "bilingual" programs are highly valued by some people while others see them negatively, as just a way of erasing dependence on non-English languages as quickly as possible. Later, the same language may be seen as desirable, even elitist in character, as when high school students take up "foreign" language studies: "Elite bilingualism is a voluntary learning of a second language whereas folk bilingualism is typical of immigrants and refugees who are required to learn a second language, that of the majority or host culture" (Shannon and Hakuta, 1991, p. 218).

The willingness of students and parents to bear labels is enhanced, of course, if there is clear evidence that the related "special" programs have true value. It seems likely, for example, that the *Larry P. v. Riles* case would never have occurred if there were strong evidence that special classes for retarded pupils really "worked" well. Sadly, that was not and is not the case. In the case of bilingual programs, the testimony is mixed, with some people believing that "bilingual education retards rather than expedites the movement of Hispanic children into the English-speaking world and that it promotes segregation more than it does integration" (Schlesinger, 1992, p. 108). The situation faced by bilingual students is very complex, involving factors besides language. When instruction takes into account specific cultural differences, as well as language differences, academic success appears to improve (Moll and Diaz, 1987).

## A RESPONSE TO DIVERSITY

Until World War II, the structure, power arrangements, social position, and financing arrangements of public education in the United States had persisted with few basic changes from the nineteenth century. It survived, in part, by permitting students who were reluctant attenders to withdraw or by excluding those who were inconvenient to teach. But since World War II the system has been assaulted by new demands to serve all children, including ethnic, cultural, and linguistic minorities, the poor, the handicapped, children of migrant families, and poorly motivated students. As public attention focused on each category of students, a separate program was often created, each with its own bureaucracy, funding system, and monitoring system. The typical state now has eight or nine different categories of special education, the Chapter I program, bilingual programs, migrant education programs, and more. In 1982, 381 varieties of "special" programs were coded in the Migrant Student Record Transfer System (Barresi, 1982).

There can be no doubt about the increasing diversity of public school students in the post-war period. Sheila Shannon and Kenji Hakuta (1991) wrote that "in the last two decades [early 1960s to early 1980s] immigration from Mexico, Central America, Southeast Asia and Pacific islands has increased dramatically. The Mexican origin population . . . has grown at a rate eight times that of the total population" (p. 216).

In 1977 alone, 3,700 school-age children and youth in the United States moved from residential institutions back to community residential facilities, and 2,900 more moved back to their own or to adoptive homes (Bruininks, Hauber, and Kudla, 1979). Many of the thousands of children coming back to day schools in each year of the last two decades were severely and profoundly disabled. Unfortunately for the schools, funds formerly directed to institutions were not transferred to the local schools along with these very complex children and youth. The transfers also involved a shift from support through progressive tax bases (often income taxes) to more regressive ones (usually a property tax).

Approximately 6 percent of the newborn of the nation, many showing low birth weight, are now placed in neonatal intensive care units. Such children are kept alive at sharply increasing rates, but a high percentage of them (12 percent is one estimate [Zill, 1985]) show significant life impairments and require highly expensive school programs. All such children now come into the school, along with growing numbers of children in grief because of family problems and many who are abused, neglected, and afraid.

A pervasive set of changes in the demographics of students have occurred simply because of the expanding importance of education and the attempt to serve literally all children. Advanced literacy is no longer an ornament for the few; it is an essential for all who expect to be employed in a complex global economy. That was part of the message of the U.S. Supreme Court in *Brown v. Board of Education* (1954). Ralph Tyler (1987) recounts that as late as 1900, more than 60 percent of the U.S. labor force were employed in unskilled jobs and that "in 1910 more than half the children had dropped out [of school] before completing sixth grade" (p. ix). Now, less than 5 percent of the employed are in unskilled work: "Today, most uneducated youth are unemployed" (p. viii). As late as 1975, it was estimated by the Children's Defense Fund that as many as two million children of the nation were still not in school, but progress was being made (Featherstone, 1975). The new demographics show increasing numbers of students who come from disadvantaged backgrounds and from families and communities showing high rates of disorder—as in crime, drug abuse, homelessness, and general despair. Now we are engaged in widespread efforts to enroll all students in the schools, and to hold them at least through to high school graduation; the national success rate now for high school graduation is about 75 percent.

## ECONOMIC CHANGES

The changing demographics have been associated with increasing school costs, not just because of higher numbers of enrollees but also because of the growing numbers of high-cost categorical programs. It seems unlikely that the nation could have afforded the rising school costs in the period since World War II without the expanding national economy of the 1950s and 1960s. The mixed economic climate of the 1970s occurred just at a time of decline in the general child population. The "baby boomers" of the late 1940s and the 1950s completed their schooling and fewer children were entering the lower grades. In 1975, there were approximately 51 million school-age children in the United States, a figure that dropped to 44 million a decade later.

The reduced child count translates to declining demands for school funds and for new teachers (actually many teachers lost jobs in this period), but this reversal of trends came exactly in a period of rapidly growing categorical programs. In Minnesota, for example, the number of special teachers for various categories of handicapped students increased by 95 percent from 1974 through 1983. In the same period, the number of regular secondary and elementary teachers decreased by 25 percent and 9.5 percent, respectively (Newsletter, 1984). Significant numbers of the teachers released from regular education positions took training to qualify for openings in categorical programs.

In 1985, a small increase in the national school-age population was observed and predictions suggested another reversal of trends, moving the count back up to about 50 million school-age children and youth by the year 2000. The period of the 1990s is one of general expansion in education; but now many categorical programs are in place and they compete with regular education for funds and for teachers. The current (1990s) press for resources has come at a time of recession (late 1980s and 1990s), of enormous public debt, and of general resistance to tax increases. This creates a troubled context for education and a cause for reexamination of categorical programs. For example, it was observed in 1991 that 25 percent of New York City's total expenditures in the public schools is tied to categorical programs in special education (Berger, 1991). Furthermore, "in the current fiscal crisis when savings of $505 million must be found, cutbacks are being confined almost entirely to regular classrooms. Special education is protected against reductions by a web of state mandates and court rulings" (p. 1). Clearly, the economics of categorical programs and their rigid management are important in causing the current reappraisal of them.

## THE EQUITY ISSUE

In an eloquent dissent to the "separate but equal" doctrine as established in *Plessy v. Ferguson* (1896), Justice Harlan wrote: "Our constitution is color-blind, and neither knows nor tolerates classes among citizens. In respect of civil rights, all citizens are equal before the law." That view was unanimously expressed by the U.S. Supreme Court only half a century later. In *Brown v. Board of Education of Topeka* (1954), separate schooling by race was declared unconstitutional and the importance of education for all students was acknowledged in Chief Justice Warren's words: "It is doubtful that any child may reasonably be expected to succeed in life if he is denied the opportunity of an education."

John W. Davis, a counselor representing defendants in *Brown*, said in his opening argument to the Court:

If the appellants' construction of the 14th Amendment should prevail here, there is no doubt in my mind that it would catch the Indian within its grasp just as much as the Negro. If it should prevail, I am unable to see why a state would have any further right to segregate its pupils on the ground of sex or on the ground of age or on the ground of mental capacity." [Friedman, 1969, p. 51]

Davis was surely right in his prognostics: "The analogies between the black and the handicapped and their respective experiences in our society are strikingly exact, and thus their legal posture is startlingly similar. Both have been subjected to a history of purposeful discrimination and segregation, and relegated to a position of powerlessness" (Gilhool, 1976, p. 12). By such reasoning, the *Brown* decision has been extended to Native Americans, to Hispanics, to women, to the poor, and to the disabled.

Most of the events listed in Table 1-1 have origins in the *Brown* decision. Each event represents a move to redress past injustices of inequality; and they tell of the rapidly expanding role of the federal government in education as a means of achieving equality of opportunity for all children. A point of much soreness for state and local officials is that the federal role has been heavy on mandates but light on funding.

The largest single federal action to provide equality of opportunities for education came in 1965 in provisions for Chapter I programs targeted on children of the poor. In the early 1960s, President Kennedy was much criticized for his advocacy of federal aids (or what Bernard Baruch preferred to call "supports") to education because funds were proposed to go only to public education and to desegregated schools. Issues concerning separation of church and state were at high pitch in that period. However, it became acceptable that federal supports could go to categorical programs, especially for children of the poor. It was thought that one might even expect public and private/parochial schools to cooperate in categorical programs that operated at their programmatic edges if not across mainstream elements. The Elementary and Secondary Education Act of 1965, including its major provisions in Title I (in later reviews it became known as Chapter I) of the act for programs serving economically disadvantaged students, was a major part of the War on Poverty program led by President Johnson.

Title I/Chapter I programs have operated over the years mainly by "pull-out" procedures whereby selected children received intensive tutoring in basic subjects, mainly reading and arithmetic. Evaluations of the programs have been mixed; but the latest versions of these programs have tended to show positive results (Carter, 1984; Slavin, Karweit, and Madden, 1989). However, a new wave of criticisms suggests that the Title I/Chapter I program, its evaluations, and its organizational structure have been framed too narrowly (Commission on Chapter I, 1992). Children of the poor need more than basic skills, it is argued. They need help in learning at more complex levels, such as in problem solving and communications. They need help in restructured total schools, rather than just in special enclaves, and they need aggressive teaching that expresses high expectations for learning:

> Chapter I was part of a powerful demand that American society live up to its ideals by extending equal opportunity to all: . . . it has distributed more than $70 billion to schools with concentrations of poor children; . . . it touches one of every nine children; it influences what happens in over one-half of the schools in the country. [Commission on Chapter I, 1992, p. 3]

The federal functions in education have involved much monitoring of compliance in state and local education. But does such monitoring make things better or worse? Much of the monitoring has been procedural rather than substantive, which is to say that norms for procedures (e.g., did the parents give agreement in writing before the child was tested?) have tended to surpass real checks on learning progress. Even some of the advocacy groups, such as the Children's Defense Fund (1983), have advanced mainly procedural approaches for the monitoring of programs.

Satisfying the new mandates expressed in categorical programs, with all their associated rules and regulations, is no simple matter. Schools that had been quite standardized are now expected to diversify programs, to make adaptations to individual needs, and to admit new voices in planning for groups and even for individuals. Educators are now expected to serve new groups and even place "the needs of individual children at the center of school activity [in ways] that would require a complete overhaul of our current ways of schooling children" (Lortie, 1976, p. 18).

There is the matter of mutual trust as well. Dan Lortie was heard saying in a 1975 conference that the new federal mandates "leave classroom teachers at the far tail end of a long chain of moral insight." That view of the matter is illustrated in the case of rules and regulations for special education, following PL 94–142, which require an essentially judicial model in making plans for individual pupils. The principle of teachers acting in *loco parentis* was essentially "undone" in favor of giving parents an extraordinary role, if they wished to take it, in planning how resources of the school would be organized to meet needs of their particular child— and a right to appeal to higher authorities and the courts when plans or the delivery of them were judged to be deficient. Mutual trust among parents, teachers, and pupils may well be the first requirement for effective teaching, but such trust probably has not been advanced by new mandates from Washington, D.C.

Dissatisfaction with the curricular aspects of categorical programs created to meet emerging federal mandates has been widespread. One extreme view proposed after the *Brown* decision was that "the bare minimum is all that is needed, just enough to read the instructions on the fertilizer sack" (Atkinson, 1984, p. 9).

Marlene Scardamalia and Carl Bereiter (1989) contrast teaching described as "progressive problem solving" with "problem-minimizing" teaching. In the latter approach, the teacher fixates on management problems rather than advancing student learning. In such teaching, one eliminates difficult content, uses much decontextualized skill practice, and may give primary attention to enjoyment rather than to learning. Avoiding referrals of behavioral problems to the principal's office is a critical concern. It is to problem-minimizing approaches in programs for poor and handicapped children that objection is rising; and the call is for more aggressive teaching for conceptual changes, problem solving, complex communications abilities, and students' ability to advance their own learning and social behavior. That is the message of Henry Levin (1985) and his accelerated learning projects and of the Commission on Chapter I (1992).

There can be little doubt, in spite of all the problems of change, that something revolutionary has been occurring in the schools over the last half century, much of it centered on a concept of "equality." Following his visit to the United States more than a century ago, Alexis de Tocqueville described such a time of change:

> Democratic nations are at all times fond of equality, but there are certain epochs at which the passion they entertain for it swells to the height of fury. This occurs at the moment when the old social system, long menaced, is overthrown after a severe intestine struggle, and the barriers of rank are at length thrown down. At such times, men pounce upon equality as their booty. [As cited in Jarrett, 1972, p. 1]

The principle of equality, bound up with a concept of justice, has stirred much passion and many programs in education in recent years, even though doubts remain about how to turn precepts and process into truly fulfilling outcomes.

## INCLUSION

The extension of educational opportunities to formerly excluded students can be described as a story of progressive inclusion.
In special education, in particular, the historical sequence of
arrangements for schooling is quite clear: first came total exclusion,
then only distal arrangements (residential schools, usually placed
at a distance from most homes), then local special schools (students
still segregated by category, but living at home), followed by development of local special classes (segregated by class but not by
school), then resource rooms (labeled students enrolled in regular
classes but "pulled out" part time for "special" instruction), then
full-time mainstreaming with help by teams of educators.

Major developments since World War II have been in special
classes, resource rooms, and mainstreaming. However, many states
still maintain all of these several kinds of "special" administrative
arrangements, but with increasing pressure to favor provisions
at the mainstream side of the continuum. This policy of bias
toward "mainstreaming" was made explicit in the 1975 Education
for All Handicapped Children Act (Public Law 94–142, 1975),
by requiring each state to adopt procedures "to insure that to
the maximum extent appropriate, handicapped children . . . are
educated with children who are not handicapped, and that separate
classes, separate schooling, or other removal of handicapped children from the regular education environment occurs only when . . .
education . . . cannot [otherwise] be achieved satisfactorily."

The *Brown* decision of 1954 provided some of the rationale
for inclusiveness: "To separate them . . . generates a feeling of
inferiority . . . that may affect their hearts and minds in a way
unlikely ever to be undone. Segregation . . . has a detrimental
effect. . . . The policy of separating [them] is usually interpreted
as denoting inferiority" (*Brown v. Board of Education*, 1954).

The policy requiring inclusive arrangements follows the *least
restrictive environment* (LRE) principle, which is that when a public
agency intervenes in the life of an individual, the preferred "treatment" is always to try first for adjustments in the normal or natural
environment of the individual and to move the individual to other
environments for treatment for compelling reasons only. This
policy had origins in health care, particularly mental health, and
is associated with a move of some clinical professions (psychology,
psychiatry) out of their special offices and clinics and into the
community. In the mid-1970s, the policy was spread to schools

and the ways they deal with students who have special needs.

Implementation of the LRE policy is made very complex because the law, at least in the case of handicapped students, requires programs to be "appropriate" also. Adherence to LRE and to appropriateness principles opens doors for many and varied views and debates. A case for emphasis on strengthening "regular" education as a resource for handicapped children led in the late 1980s to a raging debate on the so-called "Regular Education Initiative" (REI) (Reynolds, Wang, and Walberg, 1987; Will, 1986). The idea was that the needs of marginal students were unlikely to be met just by services in special stations or enclaves and that more initiatives by the regular school system were required. It was hoped that specialized teachers and other staff associated with categorical programs would join in REI activities, making them broad teamwork efforts. Leadership in the REI arena has come lately from the Council of Chief State School Officers (1992), the National Association of State Boards of Education (1993), and the Commission on Chapter I (1992).

A particular facet of the LRE movement concerns children and youth who are severely and profoundly disabled. Pressing the case for their inclusion in mainstream schools and classes is a relatively new organization of professionals and parents, The Association for the Severely Handicapped (TASH). Among all of the advocacy groups concerned with "categories" of students, TASH has been most effective in producing a full array of trainers, researchers, and policy advocates from within its own ranks. They conduct research, develop policies, and advocate very aggressively for their policies. It is of interest that this group, while pressing for inclusive arrangements in the schools, has itself operated quite independently of other professional groups. A common feature in work with severely and profoundly disabled children is reliance on behavioral methods. Other educators and researchers have been content to leave work with the most complex and needful children to the behavior analysts (Meyer, Peck, and Brown, 1991).

## TEACHER EDUCATION

Fulfillment of the promises to students that inhere in categorical mandates depends on the quality of teachers. But the federal courts, and the Congress, have no teachers and no teacher educators directly at their command. Even at the state level, teacher preparation is carried on mainly in colleges, both public and

private, that are connected by only a few threads to the new
bureaucracies responsible for Chapter I, migrant education,
bilingual education, special education, and other categorical
programs. In some cases, state agencies for the licensing of teachers
have set standards requiring that teachers obtain special licenses
to teach in categorical programs. But training standards have
been reduced to bargain level for provisional licenses in most
states when teacher shortages existed.

The makers of the Education for All Handicapped Children
Act anticipated the teacher preparation challenges and took prece-
dent-setting action in a mandate to states for:

> (A) the development and implementation of a comprehensive sys-
> tem of personnel development which shall include . . . detailed pro-
> cedures to assure that all personnel necessary to carry out the purposes
> of this Act are appropriately and adequately prepared and trained
> and [that] effective procedures for acquiring and disseminating . . .
> significant information derived from educational research, demon-
> stration and similar projects [are developed] and (B) adapting, where
> appropriate, promising educational practices and materials developed
> through such projects.

It stretches the matter only slightly to describe the teacher
education provisions of PL 94–142 as a call for "sovietizing" teacher
education, at least in a range of certain categorical programs.
The assumption was that state government, colleges, and
universities could all be "systematized" by federal mandate to
prepare special teachers at a "state-of-the-art" level and manage
their placement where needed—whether in rural Idaho or central
Philadelphia. Even the U.S. Department of Education has never
faced up fully in its own operations to the requirements of such
a system, although it helped to establish a network of state agencies
for planning a Comprehensive System for Personnel Development
(Schofer, 1978). Some progress in systematizing specialized teacher
preparation was made voluntarily in southeastern states through
the Southern Regional Education Board (SREB). A concentration
of programs at the George Peabody College for Teachers (later
part of Vanderbilt University) was one outcome of the work of
SREB. But in large part, the teacher education aspect of PL 94–
142 has been regarded lightly.

B. O. Smith, a leader in teacher education, wrote in 1975, a
period of slowed demand for new teachers, that "teacher training institutions have never before been in a period so favorable

to improvement of their programs. . . . [The] focus [must be] on children who have problems in learning. This will turn teacher training right side up and require the inclusion of skills and concepts now almost completely neglected" (p. 104). By 1980, Smith despaired of change: "Let's face it. Colleges of pedagogy will in all probability never overhaul their programs if each college is to do it alone" (Smith, 1980, p. 90).

When education is a right, it is a present right and it is a duty of educators to deliver on that right. The situation becomes more complex by a placement policy of "least restrictive environment." This means that literally all teachers need to extend themselves directly in work with students whose school achievement, social behavior, and life situation is marginal in various ways. Work with such students requires more teamwork among teachers and other specialists employed in the schools. Only the barest beginnings have been made in revising teacher preparation, taking into account the new realities of serving literally all children and youth in the schools.

## EMERGING PROBLEMS AND TRENDS

### School Integration with Other Community Agencies

Students enrolled in categorical programs and their families often face problems that go well beyond what educators can be expected to treat or even to understand. Already, large numbers of students come to school for breakfast as well as for lunch; and many schools provide after-school activities for children who would otherwise return alone to isolated and unsupervised homes and apartments. Especially in inner cities and in deprived rural areas, many families are in disorder and children lead fearful lives. It is not unusual for families to have contacts with three or four community agencies besides the schools. This will have involved several "intake" interviews at different agencies that are forbidden by privacy laws from communicating with one another.

Educators are beginning to seek linkages with other human services groups and agencies so that more coordinated services can be provided and to simplify for families the many problems of travel, intake procedures, service eligibility, and agency fragmentation. In effect, schools that in the past sought to be "independent" are now moving to a new strategy of cooperation and coordination, recognizing that their interests overlap with other human service groups. Table 1-2 lists some of these groups and agencies.

Integration programs of broad kinds have been of particular interest to foundations—such as Casey and Kellogg—but broad public interest and support is growing as well. In California, for example, a Healthy Start program, which brings health professionals into teamwork with educators in serving young children, has been launched as a companion piece with Head Start, and the schools are providing the central coordinating offices. There is much uncertainty about how all of these linkages will and should develop.

## Some Current Problem Areas

Trends toward inclusiveness and equality of opportunity have not always been steady and positive. Percy Bates (1990) tells us that "there is evidence that the number of U.S. students attending racially isolated schools is now on the rise" (p. 9). That can be confirmed by visits to schools in the inner-city environments

Table 1-2

**Agencies with Interests that Overlap with Those of Categorical Programs in Education and Education in General**

| Agency | Program or Account |
| --- | --- |
| Public Welfare | Social Services, Aid to Families with Dependent Children, Foster Care, Child Welfare, Medicaid, SSI, Day Care Systems |
| Health | Maternal and Child Health Programs, Crippled Children's Program, Wellness Programs, Institutional Licensing and Monitoring Programs, Migrant Health Centers |
| Mental Health and Developmental Disabilities | Institutional Programs, Community Grants, Foster Care, Family Support and Subsidy Programs, Mental Health Systems, Medicaid Waiver Programs |
| Vocational Rehabilitation | Medical Rehabilitation, Vocational Rehabilitation, Disability Determination Unit (for SSI and SSDI), Deaf and Blind Rehabilitation Programs |
| Corrections | Juvenile Programs in Institutions and Communities, Court Services Systems |
| Agriculture | Subsidized school breakfast and lunch programs |
| Private | Churches, ethnic and linguistic service groups, parent associations |

of many of our largest cities; in some cities the isolation is for Hispanic students and in other places for black students.

In many schools, one sees increases in rates of suspension and exclusion, which inevitably complicates instructional problems. There are disturbing disproportionalities in these several demission procedures, with some racial minority students and special education students showing the highest rates (Williams, 1989).

There is a disturbing and challenging theory about why some minority groups have high rates of low achievement, poor school attendance, and frequent suspension. John Ogbu (1992) proposes that a useful distinction can be made between voluntary and involuntary minority groups. In the case of involuntary minorities (in the United States mainly black and Native American students), it is argued that their history, involving castelike status for a period of time, has disposed many children to be "oppositional" or to resist teaching advanced on them by the "white" community. Murray Wax (1971) at Pine Ridge observed:

> In these classrooms [of Native American children] what I and other observers have repeatedly discovered is that the children simply organize themselves so that effective control of the classroom passes in a subtle fashion into their hands.... The reticence of the ... children has nothing to do with personal shyness and everything to do with the relationship between the child and his peers in that classroom. For [they] exert on each other a quiet but powerful pressure so that no one of them is willing to collaborate with the teacher.... What the children primarily resist is the authority of the teacher and his (or her) intervention into their collective lives. [Pp. 63–64]

To the extent that Ogbu is correct, the challenge of serving some minority students has extra complications and will require extraordinary sensitivity.

Perhaps oppositional behavior is reflected also in what Arthur Schlesinger (1992) refers to as the rising "cult of ethnicity." In curriculum as well as in school organization, one sees claims for revising curricula beyond the so-called Eurocentric boundaries. In public schools, some small number of separate Afrocentric programs are in evidence, and at the collegiate level, one sees a variety of ethnic and racial centers plus curricular revisions (Vann and Kunjufu, 1993).

Proposals for school voucher systems are regarded at least by some as a threat to the unity and essential purposes of the public schools. In its broadest version, as recommended by former

President Bush, a voucher system would give to individual parents control of public dollars as they choose the schools, public or private, to be attended by their children. A narrower version, one favored by President Clinton, would give  parents choices but only within public schools. Advocates propose that by giving parents choices and creating a "market" of schools, the competition would cause improvements—much as is claimed for the market economy of business. Opponents of voucher systems of the broadest kind foresee violations of constitutional requirements of separation between church and state and also tendencies toward a kind of tribalism, in the sense that parents would seek out schools favored by like-minded parents. This, the argument goes, would cause a kind of provincialism in the experience of children that is incompatible with giving children authentic experiences with diversity and in creating environments and values that appreciate diversity. It appears that the public schools are developing alternative programs and giving choices to parents in ways that provide a middle ground on issues of vouchers and "choice," but this is an area of change worthy of much continuing attention (Raywid, 1987).

In an administrative vein, there are major continuing problems. For example, in school finance there is a disparity between rhetoric on program policy and facts of money flow. Categorical money usually flows to school districts when pupils are labeled and placed in special programs. It is all input-oriented. Actually financial incentives operate on the "bounty hunt" side; more students in trouble begets more categorical programs and money. Somehow, this practice needs to be turned to give more attention to outcome variables and to bring fiscal incentives into accord with policy preferences. The change required is not difficult conceptually. Years ago, Nicholas Hobbs (1975) suggested that funding for "special" programs should be switched over to the program side rather than to the labeled child-count side. Arrange to pay for "two square meals" per day or for intensive tutoring if that is what the student needs, he proposed; but do not label the children. It is clear that services are provided where there is money and so changes in money flow are required if programs are to change.

In troubled economic times, one sees insecurity; and it can be escalated to turbulence when deep changes are required. So it is among educators in the schools today. There is much turf-protecting behavior, but at the same time there are calls for collaboration and efficiency. Clear vision and strong leadership are required to avoid destructive turbulence as a result of these conflicting policies and trends, and to cause the needed integration and efficiency of programs within the schools. And we hope that enhanced inclusiveness, as categorical boundaries are opened and more coherent school structures are designed, will not lead to "fighting under a collapsed tent." It seems unlikely that broad integration of school and community agencies will succeed unless and until integration of programs within the school is achieved, and even then it will be difficult.

## CONCLUDING OBSERVATIONS

There have been many gains in schooling over the past half century, and the categorical programs have had a part in this story of progress. One positive outcome is the enrollment of virtually every child in school for at least some minimal period. It is doubtful that a replication of the Children's Defense Fund study of the 1970s would again find two million children out of school (Featherstone, 1975). Continuing attention is required, of course, to find and enroll all children in school, to cut down on suspensions and expulsions, and to improve school attendance by migrants and others. But access to education is no longer a major catalyzing idea for school improvement: "The goal of universal access to education has met with such great success that it now lacks power as a national ideal" (Bakalis, 1987, p. 10). Improvements in schools and in children's learning are the essential targets for the 1990s.

Similarly, the call for parent participation in school planning has been heard widely, if not always clearly. The schools are unlikely to soon again make plans for the education of a child with disabilities without involving the parents. Much remains to be done in assisting parents to become well informed and active in making their plans and choices; but the concept of teachers operating in *loco parentis* is passé as a policy matter.

There are very few, if any, rewards remaining in classification, labeling, "special placements," and categorical programs in the schools. Writing from a lawyer's point of view, David Kirp (1974) reported, "The research indicates that most school classifications [of students] have marginal and sometimes adverse impact on both student achievement and psychological development" (p. 18). Research since 1974 echoes that conclusion. This is a domain in which the schools have a very large chore—to undo and restructure most of the categorical programs and to do this in a framework that refashions the regular or general education program as a resource for children, all of them! Perhaps progress can be made. The Council of Chief State School Officers (1992) has proposed that in schoolwide projects, federal funds for special education and Chapter I be merged to serve students in both programs. A special panel of the National Association of State Boards of Education (1993) has suggested that "having insured access to public schools, we must now focus on the outcomes of that guaranteed education. . . . [E]mphasis [should be] placed on improved instruction rather than the processes of classifying and labeling students" (p. 4). Changes in categorical programs appear to fit the political and economic frame of today.

## REFERENCES

Atkinson, R. "New Segregation in the Old South," *Washington Post*, National Weekly Edition, 16 April 1984, p. 9.

Bakalis, Michael J. "Power and Purpose in American Education," *Phi Delta Kappan* 65, no. 1 (1987): 7–13.

Barresi, Josephine G. "Educating Handicapped Migrants: Issues and Options," *Exceptional Children* 48, no. 6 (1982): 473–488.

Bates, Percy. "Desegregation: Can We Get There from Here?" *Phi Delta Kappan* 72, no. 1 (1990): 8–17.

Berger, J. "Costly Special Classes Serve Many with Minimal Needs," *New York Times*, 30 April 1991, pp. 1, A12.

*Brown v. Board of Education of Topeka* (1954), 347 U.S. 483, 493.

Bruininks, Robert H.; Hauber, F.; and Kudla, M. *National Survey of Community Residential Facilities: A Profile of Facilities and Residents in 1977*. Minneapolis: University of Minnesota, Department of Psychoeducational Studies, 1979.

Carter, Launor F. "The Sustaining Effects Study of Compensatory and Elementary Education," *Educational Researcher* 13, no. 7 (1984): 4–13.

Children's Defense Fund. *Title I . . . Chapter I . . . A Monitoring Guide*. Washington, D.C.: Children's Defense Fund, 1983.

Commission on Chapter I. *Making Schools Work for Children in Poverty*. Washington, D.C.: Council of Chief State School Officers, 1992.

Council of Chief State School Officers. *Education Daily* 25, no. 20 (17 November 1992): 1, 3.

Cronbach, Lee J. "How Can Instruction Be Adapted to Individual Differences?" In *Learning and Individual Differences*, edited by Robert M. Gagné, pp. 23–39. Columbus, Ohio: Merrill, 1967.

Featherstone, Joseph. "Children Out of School: The Expendables," *New Republic*, 29 March 1975, pp. 13–16.

Friedman, Lawrence, Ed. *Argument: The Oral Argument before the Supreme Court in Brown v. Board of Education of Topeka*. New York: Chelsea House, 1969.

Gilhool, Thomas K. "Changing Public Policies: Roots and Forces," *Minnesota Education* 2, no. 2 (1976): 8–13.

Hobbs, Nicholas. *The Futures of Children.* San Francisco: Jossey-Bass, 1975.

Jarrett, James L. "The Meanings of Equality," *Minnesota Education* 1, no. 1 (1972): 1–12.

Kirp, David L. "Student Classification, Public Policy, and the Courts," *Harvard Educational Review* 44, no. 1 (1974): 7–52.

*Larry P. v. Riles.* Civil Action, No. C-71-2270, 343 F. Supp. 1306. (N.D. Cal.), 1972.

Levin, Henry M. *The Educationally Disadvantaged: A National Crisis.* Philadelphia: Public/Private Ventures, 1985.

Lortie, Dan. "Discussion," *Minnesota Education* 2, no. 2 (1976): 16–18.

Meyer, Luanna H.; Peck, Charles A.; and Brown, Lou. *Critical Issues in the Lives of People with Severe Disabilities.* Baltimore, Md.: Brookes, 1991.

*Mills v. Board of Education of District of Columbia.* 384 F. Supp. 866 (D.D.C., 1972).

Moll, Luis C., and Diaz, Stephen. "Change as the Goal of Educational Research," *Anthropology and Education Quarterly* 18 (1987): 300–311.

National Association of State Boards of Education. *Winners All: A Call for Inclusive Schools.* Alexandria, Va.: National Association of State Boards of Education, 1993.

*Newsletter.* Minneapolis, Minn.: Education Student Affairs Office, College of Education, University of Minnesota, 1984.

Ogbu, John U. "Understanding Cultural Diversity and Learning," *Educational Researcher* 21, no. 8 (1992): 5–14.

*Pennsylvania Association for Retarded Children (PARC) v. Commonwealth of Pennsylvania,* 334 F. Supp. 1257 (E.D. Pa.), 1971.

*Plessy v. Ferguson,* 163 U.S. 537 (1896).

Public Law 94–142. The Education for All Handicapped Children Act, 1975.

Raywid, Mary Anne. "The Dynamics of Success and Public Schools of Choice," *Equity and Choice* 4 (Fall 1987): 35–41.

Reynolds, Maynard C.; Wang, Margaret C.; and Walberg, Herbert J. "The Necessary Restructuring of Special and Regular Education," *Exceptional Children* 53, no. 5 (1987): 391–398.

Scardamalia, Marlene, and Bereiter, Carl. "Conceptions of Teaching and Approaches to Core Problems." In *Knowledge Base for the Beginning Teacher,* edited by Maynard Reynolds, pp. 37–46. Oxford: Pergamon, 1989.

Schlesinger, Arthur M., Jr. *The Disuniting of America.* New York: Norton, 1992.

Schofer, Richard. "Cooperative Manpower Planning," *Teacher Education and Special Education* 2, no. 1 (1978): 7–11.

Shannon, Sheila M., and Hakuta, Kenji. "Challenges for Limited English Proficient Students and the Schools." In *Handbook of Special Education: Research and Practice,* Vol. 4, edited by Margaret C. Wang, Maynard Reynolds, and Herbert J. Walberg, pp. 215–233. Oxford: Pergamon, 1991.

Slavin, Robert E.; Karweit, Nancy L.; and Madden, Nancy A. *Effective Programs for Students at Risk.* Boston: Allyn and Bacon, 1989.

Smith, B. Othanel. "The Growth of Teacher Education: Where To from Here?" *Journal of Teacher Education* 26, no. 2 (1975): 102–104.

Smith, B. Othanel. "Pedagogical Education: How about Reform?" *Phi Delta Kappan* 62 (1980): 87–93.

Smith, Hedrick. *The Power Game.* New York: Ballantine, 1988.

Tyler, Ralph W. "Foreword: Marginality in Schools." In *Reaching Marginal Students*, edited by Robert L. Sinclair and Ward J. Ghory, pp. vii–xviii. Berkeley, Calif.: McCutchan, 1987.

Vann, Kimberly R., and Kunjufu, Jawanza. "The Importance of an Afrocentric, Multicultural Curriculum," *Phi Delta Kappan* 74, no. 6 (1993): 490–491.

Wax, Murray. "How Should Schools Be Held Accountable?" In *Education for 1984 and After*. Lincoln, Nebr.: Study Commission, 1971.

Will, Madeleine C. "Educating Children with Learning Problems: A Shared Responsibility," *Exceptional Children* 51, no. 1 (1986): 11–16.

Williams, Junious. "Reducing the Disproportionately High Frequency of Disciplinary Actions against Minority Students: An Assessment-based Policy Approach," *Equity and Excellence* 24, no. 2 (1989): 31–37.

Zill, N. "How Is the Number of Children with Severe Handicaps Likely to Change Over Time?" Testimony prepared for the Subcommittee on Select Education of the Committee on Education and Labor, U.S. House of Representatives, June 25, 1985.

# 2

# The Changing Politics of Federal Educational Policy and Resource Allocation

## *Kenneth K. Wong*

Since the mid-1960s the federal government has used categorical programs as the primary tools to address equity issues in elementary and secondary education. Categorical programs have clearly focused on social equity issues by promoting racial integration, protecting the educational rights of the handicapped, funding compensatory education, and assisting those with limited English proficiency (Peterson, Rabe, and Wong, 1986). These "redistributive" programs allocate resources to address inequities that primarily arise from class, status, and racial cleavages (Lowi, 1964; Ripley and Franklin, 1984).

Categorical programs have survived partisan shifts in national governmental institutions. For almost thirty years, the federal government has spent billions of dollars in redistributive educational programs. In 1991, the federal government allocated $6.2 billion to compensatory education, $2.4 billion to special education, and $200 million to bilingual projects. The Chapter 1 (compensatory) programs, for example, are providing services to over five million disadvantaged pupils in prekindergarten through grade 12. Between 1965 and 1992, the federal government disbursed over $80 billion to compensatory education.

To be sure, federal funding for educational programs has fluctuated over time. Between 1965 and 1980, federal aid to elementary and secondary schools showed persistent growth in real dollars. However, federal support for elementary and secondary education declined during the Reagan years, dropping in constant dollars by 17 percent between 1980 and 1989. Toward the mid and late 1980s, however, major categorical programs began to receive more federal support. As we approach the mid-1990s, the Clinton administration is likely to rely heavily on continued support of existing categorical programs in addressing educational inequity.

## AN INSTITUTIONAL PERSPECTIVE ON RESOURCE ALLOCATION

Given the importance of the federal role, researchers have examined the politics that centers on the allocation of federal aid. Federal categorical programs in education, in my view, involve decisions in resource allocation in three distinct but interrelated phases. In this chapter, I argue that the three decisional phases can be differentiated by the key actors involved, the institutional location within which resource allocation takes place, and the politics that emerges.

More specifically, federal categorical programs involve resource allocation at three different levels of the policymaking system, each of which focuses on a distinct set of policy and political issues. First, in the national legislative process, which features prominently both the President and the Congress, national policy objectives are determined and federal funds are appropriated to states and localities to implement federal programs. National educational policy is clearly embedded in the political dynamics between the legislative and the executive branches. Second, in receiving federal aid, state and local educational agencies play a pivotal role in carrying out national policy objectives. Policy implementation in our federal system is far from straightforward. Instead, intergovernmental politics defines the use of federal aid at the state and district levels. Whether local administrative agencies are in compliance with federal fiscal regulations has been an important topic. At issue is whether federal resources are targeted on the intended beneficiaries. Third, at the school and the classroom levels, federal resources are likely to shape curricular and instructional organization. Policy analysts are paying particular attention to curricular fragmentation and the separation of special-needs students from their peers in regular classrooms.

Indeed, our focus on the three kinds of resource allocation in federal programs is indicative of a broadened research agenda. Over the years, researchers and policymakers have developed an increasingly comprehensive and realistic understanding of the role of federal categorical programs in addressing educational inequities. There has been a gradual shift of attention from the national level to the instructional setting at the micro level. During the mid and late 1960s, in the initial period of federal categorical involvement, much attention was focused on an allocative formula that disbursed federal aid according to a count of students in poverty on a state-by-state and county-by-county basis. During the 1970s, the federal government became more concerned about implementation—making sure that local agencies complied with federal targeting guidelines. Since the late 1980s the federal government has paid greater attention to the impact of categorical funding on classroom organization and student learning.

A broadened scope of inquiry notwithstanding, researchers are not always in agreement on matters of resource allocation. Disagreement is clearly due in part to analytical perspectives that are often time bound and context specific. As I shall discuss later in this chapter, the roles of the Congress and the President in the legislative process were reversed between the 1960s and the 1980s with respect to federal involvement in education. On policy implementation, the earlier view on conflictual federal-local relations is gradually being replaced by an emphasis on intergovernmental accommodation. On resource allocation within the school, the earlier concern about administrative compliance is now overshadowed by serious debate that centers on fragmentation in the school curriculum and especially on the need for integrating programs for children with special needs with the program in the regular core curriculum.

In this chapter, I shall synthesize the literature on politics and policy in each of the three kinds of resource allocation. First, I examine the changing legislative politics in the federal role to promote a redistributive policy in education to remedy social inequities. Second, I shall specify the political and institutional factors that have facilitated administrative compliance from districts and states. Third, I review recent federal efforts to promote learning among disadvantaged students. In the concluding section, I explore briefly the implications of this analysis for policy and research.

## THE POLITICS OF EDUCATIONAL EQUITY AT THE FEDERAL LEVEL

### Federal Redistributive Role

The literature on federalism has provided a number of reasons why a redistribution of funds to address social inequities is more likely to come from the national government. The federal government enjoys a broader revenue base in which taxes are raised on the ability-to-pay principle, and it represents a constituency with heterogeneous demands (Reagan and Sanzone, 1981; Peterson, 1981; Wong, 1990; Tiebout, 1956). In other words, it has both the fiscal capacity and the political resources (often facilitated by interest groups) to respond to social needs. In contrast, localities are more constrained in responding to social needs because their most active voters come from the middle class. Local communities have to compete with one another for investment in an open system where business and labor can move freely. Unlike the federal government, local governments have a restricted tax base (namely, property values) as their major source of income. Compared to local governments, states are somewhat more likely to provide redistributive services because they enjoy a broader tax base, they command a larger pool of resources, and they encompass a bigger geographical boundary that tends to reduce the threat of a decreased tax base resulting from an out-migration of residents who would rather leave the state than pay taxes for social programs that do not directly address their own needs.

Given the importance of the federal role, researchers have studied the politics that centers on social-equity issues. Two bodies of literature are prominent; one focuses on the legislative process and the other looks at presidential leadership. Based on a synthesis of these studies of the national institutions, I shall argue that we have revised our earlier understanding of the role of the national government in education.

### Presidential Activism

Numerous studies have focused on the dynamics of presidential leadership and congressional power in shaping educational policy

(Orfield, 1978; Munger and Fenno, 1962; Sundquist, 1968; Lowi, 1964; Ripley and Franklin, 1984; Cavanagh and Sundquist, 1985). A good example is the passage of a compensatory education program—Title I of the 1965 Elementary and Secondary Education Act (ESEA). This legislation significantly expanded federal involvement in public education. It offered an opportunity for analysts to appreciate the ways in which groups and actors with different interests and priorities can form legislative coalitions to overcome institutional obstacles. For years, action on this bill was deadlocked over budgetary considerations, concerns over federal aid to segregated schools and to parochial schools, and issues of local autonomy. These barriers were reinforced by the authority structure of the Congress—a committee system allowed a powerful few working behind closed doors to effectively kill a bill and the seniority practice preserved the privileges of the committee chairs at the expense of voting rights of the entire legislative body (Sundquist, 1968).

Institutional barriers were finally overcome in 1965. The legislative victory was the result of a combination of political factors. Congressional leaders overcame the concern about separation of church and state by agreeing to provide aid directly to students instead of to schools. There was a clear public mandate in support of a more "activist" federal government following the passage of the 1964 Civil Rights Act. The 1964 election produced a new cohort of liberal lawmakers who formed the rank and file of an emerging liberal majority in the Congress. But above all, the legislative success was due to presidential leadership. President Lyndon Johnson was fully behind the bill and saw compensatory education as a major strategy in his newly declared "War on Poverty."

## Institutional Safeguards

The roles of the Presidency and the Congress were in large part *reversed* during the 1970s and the 1980s. Whereas studies identified institutional obstacles in Congress that blocked activist agenda submitted by the executive branch during the 1950s and early 1960s, analysts in the 1970s and 1980s found that *congressional safeguards* were used against an administration that wanted to cut back on school and other social programs. The role reversal was in large part facilitated by divided governance throughout the 1970s and the 1980s—the Republican Party virtually secured its hold in the Presidency and the Democratic Party dominated the Congress (Mayhew, 1974; Cavanagh and Sundquist, 1985). In other words, Republican administrations have made numerous attempts to contain the federal social role. Yet even when the President claimed public mandates to reduce federal involvement in domestic programs, as in the case of Nixon's first term and the Reagan years, the Democratic-controlled Congress was able to exercise enormous restraints (Orfield, 1978; Peterson, Rabe, and Wong, 1986).

A closer look at the institutional safeguards suggests that they come from diverse sources. First, legislative restraints are rooted in the division of labor in Congress, incumbency power, and seniority privileges. For example, members of Congress who supported the passage of ESEA in 1965 subsequently held leadership positions with long tenure in the 1970s and 1980s.

Second, the educational bureaucracy has come to identify with the interest of its clients and has become an advocate for special-needs programs (Lowi, 1979). A dramatic example is provided in the conflict between the career legal professionals and the politically appointed Attorney General in the Justice Department over school desegregation policy during the first year of the Nixon administration. In August 1969, when the administration stopped the practice of cutting off funds if schools were not promoting racial integration, nine out of ten of the attorneys in the Civil Rights Division protested the White House strategy (Orfield, 1978).

Third, over time, federal programs are preserved by a fairly stable bipartisan coalition of top bureaucrats, key members of the Congress, and prominent interest groups (Anton, 1989). Major educational programs for the needy have received bipartisan support due in part to growing public concerns for investment in human capital. Indeed, over the years public support for the Head Start program for preschoolers and compensatory education has broadened. Just as important is the territorial impact of federal categorical grants. In 1990, the Chapter 1 program provided supplemental resources to 64 percent of all the schools in the nation (Millsap et al., 1992). Clearly, big districts are not the only beneficiaries of compensatory education funds—over 20 percent of the federal aid goes to districts with fewer than 2,500 students. Districts with enrollments between 2,500 and 25,000 receive almost 45 percent of the funds. Because there are Chapter 1 programs in every single congressional district, partisan conflict has been generally limited during the appropriations process

(Peterson, Rabe, and Wong, 1986, pp. 110–112).

Finally, judicial decisions cumulate in a legal framework that offers legitimacy for the national government to play a role in redressing educational inequities. Although the U.S. Supreme Court rejected federal involvement in school finance in *San Antonio Independent School District v. Rodriguez* (411 U.S. 1 [1973]), it justified national leadership in racial desegragation, civil rights, gender equity, and equal educational opportunities. Even with opposition from the Nixon administration, the Supreme Court actively pursued desegregation in the South during the late 1960s and the early 1970s. Consequently, between 1968 and 1972, racial segregation in Southern schools declined sharply—the percentage of blacks in schools with more than 90 percent minority enrollment decreased from 78 to 25 percent (Orfield, 1988). However, with a prevailing conservative mood during the Reagan years, the Supreme Court seemed ready to become less of a social agent.

Institutional safeguards clearly have policy consequences. Even in the period of federal fiscal retrenchment during the 1980s, the socially redistributive character of federal grants to states and localities had been largely preserved. During fiscal year 1984, in the midst of the Reagan retrenchment, the appropriations process in Congress made sure that over half of all the 142 federal formula grants remained targeted to those programs serving groups whose incomes fell below the poverty line. In education, training, and employment-related services, over 80 percent of the federal funds went to special-needs groups (Wong, 1989). Opposition from Congress and various interest groups resulted in the failure of the Reagan administration to deliver its campaign promise of dismantling the U.S. Department of Education, which would have substantially reduced the federal role in encouraging education equity. Instead, compensatory education received even more funds in the 1980s than it had in the 1970s: its focus on low-achieving students living in impoverished communities was retained, its administration remained with state and local programs, and its allocative practices were not replaced by a voucher arrangement (see Peterson, Rabe, and Wong, 1986). In the early 1990s, the largest federal educational program, Chapter 1, continued to distribute resources to districts with the greatest needs. Districts with the highest concentration of children living in poverty (i.e., at least 21 percent of the enrollment is poor) receive 45 percent of the total federal Chapter 1 funds, even though they enroll only one-fourth of the nation's public school students. Conversely, districts with the lowest concentration of poor students (i.e., fewer than 7.2 percent of the district's students are poor) receive only 11 percent of Chapter 1 aid, although they educate 27 percent of the nation's public school students (Millsap et al., 1992).

## Impact of the New Federalism

Although the federal role in educational equity remains largely unchanged, the Reagan administration succeeded in terminating several categorical programs, reducing funding levels in others, and consolidating many categorical programs into broadly defined block grants (Clark and Astuto, 1986). Indeed, when institutional safeguards are weak, programs can actually be eliminated.

Termination of the Emergency School Aid Act (ESAA), Title VI of which provided for desegregation programs, provides a good example of how a federal policy failed to receive either bureaucratic advocacy or bipartisan support during the Reagan years. By eliminating ESAA, the Reagan administration substantially trimmed federal fiscal support for racial integration purposes. It took four years for the federal government to enact another categorical program on racial desegregation. The Magnet Schools Assistance Program that started in 1985 became the only major program that supported racial integration in urban districts. Funding for this highly competitive grant program remained around $75 million during the Reagan years, but increased to $114 million for fiscal 1989. These grants, however, are not specifically for big urban districts. According to a study of the General Accounting Office, while four of the eleven largest school districts in the south and the west applied for a grant in 1985, only one received funding. In 1987, eight of these districts applied for a grant, but only three received funding (U.S. General Accounting Office, 1987).

Another major impact of the Reagan administration was the decentralization of decision making on federal aid (Knapp and Cooperstein, 1986). However, when states are given the responsibility for making decisions about resource allocation, they are less likely to focus on redistributive issues. At the state and local level, "policy generalists" and their constituencies tend to dominate in the decision-making process. Generalists include elected officials (e.g., state legislators) as well as top appointees in education agencies. A good example of how federal dollars can be diverted away from redistributive needs is the block grant created under Chapter 2 of the Education Consolidation and Improvement Act. The block grant consolidated twenty-eight categorical programs (including the ESAA desegregation program) and shifted allocative authority to the states. State control has weakened the redistributive focus of the antecedent programs. In their fifty-state analysis of the allocation of block grant funds, Martin Orland and Staffan Tillander (1987) found that seventeen of the twenty-six largest urban districts received fewer funds than in the immediately preceding block grant year. Virtually all the losers received a significant amount of ESAA funds before the consolidation. More important, 80 percent of the states distribute most of the federal aid without regard to any special-needs criteria. Only two states targeted the block grant at the districts with high needs factors. In other words, devolution of federal aid has resulted in lower governmental support for educational equity.

The Reagan administration also failed in several attempts to promote a nationwide voucher policy for Chapter 1 participants. Indeed, the administration tried three times to convert the federal compensatory categorical program into a voucher program. The most serious proposal was the Equity Choice Act (H.R. 3821) in November 1985, also known as "TEACH," which would have allowed Chapter 1 students, at their parents' request, to attend any schools in the district. No funding increase was proposed for Chapter 1's conversion. None of the Reagan proposals was seriously considered by the Congress, particularly after the 1986 election when the Republican Party lost its six-year majority in the Senate.

Overall, the impact of the Reagan administration is uneven among policy domains. Although Congress succeeded in preserving most of the major educational programs, the Reagan administration was able to reduce federal support in low-income housing and other social policy areas. Consequently, the federal grants-in-aid in the late 1980s have returned to the level of the early 1960s when measured as a percentage of the gross national product.

## DISTRICT COMPLIANCE WITH FEDERAL CATEGORICAL POLICY

Implementation studies focus on how federal resources are actually used in the school district. This literature offers two very distinct perspectives on the administrative effectiveness of federally funded programs. In particular, these studies focus on whether federal resources are targeted to the intended beneficiaries. In other words, a key research question is, Are districts and state agencies in compliance with federal auditing and administrative requirements? In this section, I shall summarize how over the years we have revised our understanding of policy implementation in the intergovernmental system.

## Intergovernmental Conflict

The first set of evaluation studies (or the first-generation studies) came out in the 1970s and covered a wide range of policy topics—from compensatory education and busing programs to achieve integration to job training and employment programs in economically depressed communities. The studies were highly critical of the ways federal programs operated. In reviewing the complex intergovernmental administrative structure of such programs, analysts often found confusion, conflict, and failure to complete national social objectives (Murphy, 1971; Coleman et al., 1975; Pressman and Wildavsky, 1973; Hill, 1977, Martin and McClure, 1969; National Institute of Education, 1977; Kirp and Jensen, 1985). In other words, federal resources set aside for goals of remedying social inequities seldom got into the hands of the intended beneficiaries.

The earlier studies have no doubt raised important political and policy issues—whether federal regulations provide the best way to achieve national social objectives, and whether the federal government could overcome obstacles at the subnational level to improve services for the intended beneficiaries. At the same time, these studies have several methodological shortcomings. They are predominantly single-case studies, often focused on the first couple of years when the programs had just started (and conceivably the period of greatest implementation problems), and they did not distinguish the programs that addressed social inequity from those that did not.

## Toward Accommodation

The recent (or "second-generation") implementation studies tend to overcome these methodological shortcomings. First, these studies differentiate the social-equity objectives from other purposes in federal programs. Having made explicit the differences in national purposes, the second-generation studies consider intergovernmental conflict as a function of redistribution of funds to achieve social-equity goals (Peterson, Rabe, and Wong, 1986; Odden and Marsh, 1989; Jung and Kirst, 1986; Singer and Butler, 1987; Orfield, 1969).

Programs that address the disadvantaged often require local governments to reformulate the way services are delivered. Because revenues in these programs come mostly from the U.S. Congress, the federal government tends to impose numerous and complicated standards on local schools. These regulations are intended to ensure that disadvantaged pupils directly benefit from federal dollars. In compensatory education, for example, local districts are required to use federal funds in schools with the highest concentration of students in poverty, to spend as many local dollars on these schools as on any other school in the district, and to commit at least the same level of local resources as they provided in previous years. In special education, the federal provisions in the Education for All Handicapped Children Act (PL 94–142) give service recipients an official policymaking voice within the service-delivery system. The IEP (individualized education plan) provision is designed to allow as much parental participation as possible in making evaluation and placement decisions about services for their handicapped children. During the 1970s and the early 1980s, the compensatory education program required the formation of advisory councils composed of parents of children participating in the program.

As expected, there is local opposition to federal targeting on the special-needs populations. In a comparative study of four major federal education programs in four districts, Paul Peterson, Barry Rabe, and I (Peterson, Rabe, and Wong, 1986) found that local districts were tempted, to a greater or lesser extent, to divert funds away from these redistributive programs to other purposes. Compensatory education funds, for example, were used for general operating purposes that tended to benefit the entire school population. Implementation difficulties were also found in special education. However, programs such as vocational education and ESEA Title IVB that were not primarily redistributive in focus showed minimal conflict, or even cooperation, between levels of the government.

Second, even when they conduct a single case study, the second-generation researchers adopt a longitudinal view. Policy analysts often collect information from multiple years during the implementation process, thereby enabling them to denote cycles of political compromise and programmatic accommodation in the complex intergovernmental system.

With the passage of time, a tendency toward increasing intergovernmental accommodation seems to have emerged in social-equity policy. The compensatory education program, for example, has evolved through three distinct phases (Peterson, Rabe, and Wong, 1986; Kirst and Jung, 1982). Originally it was little more than general federal school aid, with virtually no stipulations attached to the use of funds. Extensive local misuses of these resources prompted the federal government to develop tighter regulations. Most notably, a study conducted by the NAACP Legal Defense Fund during the first program years found that federal funds were being used for "general school purposes; to initiate systemwide programs; to buy books and supplies for all school children in the system; to pay general overhead and operating expenses; [and] to meet new teacher contracts which call for higher salaries" (Martin and McClure, 1969). Consequently, throughout the 1970s, the program had acquired such an exceedingly well-defined set of rules and guidelines that many state and local officials had difficulty in putting them in place. Intergovernmental conflict seemed to have tempered by the late 1970s and early 1980s, when federal, state, and local administrators worked out their differences.

This transformation from institutional conflict to accommodation has been facilitated by several factors. At the district and school level, a new professional cadre closely identified with program objectives was recruited to administer special programs, and local officials became more sensitive to federal expectations. At the federal level, policymakers began to see that detailed regulations, tight audits, and comprehensive evaluations were mixed blessings. With the state agency serving as an active mediator, appropriate changes and adjustments were made. Over time, administrators developed program identifications that transcended governmental boundaries, and a commitment to a coordinated effort gradually emerged.

The pace of moving toward federal-local cooperation in the management of special programs is not uniform—there are significant variations among districts (see McLaughlin, 1990). This leads to the third methodological characteristic of the second-generation studies—the use of comparative cases that involve multiple schools, districts, and/or states. Researchers are able to specify the sources of local compliance and resistance by taking into consideration any variation in the local context.

District-level contextual variables are seen as relevant. I (Wong, 1990) found that local reform in redistributive services depends on the district's fiscal conditions, on the political culture, and on the autonomy of the program professionals in policymaking. More severe and prolonged conflict is likely to be found in districts with a weak fiscal capacity and a program apparatus that is subject to strong political (machine-style) influence. A combination of these fiscal and political circumstances hinders local reform toward redistributive goals. In Baltimore, a 1978 federal audit faulted the local administration for the misuse of almost $15 million. Since the city's mayoral office had direct access to the Title 1 account, it was likely that federal funds were at times used for patronage employment. During fiscal year 1976, for example, the district used the federal funds to hire employees whose duties were "handling requisitions for repair of equipment, preparing reports on a state-funded driver education program, coordinating printing for the entire district, and budgeting control on personnel position and payroll authorization for the entire system" (Wong, 1990, p. 135).

At the other end of the continuum is a district with strong fiscal capacity, autonomous program professionals, and, most of all, teacher commitment to policy objectives. (On linking site-level variables to the design of macro policy, see McLaughlin, 1987; Elmore, 1980; McLaughlin and Berman, 1978). In these circumstances, one expects to find rapid transformation from the conflictual to the accommodative phase in special-needs programs. This institutional process of adaptation (e.g., targeting resources to those who are eligible to receive them) is a necessary condition for instructional and academic improvement in disadvantaged schools.

## ALLOCATION OF FEDERAL RESOURCES TO PROMOTE CLASSROOM LEARNING

### Beyond Administrative Compliance

Fiscal accountability is clearly becoming less of a problem than classroom issues. Based on a national survey of Chapter 1 district-level coordinators in 1990, a major evaluation study (Millsap et al., 1992) found that federal requirements on funding compliance—supplementing (not supplanting) existing services, maintenance of efforts, and comparability provisions—are all ranked as far less burdensome than procedures that affect instructional practices. Indeed, evaluation procedures, needs assessment, and student selection are viewed as the three most burdensome federal regulations that govern Chapter 1 (Millsap et al., 1992). For example, very few districts develop reliable procedures for assessing the educational needs of students who remain in compensatory education for more than two years (Millsap et al., 1992, pp. 2–44).

As local noncompliance over funding use became less of a problem, the federal government and local school professionals began to look for ways to improve program effectiveness. Recent federal and local reform efforts are directed at issues that would forge a better linkage between community setting and instructional strategies in compensatory education.

## Addressing "Concentration Effects"

The first issue is related to the "concentration effects" of disadvantaged pupils in poor neighborhoods (Wilson, 1987). According to the National Assessment of Chapter 1, educational performance is just as adversely affected by living in a low-income neighborhood as by coming from a poor family. As the report pointed out, "[S]tudents were increasingly likely to fall behind grade levels as their families experienced longer spells of poverty, and that achievement scores of all students—not just poor students—declined as the proportion of poor students in a school increases" (Kennedy, Jung, and Orland, 1986, p. 107). In other words, if both factors are combined (i.e., if a child comes from a poor family and lives in an impoverished neighborhood) the incidence of educational disadvantage (e.g., doing poorly on tests, failure to move on to the next grade level) is approximately twice as high as when neither factor is present. Similarly, a 1992 General Accounting Office report found that schools with a high concentration of children living in poverty "have disproportionately more low achievers than schools with fewer children in poverty" (U.S. General Accounting Office, 1992b).

Clearly, compensatory education is especially needed in those neighborhoods where the incidence of poverty is very high. However, resources intended for the needy students become diffused in the multilayered system of school policy. Schools with over 25 percent of their students from low-income families are eligible for Chapter 1 aid. Consequently, federal Chapter 1 funds are distributed to 64 percent of the nation's public schools instead of concentrating on the schools with the highest proportion of disadvantaged pupils. At the school level, the principal and teachers enjoy discretion in student selection. While most of the students receiving Chapter 1 reading services are either low-income or low achievers, a number of them do not fall in the disadvantaged categories. Indeed, according to the National Assessment report, almost 10 percent of the program participants are nonpoor who achieved above-average performance (Kennedy, Jung, and Orland, 1986). Because of the diffused resource allocation pattern, the National Assessment estimated that as high as 60 percent of students eligible for receiving Chapter 1 services remained unserved in the poor community.

While the Congress has become increasingly aware of the "concentration effects," it remains to be seen whether the federal government will move to allocate significantly more resources to the neediest schools. Though short of allocating additional resources to the neediest schools, the Congress enacted the Hawkins-Stafford Amendments in 1988 that allow for a schoolwide project in schools where at least 75 percent of their students come from families whose incomes fall below the poverty line. The new flexibility seems to have encouraged schoolwide projects, which increased from 621 in 1989 to 1,362 in 1990 (Millsap et al., 1992). Schools with many children from poor families are permitted to use federal Chapter 1 funds to reduce class size, develop staff training, support parent involvement, and recruit new professional support personnel. Equally important is that schoolwide projects have, in some cases, contributed to instructional innovation. For example, in a 1990 survey of district coordinators, over 50 percent of the respondents reported that schoolwide projects strengthened parent education programs and helped to change practices in student placement in reading and mathematics classes so as to have more heterogeneous student groups.

### Strategies to Reduce Classroom Fragmentation

The second issue taken up by federal policymakers relates to improving curricular and instructional coordination within the classroom, which thereby facilitates higher performance among participants in the Chapter 1 program. Fragmentation is nothing new and it has very little to do with meeting the educational needs of the disadvantaged pupils. Schools that receive Chapter 1 funding often "pull out" the program participants for special instructional purposes as a way to meet the accounting requirements. A 1983 survey of district-level program coordinators found that 73 percent of the respondents used pull-outs mainly to comply with auditing regulations, and "only 18 percent of district administrators who used a pull-out design indicated they believed it was educationally superior to any other mode of delivery" (Smith, 1988, p. 130).

In the context of increasing public concerns about competitiveness and reform, policymakers and local school professionals are beginning to shift their focus from administrative compliance to program effectiveness. Indeed, as Michael Kirst observed, the publication of *A Nation at Risk* in 1983 renewed concerns for blending Chapter 1 with a core academic curriculum (Kirst, 1988, p. 110). There is now a call to redesign programs at the school level in ways that will strengthen the school's overall organizational capacity to develop more comprehensive (instead of fragmentary) strategies for helping the disadvantaged. (See Chapter 4 in this volume.)

As we know more about the learning pattern among disadvantaged students in Chapter 1 programs, there is a heightened concern for better coordination at the classroom level. Evaluation studies have shown that Chapter 1 participants make greater progress in mathematics than in reading. Participants in the later grades generally made slower progress than their peers in the earlier grades (see Heid, 1991). To enhance program quality, Congress passed in 1988 the Hawkins-Stafford Elementary and Secondary School Improvement Amendments to Chapter 1, which in addition to allowing schoolwide projects in schools with a high concentration of children in poverty, required coordination of Chapter 1 programs with the regular instructional program and encouraged parental involvement.

To promote these reforms, each state was given a modest grant of $90,000, which on average amounted to a grant of only $2,000 per district to districts with large concentrations of children in poverty. While the effects of these federal initiatives remained uncertain in the short run (Herrington and Orland, 1992), some schools already showed positive results (de Baca et al., 1991).

Several national trends on classroom organization seem to have emerged following the implementation of the Hawkins-Stafford Amendments. First, an increasing number of Chapter 1 schools are beginning to combine pull-out programs with in-class strategies, although the latter remain by far the most popular instructional arrangements. Between 1985 and 1990, one study found that "there has been almost a 50 percent increase in the number of districts offering in-class instruction" (Millsap et al., 1992). Another study reported that several districts have adopted computer-assisted instruction (Stringfield, Billig, and Davis, 1991).

Second, while schoolwide projects have become more popular in schools that have many students living in poverty, as discussed above, coordination between Chapter 1 and the regular curriculum remains a challenge in most Chapter 1 schools. In most schools, coordination relies almost entirely on informal meetings, and staff planning sessions rarely occur. Third, the recent federal reform effort has facilitated district activities to promote parental involvement. Between 1987 and 1990, more districts reported "disseminating home-based education activities to reinforce classroom instruction," and using liaison staff to coordinate parent activities (Millsap et al., 1992). Finally, local districts remain largely uncertain with regard to student needs assessment and program evaluation, areas where the federal and state agencies can provide crucial technical assistance. Overall, given the climate of programmatic reform, local professionals are directing greater attention to instructional issues, such as whether pull-out practices are educationally sound (Slavin et al., 1989). In short, the federal categorical role seems to have moved from excessive regulatory oversight in the 1970s to facilitating instructional effectiveness in the late 1980s and early 1990s.

## CONCLUSIONS: POLICY IMPLICATIONS

The federal government has relied primarily on categorical programs to address educational inequities. Given our multilayered policymaking system in education, we have identified three phases in the allocation of federal categorical aid. This more differentiated understanding offers a useful way to analyze resource allocation, because each level involves different actors, issues, and politics. Legislative politics is clearly embedded in the partisan and institutional interplay between the Congress and the presidency. Policy implementation is substantially shaped by professionalism, fiscal capacity, and other institutional factors at the state and district levels. At the school and classroom levels, federal resources are likely to affect how teachers organize the curriculum and the instructional strategies they use. Over the years, our understanding of the federal categorical role has been broadened to include policy issues at both the macro (district) and the micro (school, classroom, and instructional groups) levels.

As we enter the last decade of the twentieth century, categorical programs as a federal redistributive policy tool seem far more secure than when they began thirty years ago. With broadened public support for education and a unified national government controlled by the Democratic Party, the Clinton administration is likely to expand the federal categorical role in addressing social inequities. We may see a significant increase in federal funding in Head Start, Chapter 1, bilingual education, and programs for the handicapped.

A major challenge for the federal policymakers is to decide where to allocate resources that would bring about better life chances for the disadvantaged. Recent literature suggests two areas for additional federal funding. First, additional funds should be allocated to deal with the "concentration effects" in inner-city schools. Clearly, the ecological context of urban schools has changed significantly since the enactment of the original legislation for compensatory education (ESEA Title I) in 1965. At that time, the nation had extensive rural poverty, its central cities were economically stable, and suburbs were emerging as viable communities. By the 1990s, we see a widening educational gap between the central city and its surrounding suburbs. This is especially evident in major metropolitan areas, where most students in schools in outlying suburban communities are white and most students in schools in the central cities are minority and from low-income families. In 1990, while minority groups made up over 60 percent of the central-city school enrollment, whites accounted for almost 80 percent of the suburban school population in major metropolitan areas. In the metropolitan Chicago area, a typical Chicago public school has 73 percent of its students classified as low-income, as compared to only 12 percent in suburban schools (Scheirer, 1989). As a 1985 report on metropolitan Milwaukee concluded, "[Our] study revealed two very different worlds of educational achievement; worlds separated by but a few miles, yet by much greater distances in terms of acquired skills, institutional success, and future prospects" (Witte and Walsh, 1985). Similarly, Gary Orfield and Sean Reardon (1992) observed "a structure of educational opportunity that is highly stratified at every level by both race and class" and by residential choices. They found that students in central-city districts "have a narrower range of course offerings and fewer opportunities for advanced and college-preparatory coursework than their suburban counterparts."

Given the pervasiveness of metropolitan inequality, federal categorical programs are particularly needed in narrowing the educational gap between the haves and the have-nots. For example, to combat "concentration effects" in the classroom, schools in major urban centers need additional federal resources to provide support services for the targeted population. In an eight-district study on Chapter 1 resource allocation, large urban districts were found to spend fewer dollars on the classroom because their students need noninstructional support services. For example, Dade County and Detroit were found to have spent 14 percent and 22 percent, respectively, of the program funds for parental involvement, in-house training, educational specialists, and supplies and equipment. In contrast, the smaller districts merely allocated between 1 to 6 percent of the Chapter 1 money for support services (U.S. General Accounting Office, 1992a).

The second area where the federal role can make a difference is in helping needy schools to build up their organizational capacity. In this regard, federal categorical programs should focus less on auditing compliance but more on within-school coordination. Michael Kirst (1988) has suggested a federal role that is less regulatory but more supportive in technical areas. In schools with many children from low-income families, federal initiative to promote schoolwide projects is a good example. To that end, disadvantaged children would be better served if they were taught the core academic curriculum in the regular classroom, placed in heterogeneous groups, and asked to perform to higher academic expectations (see Dreeben and Barr, 1988). In sum, federal categorical programs can be redesigned to make a real difference in classroom learning.

## REFERENCES

Anton, Thomas. *American Federalism and Public Policy.* New York: Random House, 1989.

Cavanagh, Thomas E., and Sundquist, James L. "The New Two-Party System." In *The New Direction in American Politics*, edited by John Chubb and Paul Peterson. Washington, D.C.: Brookings Institution, 1985.

Clark, David L., and Astuto, Terry A. "The Significance and Permanence of Changes in Federal Education Policy." *Educational Researcher* 15, no. 8 (1986): 4–13.

Coleman, James, et al. *Trends in School Desegregation, 1968–73.* Washington, D.C.: Urban Institute, 1975.

de Baca, Mary Rose C., et al. "Santo Domingo School: A Rural Schoolwide Project Success," *Educational Evaluation and Policy Analysis* 13, no. 4 (1991): 363–368.

Dreeben, Robert, and Barr, Rebecca. "The Formation and Instruction of Ability Groups," *American Journal of Education* 97, no. 1 (1988): 34–64.

Elmore, Richard. "Backward Mapping: Implementation Research and Policy Decisions," *Political Science Quarterly* 94, no. 4 (1980): 601–616.

Heid, Camilla A. "The Dilemma of Chapter 1 Program Improvement," *Educational Evaluation and Policy Analysis* 13, no. 4 (1991): 394–398.

Herrington, Carolyn, and Orland, Martin. "Politics and Federal Aid to Urban School Systems: The Case of Chapter One." In *The Politics of Urban Education in the United States,* edited by James Cibulka, Rodney Reed, and Kenneth Wong, Chapter 11. London: Falmer Press, 1992.

Hill, Paul. *Compensatory Education Services: A Report Prepared for the U.S. Office of Education.* Washington, D.C.: U.S. Department of Health, Education, and Welfare, 1977.

Jung, Richard, and Kirst, Michael. "Beyond Mutual Adaptation, Into the Bully Pulpit: Recent Research on the Federal Role in Education," *Educational Administration Quarterly* 22 (Summer 1986): 80–109.

Kennedy, Mary; Jung, Richard; and Orland, Martin. *Poverty, Achievement and the Distribution of Compensatory Education Services.* Washington, D.C.: U.S. Department of Education, 1986.

Kirp, David, and Jensen, Donald N. *School Days, Rule Days.* Philadelphia: Falmer, 1985.

Kirst, Michael. "The Federal Role and Chapter 1: Rethinking Some Basic Assumptions." In *Federal Aid to the Disadvantaged: What Future for Chapter 1?* edited by Denis Doyle and Bruce Cooper, pp. 97–115. London: Falmer Press, 1988.

Kirst, Michael, and Jung, Richard. "The Utility of a Longitudinal Approach in Assessing Implementation: A Thirteen-Year View of Title I, ESEA." In *Studying Implementation: Methodological and Administrative Issues,* edited by Walter Williams et al. New York: Chatham House, 1982.

Knapp, Michael, and Cooperstein, R. A. "Early Research on the Federal Education Block Grant: Themes and Unanswered Questions," *Educational Evaluation and Policy Analysis* 8, no. 2 (1986): 121–137.

Lowi, Theodore. "American Business, Public Policy, Case Studies, and Political Theory," *World Politics* 16, no. 4 (1964): 677–715.

Lowi, Theodore. *The End of Liberalism,* 2d ed. New York: W. W. Norton, 1979.

Martin, Ruby, and McClure, Phyllis. *Title I of ESEA: Is It Helping Poor Children?* Washington, D.C.: Washington Research Project of the Southern Center for Studies in Public Policy and the NAACP Legal Defense of Education Fund, 1969.

Mayhew, David R. *Congress: The Electoral Connection.* New Haven: Yale University Press, 1974.

McLaughlin, Milbrey. "Learning from Experience: Lessons from Policy Implementation," *Educational Evaluation and Policy Analysis* 9, no. 2 (1987): 171–178.

McLaughlin, Milbrey. "The Rand Change Agent Study Revisited: Macro Perspectives and Realities," *Educational Researcher* 19, no. 9 (1990): 11–16.

McLaughlin, Milbrey, and Berman, Paul. *Federal Programs Supporting Educational Change. Vol. 8: Implementing and Sustaining Innovation.* Santa Monica, Calif.: Rand, 1978.

Millsap, Mary Ann, et al. *The Chapter 1 Implementation Study: Interim Report.* Washington, D.C.: U.S. Department of Education, 1992.

Munger, Frank J., and Fenno, Richard F. *National Politics and Federal Aid to Education.* Syracuse, N.Y.: Syracuse University Press, 1962.

Murphy, Jerome. "Title I of ESEA: The Politics of Implementing Federal Education Reform," *Harvard Educational Review* 41 (February, 1971): 35–63.

National Institute of Education. *Administration of Compensatory Education.* Washington, D.C.: U.S. Department of Health, Education, and Welfare, 1977.

Odden, Allan, and Marsh, David. "State Education Reform Implementation: A Framework for Analysis." In *The Politics of Reforming School Administration,* edited by Jane Hannaway and Robert Crowson, London: Falmer, 1989.

Orfield, Gary. *The Reconstruction of Southern Education: The Schools and the 1964 Civil Rights Act.* New York: John Wiley, 1969.

Orfield, Gary. *Must We Bus?* Washington, D.C.: Brookings Institution, 1978.

Orfield, Gary. "Race, Income, and Educational Inequality: Students and Schools at Risk in the 1980s." In Council of Chief State School Officers, *School Success for Students at Risk.* Orlando, Fla.: Harcourt Brace Jovanovich, 1988.

Orfield, Gary, and Reardon, Sean. "Separate and Unequal Schools: Political Change and the Shrinking Agenda of Urban School Reform." Paper presented at the Annual Meeting of the American Political Science Association, Chicago, 1992.

Orland, Martin E., and Tillander, Staffan. "Redistribution and the Education Block Grant: An Analysis of State Chapter 2 Allocation Formulas," *Educational Evaluation and Policy Analysis* 9, no. 3 (1987): 245–257.

Peterson, Paul E. *City Limits.* Chicago: University of Chicago Press, 1981.

Peterson, Paul E.; Rabe, Barry; and Wong, Kenneth. *When Federalism Works.* Washington, D.C.: Brookings Institution, 1986.

Pressman, Jeffrey, and Wildavsky, Aaron. *Implementation.* Berkeley, Calif.: University of California Press, 1973.

Reagan, Michael, and Sanzone, John. *The New Federalism,* 2d ed. New York: Oxford University Press, 1981.

Ripley, Randall, and Franklin, Grace. *Congress, the Bureaucracy, and Public Policy.* Homewood, Ill.: Dorsey Press, 1984.

*San Antonio Independent School District v. Rodriguez.* 411 U.S1 (1973).

Scheirer, Peter. "Metropolitan Chicago Public Schools: Concerto for Grades, Schools, and Students in F Major." Draft paper, Metropolitan Opportunity Project. Chicago: Metropolitan Opportunity Project, University of Chicago, 1989.

Singer, Judith, and Butler, John. "The Education of All Handicapped Children Act: Schools as Agents of Social Reform," *Harvard Educational Review* 57, no. 2 (1987): 125–152.

Slavin, Robert, et al., Editors. *Effective Programs for Students at Risk.* Boston: Allyn and Bacon, 1989.

Smith, Marshall S. "Selecting Students and Services for Chapter 1." In *Federal*

*Aid to the Disadvantaged: What Future for Chapter 1?* edited by Denis Doyle and Bruce Cooper, pp. 119–145. London: Falmer Press, 1988.

Stringfield, Sam; Billig, Shelley; and Davis, Alan. "Chapter 1 Program Improvement: Cause for Cautious Optimism and a Call for Much More Research," *Educational Evaluation and Policy Analysis* 13, no. 4 (1991): 399–406.

Sundquist, James L. *Politics and Policy.* Washington, D.C.: Brookings Institution, 1968.

Tiebout, Charles. "A Pure Theory of Local Expenditures," *Journal of Political Economy* 64 (October 1956): 416–424.

U.S. General Accounting Office. *Magnet Schools: Information on the Grant Award Process.* Washington, D.C.: U.S. General Accounting Office, 1987.

U.S. General Accounting Office. *Compensatory Education: Most Chapter 1 Funds in Eight Districts Used for Classroom Services.* Washington, D.C.: U.S. General Accounting Office, 1992a.

U.S. General Accounting Office. *Remedial Education: Modifying Chapter 1 Formula Would Target More Funds to Those Most in Need.* Washington, D.C.: U.S. General Accounting Office, 1992b.

Wilson, William J. *The Truly Disadvantaged.* Chicago: University of Chicago Press, 1987.

Witte, John, and Walsh, Daniel. "Metropolitan Milwaukee District Performance Assessment Report." Staff report to the Study Commission on the Quality of Education in the Metropolitan Milwaukee Public Schools, Report no. 4. Milwaukee: The Commission, 1985.

Wong, Kenneth K. "City Implementation of Federal Antipoverty Programs: Proposing a Framework," *Urban Resources* 5, no. 2 (1989): 27–31.

Wong, Kenneth K. *City Choices: Education and Housing.* Albany, N.Y.: State University of New York Press, 1990.

# Section II
## PROGRAM IMPLEMENTATION AND CLASSROOM EFFECTIVENESS

# 3

# Educational Experiences and Needs of Middle School Students in Poverty

## *Samuel S. Peng and Ralph M. Lee*

Over the years, improving the performance of students from low-income families has been a top national education priority. Under Chapter 1, formerly Title 1, of the Elementary and Secondary Education Act of 1965 (ESEA), as amended by the Hawkins-Stafford Elementary and Secondary School Improvement Amendments of 1988, the federal government has provided a significant amount of financial assistance to local education agencies to meet special needs of these students. In 1992 alone, Congress appropriated $6.1 billion for basic Chapter 1 services, the federal government's largest investment in elementary and secondary education, which accounts for 19 percent of the total budget of the U.S. Department of Education (Commission on Chapter 1, 1992, p. vii). As a result of this assistance, the majority of school districts and schools have Chapter 1 programs. Estimates are that in 1987–88 over 90 percent of school districts and 60 percent of public schools provided such services (Anderson, 1992).

But does this significant amount of government assistance lead to substantial improvement in the school performance of these students? Unfortunately, students in poverty still perform poorly on achievement tests, have high dropout rates, and have not received the kind of assistance they need. As summarized in *Making Schools Work for Children in Poverty*, "To those who need the best our education system has to offer, we give the least. . . . Less, indeed, of everything that we believe makes a difference" (Commission on Chapter 1, 1992, p. 4).

Thus, the method of assisting students in poverty is still a highly contested question, and a clearer understanding of the current educational experiences and specific needs of these students is needed before devising strategies for future assistance. This need is particularly urgent for students in secondary schools because data on the implementation of federal programs at the secondary education level are scarce. Although most programs that work in elementary schools may also work in secondary schools, secondary school students may have unique needs because they are at different stages of physical, psychological, and social development. Any successful instructional strategies and program emphases must match student needs.

The purpose of this chapter is, therefore, to report the educational experiences and needs of middle-school students in poverty. Specific topics covered include: (a) the distribution of students in poverty by social background, community type, and geographic region; (b) educational opportunities as measured by school characteristics, curriculum, teacher qualifications, and special services; (c) deficiencies in student performance in school; and (d) educational emphases in the future. In addressing most of these topics, students in poverty were compared with students not in poverty.

## DATA SOURCE

The discussion in this chapter is based on the base-year data of the National Education Longitudinal Study of eighth graders in 1988 (NELS:88), administered by the National Center for Education Statistics, U.S. Department of Education. NELS:88 involved a national representative sample of 24,599 students from 1,051 schools across the country. Students were selected with a highly stratified, two-stage sample design—the schools were selected first, and then an average of twenty-six students were selected within each school. Certain schools and certain students, such as Asian Americans, were oversampled with a higher selection probability (Ingels et al., 1992).

The base-year data were collected in the spring of 1988. Over 93 percent of the sampled students completed a questionnaire that tapped information about their backgrounds and educational experiences. Students also took achievement tests designed for the study. Additionally, parents were surveyed to obtain information about family characteristics and home educational activities, and school administrators were asked to complete a questionnaire about school practices, curriculum requirements, and school environments. Selected English, mathematics, science, and social studies teachers of the sampled students were also asked to provide information about their own backgrounds and to rate their students' behavior in the classroom. The response rates for all these surveys were over 90 percent (see Ingels et al., 1992). The sample sizes for major subgroups used in this study are presented in Table 3-1.

Table 3-1
**Sample Sizes for Major Subgroups***

| Subgroup | Sample Size |
| --- | --- |
| Community type | |
| Urban | 6,509 |
| Suburban | 8,925 |
| Rural | 6,160 |
| Region | |
| Northeast | 3,915 |
| North Central | 5,634 |
| South | 7,670 |
| West | 4,342 |
| Race-ethnicity | |
| Asian American | 1,304 |
| Hispanic | 2,603 |
| African American | 2,591 |
| White | 14,667 |
| American Indian | 206 |

Note: "Hispanic" includes all races.

*The source of data reported in all tables in this chapter is Ingels et al., *National Education Longitudinal Study of 1988 First Follow-Up: Student Component Data File User's Manual.* Washington, D.C.: National Center for Education Statistics, U.S. Department of Education, 1992.

It should be noted that this chapter is based on a secondary analysis of an existing national data base. One strength of such an analysis is the ability to examine multiple topics of interest. However, the data may be insufficient for in-depth analyses because some desirable variables may be missing. So while this analysis tried to take advantage of the strength of the data base by including a number of topical areas of interest, it remains descriptive rather than analytical.

## PREVALENCE AND DISTRIBUTION OF STUDENTS IN POVERTY

Parents of the sampled students provided information on family income in categories. Based on this information, students were classified into two categories: *in poverty* if their family income was less than $15,000; *not in poverty*, otherwise. This classification matched quite closely the poverty definition provided by the U.S. Bureau of the Census. In 1988, the poverty threshold was $12,092 for a family of four and $16,149 for a family of six (U.S. Bureau of the Census, 1989).

Based on this classification, it was estimated that over 21 percent of the eighth graders in 1988 were from families below the poverty level. Assuming this rate is consistent across grades K through 12, there were over 7 million students in poverty in this country who generally needed special assistance in school in 1988.

The prevalent rate of students in poverty, as expected, varied somewhat by geographic regions, ranging from 25.7 percent in the South and 20.2 percent in the West to 18.5 percent in the North Central and 17 percent in the Northeast. Similarly, the rate varied by the type of community, with the urban community showing 26.9 percent, rural community, 25.8 percent, and suburban community, 14.5 percent. These results indicate that the need for assistance was greatest among students in the South and in the urban and rural areas.

Further analyses revealed that students in poverty were likely to be minorities—51 percent (see Table 3-2). In contrast, about 80 percent of students not in poverty were white.

Students in poverty were also more likely to have parents with low education levels—27 percent of these students' parents did not complete high school and 29 percent had only a high school education. In contrast, only 5 percent of the parents of students not in poverty had less than a high school education, 44 percent had some college education, and 32 percent had a college education (see Table 3-2).

Moreover, students in poverty were more likely to come from single-parent families. Some 36 percent of these students came from two-parent families, another 44 percent came from single-parent families, and the remaining 21 percent came from families of other arrangements (e.g., mother with male companion). In contrast, 72 percent of students not in poverty came from two-parent families (see Table 3-2). The percentage of students in poverty from single-parent families was highest among African-American students—55 percent as compared to 43 percent for white students and 32 percent for Hispanic students (not shown in the table).

Table 3-2

**Percentage Distribution of Students by Social Background and Poverty Status**

| Social Background | Poverty Status | |
|---|---|---|
| | In Poverty | Not in Poverty |
| Race-ethnicity | 100.0 | 100.0 |
|   Asian American | 2.8 | 3.5 |
|   Hispanic | 17.3 | 7.6 |
|   African American | 28.6 | 8.6 |
|   White | 49.1 | 79.5 |
|   American Indian | 2.0 | .8 |
| Parental education | 100.0 | 100.0 |
|   Less than high school | 27.4 | 5.2 |
|   High school only | 28.6 | 18.0 |
|   Some post high school education | 40.0 | 44.4 |
|   College and above | 4.1 | 32.3 |
| Family composition | 100.0 | 100.0 |
|   Two-parent family | 35.9 | 71.8 |
|   Single-parent family | 43.5 | 12.0 |
|   Other | 20.6 | 16.1 |

Note: Poverty—family income < $15,000.
    Hispanic includes all races.

Consistent with the population distribution pattern, the racial-ethnic composition of the students in poverty varied by community type. In the urban community, the majority of students in poverty were minorities—46 percent African American, 25 percent Hispanic, and 4 percent Asian American, as compared to 24 percent white. In contrast, the majority (54 percent) of poor students in the suburban community were white—compared to 21 percent African American, 19 percent Hispanic, and 4 percent Asian American. Similarly, in the rural community, the majority of students (65 percent) in poverty were white—compared to 21 percent African American, 10 percent Hispanic, and 1 percent Asian American. American Indians represented about 2 percent of the poor students in each type of community.

Likewise, the racial-ethnic composition of students in poverty also varied by geographic region. For example, there was a higher percentage of African Americans in the South (43.2 percent) and a higher percentage of Hispanics and American Indians in the West (35.7 percent Hispanic and 6.1 percent American Indian).

It is interesting to note that students in poverty were likely to concentrate in certain areas within a community (i.e., disadvantaged areas). As shown in Table 3-3, a substantially higher percentage of urban students in poverty than students not in poverty were enrolled in schools where over 50 percent of the students participated in free or reduced-price lunch programs. The suburban and rural communities in the South and West also had a high concentration of poverty students in disadvantaged areas. Schools with a high concentration of poor students would have more problems and thus require greater assistance than schools with a low concentration of poor students.

Table 3-3

**Percentage of Students Enrolled in Schools Where over 50 Percent of Students Participated in Free or Reduced-price Lunch Programs, by Region, Community Type, and Poverty Status**

| Region | Urban | | Suburban | | Rural | |
|---|---|---|---|---|---|---|
| | P | NP | P | NP | P | NP |
| Northeast | 70.4 | 41.4 | 13.7 | 3.7 | 20.5 | 19.2 |
| North Central | 58.0 | 15.5 | 6.2 | 1.4 | 1.3 | .8 |
| South | 44.9 | 16.3 | 33.8 | 7.4 | 30.0 | 14.4 |
| West | 31.7 | 10.0 | 20.7 | 7.2 | 46.3 | 23.9 |
| Average | 51.3 | 20.8 | 18.6 | 4.9 | 24.5 | 14.6 |

Note: P—students in poverty, NP—students not in poverty

## EQUALITY OF EDUCATIONAL OPPORTUNITY

Did students in poverty receive the same quality of education as students not in poverty? To answer this question, the type of schools students attended, the environments of the school, curriculum requirements, instructional practices, and teachers' qualifications and attitudes toward students were compared. Results showed that although there were not obvious differences in most of the school characteristics and curriculum requirements, there were some differences in the type of services students received and in the environments the students were exposed to. These results are described next.

### Type of School Attended

Overall, 96 percent of students in poverty as compared to 87 percent of students not in poverty attended public schools. This difference was most marked in the urban community, where 93 percent of students in poverty attended public schools and 6 percent attended Catholic schools. In contrast, only 72 percent of students not in poverty enrolled in public schools, while 17 percent enrolled in Catholic schools and the remaining 11 percent enrolled in other private schools. In the suburban community, 95 percent of students in poverty attended public schools and 4 percent attended Catholic schools, while 88 percent of students not in poverty were enrolled in public schools and 8 percent in Catholic schools. In the rural community, almost all students in poverty (99 percent) attended public schools (see Table 3-4). Thus, public schools, as one would expect, assume a greater responsibility and burden than private schools for providing education and services to students in poverty. If the services of public schools were reduced and quality consequently declined, students in poverty would be hurt more than students not in poverty.

Moreover, students in poverty in the urban and suburban communities were more likely to attend schools where safety and discipline were a major concern. For example, over 90 percent of the students in poverty, as compared to 80 percent of the students not in poverty, attended schools where hall passes were required to visit libraries, lavatories, or the school office (see Table 3-5). These students were also more likely to attend schools where robbery or theft, vandalism and weapons, student tardiness, absenteeism, class cutting, physical conflicts, and verbal abuse

Table 3-4
**Percentage Distribution of Students by School Type, Community Type, and Poverty Status**

| Student Type | Public | School Type Catholic | Other Private |
|---|---|---|---|
| All students | | | |
| In poverty | 95.9 | 3.3 | 0.8 |
| Not in poverty | 86.7 | 8.1 | 5.2 |
| By community type | | | |
| Urban | | | |
| In poverty | 93.0 | 5.9 | 1.1 |
| Not in poverty | 72.1 | 17.0 | 10.9 |
| Suburban | | | |
| In poverty | 94.8 | 4.3 | 0.9 |
| Not in poverty | 87.5 | 8.2 | 4.3 |
| Rural | | | |
| In poverty | 99.1 | 0.6 | 0.3 |
| Not in poverty | 96.2 | 1.5 | 2.4 |

Note: Poverty—family income < $15,000

of teachers were serious problems (see Tables 3-5 and 3-6). Although it is not clear whether such practices and problems reflect the students' lack of discipline or motivation for learning, they nevertheless point out areas of deficiencies that may affect student learning and thus should be emphasized in any future improvement efforts.

### Curriculum Requirements and Offerings

Did students in poverty receive the same kind of curriculum and offerings as students not in poverty? In terms of curriculum requirements, the data did not show any substandard schools. For example, the number of courses required in English, mathematics, science, and social studies was basically the same for all students. This was not surprising, since the school district office usually sets curriculum requirements and standards for all students.

Similarly, students in poverty had access to the same kind of extracurricular activities as students not in poverty. These activities included band, computer clubs, drama clubs, subject matter clubs, student council, student newspaper, interscholastic sports, and intramural sports.

However, in urban and suburban communities, students in

Table 3-5
## Percentages of Students Attending Schools with Specified Characteristics, by Community Type and Poverty Status

| School Practice | Urban | | Suburban | | Rural | |
|---|---|---|---|---|---|---|
| | P | NP | P | NP | P | NP |
| Hall passes required to | | | | | | |
| a. visit library | 90.3 | 80.9 | 87.2 | 84.5 | 81.5 | 79.8 |
| b. visit lavatory | 91.4 | 80.1 | 90.9 | 86.1 | 78.0 | 79.3 |
| c. visit office | 90.3 | 78.4 | 89.8 | 80.5 | 76.5 | 76.8 |
| d. visit counselor | 86.0 | 73.2 | 86.4 | 80.8 | 74.8 | 74.2 |
| Schools had a problem of | | | | | | |
| a. Robbery or theft | 75.7 | 63.9 | 73.0 | 62.0 | 69.7 | 67.2 |
| b. Vandalism | 74.2 | 62.0 | 70.2 | 58.2 | 61.6 | 57.6 |
| c. Weapon use | 41.9 | 25.2 | 21.7 | 15.9 | 17.5 | 15.1 |

Note: P—students in poverty; NP—students not in poverty

Table 3-6
## Percentages of Students Attending Schools with Specified Problems, by Community Type and Poverty Status

| Student Problem | Urban | | Suburban | | Rural | |
|---|---|---|---|---|---|---|
| | P | NP | P | NP | P | NP |
| Teachers had difficulty motivating students | 91.4 | 85.8 | 96.7 | 88.1 | 94.3 | 92.5 |
| School had a moderate or serious problems in student | | | | | | |
| a. tardiness | 57.5 | 36.5 | 44.3 | 29.8 | 32.2 | 26.7 |
| b. absenteeism | 47.7 | 26.8 | 42.7 | 26.5 | 36.8 | 28.3 |
| c. class cutting | 23.2 | 10.3 | 10.6 | 4.8 | 8.6 | 5.2 |
| d. physical conflict | 33.9 | 16.9 | 22.3 | 15.3 | 18.3 | 14.8 |
| e. verbal abuse of teachers | 13.7 | 5.5 | 10.3 | 5.8 | 3.7 | 2.1 |

Note: P—students in poverty; NP—students not in poverty

poverty unless enrolled in private schools were less likely than students not in poverty to receive moral/ethical and religious instruction. This difference may reflect the fact that more nonpoverty students enrolled in private schools where instruction in these subjects is often offered.

## Teachers' Qualifications and Attitudes

There were slight differences in educational preparation and experiences between teachers of students in poverty and teachers of students not in poverty. As shown in Table 3-7, slightly more students in poverty in *public schools* were taught by new teachers (two years or fewer in the school) and by teachers who were either without any certification or not certified to teach the subject they were teaching. This pattern is consistent across the four subject matters—English, mathematics, science, and social studies—and across the three community types, even though some of the individual differences are not statistically significant. Furthermore, as reported by school administrators in the urban and suburban schools, more students in poverty than students not in poverty were taught by teachers who had negative attitudes toward students and were less likely to encourage students to do their best or to do homework (see Table 3-8).

Table 3-7

**Percentage of Public School Students Taught by New Teachers (Two Years or Fewer in the School) and by Noncertified Teachers**

|  | Urban | | Suburban | | Rural | |
|---|---|---|---|---|---|---|
|  | P | NP | P | NP | P | NP |
| New teachers |  |  |  |  |  |  |
| English | 19.0 | 16.7 | 16.1 | 12.9 | 20.0 | 14.9 |
| Mathematics | 27.7 | 24.2 | 26.3 | 21.0 | 16.9 | 13.3 |
| Science | 30.4 | 21.4 | 23.1 | 22.8 | 15.4 | 15.1 |
| History | 21.2 | 20.1 | 23.8 | 18.4 | 14.5 | 12.1 |
| Teachers not certified |  |  |  |  |  |  |
| English | 13.2 | 10.0 | 15.0 | 11.0 | 17.7 | 13.2 |
| Mathematics | 18.2 | 15.2 | 16.2 | 11.1 | 16.9 | 14.9 |
| Science | 11.3 | 5.8 | 11.4 | 10.1 | 15.9 | 14.3 |
| History | 16.0 | 11.0 | 10.1 | 6.8 | 11.3 | 9.3 |

Notes: P—students in poverty; NP—students not in poverty. Noncertified teachers include those certified for other subjects, but not the subject they were teaching.

Table 3-8
**Teacher Characteristics, by Community Type and Poverty Status**

| Teacher Characteristics | Urban P | Urban NP | Suburban P | Suburban NP | Rural P | Rural NP |
|---|---|---|---|---|---|---|
| Very much encouraged/expected students to | | | | | | |
| a. do their best | 45.3 | 62.3 | 47.8 | 57.4 | 52.2 | 52.8 |
| b. do homework | 57.0 | 68.5 | 52.2 | 60.4 | 51.5 | 53.2 |
| Morale was high | 22.1 | 29.0 | 27.3 | 31.3 | 25.8 | 24.5 |
| Had negative attitude about students | | | | | | |
| | 71.2 | 54.7 | 64.4 | 54.7 | 59.5 | 60.3 |
| Responded to individual needs | | | | | | |
| | 20.8 | 33.3 | 25.9 | 30.5 | 27.4 | 26.5 |

Note: P—students in poverty; NP—students not in poverty

## Special Programs and Services

Did schools provide extra services to students in poverty in response to their special needs? Based on the limited information from the data base, it was found that certain programs were more readily available to students in poverty. As shown in Table 3-9, more students in poverty attended schools where the following special programs were offered: vocational counseling, English as a second language, and mathematics, science, and social studies taught in a language other than English, reflecting the fact that more of students in poverty were language minorities.

Table 3-9
**Percentage of Students Attending Schools That Had Special Programs**

| Special Program | Urban P | Urban NP | Suburban P | Suburban NP | Rural P | Rural NP |
|---|---|---|---|---|---|---|
| Vocational counseling | 65.3 | 54.5 | 60.3 | 55.7 | 60.8 | 60.4 |
| English taught as ESL | 16.5 | 10.4 | 12.0 | 4.8 | 9.0 | 5.0 |
| Courses taught in a language other than English | | | | | | |
| Math | 15.9 | 9.7 | 8.2 | 2.4 | 2.6 | 1.8 |
| Science | 15.6 | 9.0 | 7.3 | 2.4 | 5.1 | 2.6 |
| Social studies | 16.0 | 10.3 | 8.2 | 3.2 | 6.0 | 3.3 |
| Foreign language offered | 45.4 | 51.2 | 30.3 | 41.3 | 29.5 | 30.1 |

Note: P—students in poverty; NP—students not in poverty

## STUDENTS' PERFORMANCE IN SCHOOL

### Achievement Test Scores

Previous studies have documented that students in poverty have lower test scores than other students. The results of this analysis, as expected, were consistent with this common phenomenon. Based on the standardized combined scores of reading and mathematics tests specially designed for NELS:88, a large percentage of the students in poverty were in the lowest quartile. For example, 53 percent of students in poverty living in urban communities in the South were in the lowest quartile. Similarly, over 50 percent of students in poverty living in urban communities in the Northeast and North Central regions were in the lowest quartile. The percentages in the lowest quartile among students in poverty in other communities ranged from 27 percent to 47 percent (see Table 3-10). In contrast, the percentages of students not in poverty who scored in the lowest quartile stayed around 20 percent or less except for those in Northeast urban and West rural communities.

Table 3-10

**Percentage of Students in the First (the Lowest) Quartile of the Combined Reading and Mathematics Standard Scores, by Region, Community Type, and Poverty Status**

| Region | Urban | | Suburban | | Rural | |
|---|---|---|---|---|---|---|
|  | P | NP | P | NP | P | NP |
| Northeast | 50.2 | 27.5 | 39.4 | 13.6 | 27.3 | 13.5 |
| North Central | 50.6 | 20.6 | 36.4 | 15.4 | 26.8 | 15.0 |
| South | 53.0 | 22.2 | 47.5 | 19.9 | 45.3 | 24.3 |
| West | 44.8 | 23.7 | 39.0 | 16.8 | 38.5 | 27.6 |

Note: P—students in poverty; NP—students not in poverty

A further analysis of the data revealed that students in poverty who attended schools with a low concentration of poor students had higher test scores than their counterparts in schools with a high concentration of poor students. In this analysis, schools were sorted into four categories on the basis of the percentage of students participating in free or reduced-price lunch programs: ranging from the low group (i.e., schools with no students participating in a program) to the high group (i.e., schools with more than 50 percent of their students participating in a program). As the data in Table 3-11 show, students in poverty in the low-group schools had higher achievement scores than their counterpart students in the high-group schools. The percentage of students in the lowest achievement quartile increased as the schools had more students participating in a free or reduced-price lunch program. This finding is consistent with the finding of a study by Anderson, Hollinger, and Conaty (1992).

Table 3-11

**Percentage of Students in Poverty Whose Combined Reading and Mathematics Standard Scores Were in the Lowest Quartile, by Community Type and School Socio-economic Status (SES)**

| Community Type | School SES | | | |
| | Low | Mid 1 | Mid 2 | High |
| --- | --- | --- | --- | --- |
| Urban | 30.5 | 38.7 | 51.5 | 56.1 |
| Suburban | 29.1 | 33.9 | 48.9 | 49.1 |
| Rural | 38.8 | 37.9 | 33.2 | 45.9 |
| Average | 32.8 | 36.8 | 44.5 | 50.4 |

Notes: School SES was based on the percentage of students in the free or reduced-price lunch program. Low—none; Mid 1—1 to 20 percent; Mid 2—21 to 50 percent; High—more than 50 percent.

### Students' Behavior

In each of the sample schools, four subject matter teachers—English, mathematics, science, and history—were asked about their students' behavior in the classroom. The percentages of students having the selected problems, averaged across four teachers, are presented in Table 3-12. It is quite consistent that students in poverty, regardless of the type of community, exhibited more behavioral problems than students not in poverty. For example, in urban schools 36 percent of students in poverty, as compared to 25 percent of students not in poverty, were rated as performing below their ability. The suburban and rural schools exhibited similar differences. Likewise, proportionally there were more students in poverty than students not in poverty who rarely completed homework and were frequently absent, tardy, inattentive in class, exceptionally passive/withdrawn, and frequently disruptive.

Table 3-12

**Percentage of Students Reported by Teachers as Having the Selected Behavioral Problems, by Community Type and Poverty Status**

| Student Behavior | Urban | | Suburban | | Rural | |
|---|---|---|---|---|---|---|
| | P | NP | P | NP | P | NP |
| Perform below ability | 36.0 | 24.5 | 38.3 | 23.7 | 33.3 | 22.9 |
| Rarely complete homework | 34.2 | 19.1 | 31.8 | 17.0 | 26.1 | 15.9 |
| Frequently absent | 19.3 | 9.4 | 21.0 | 9.0 | 15.4 | 8.0 |
| Frequently tardy | 13.0 | 5.8 | 9.2 | 4.8 | 7.5 | 3.6 |
| Inattentive in class | 30.2 | 19.2 | 28.7 | 19.1 | 27.1 | 18.0 |
| Exceptionally passive | 11.0 | 7.9 | 9.7 | 6.6 | 13.5 | 7.1 |
| Frequently disruptive | 20.5 | 12.1 | 17.7 | 12.6 | 15.9 | 11.1 |

Notes: Each figure is the average of ratings by English, mathematics, science, and history teachers.

P—students in poverty; NP—students not in poverty.

## SUMMARY AND DISCUSSION—EDUCATIONAL EMPHASES IN THE FUTURE

In summary, about one in five of the nation's eighth graders in 1988 was classified as being in poverty. The ratio was even higher among students in the South and in urban and rural communities. Many of these students suffered multiple disadvantages. In addition to poverty, they were likely to have parents with comparatively less education and/or to live with a single parent in an economically depressed area. As shown in previous studies (Peng, Wang, and Walberg, 1992; Peng and Lee, 1992), each of these disadvantages represents a major challenge to schools and teachers. Thus, helping these students to overcome their problems would require an extraordinary effort.

About 96 percent of students in poverty, as compared to 87 percent of students not in poverty, attended public schools. Since students in poverty generally require extra help in school, public schools would need greater resources than private schools to achieve the education goals. In many areas, particularly in urban communities, any decrease of resources in public schools would greatly affect students in poverty.

In urban communities across the country and in rural communities in the West, students in poverty were likely to concentrate in certain public schools located in areas where the majority of households were on welfare. These are "ghetto" schools that need the most assistance because the concentration of the students in poverty compounds the problems in learning and discipline. These schools would require many more resources than are currently available in order to bring forth any significant improvement in student learning.

But what can be done to help improve the quality of these schools and how would it be done? The Commission on Chapter 1 (1992) argued that the focus should be placed on improving the overall quality of the schools. To do so, one needs to examine the overall practices and environments of the schools and to determine the area of deficiencies. Results of this study do not show any significant differences in curriculum requirements and offerings; thus, no special effort would be necessary in that area. However, this study does reveal deficiencies in the qualifications of those who teach students in poverty. More qualified and experienced teachers, especially teachers with positive attitudes towards students, are needed in schools where more students are in poverty. Furthermore, this study has identified several deficiencies among students in poverty and among schools where there are more of these students. Future efforts should focus on diminishing these deficiencies. In particular, the following programs should be emphasized:

- Programs to improve the safety and discipline in the school.
- Programs that help teachers and schools place a priority on learning and encourage students to do their best.
- Programs to improve student attendance and classroom behaviors.
- Programs to improve communication with parents and to support parents in teaching students what is right.
- Programs to improve students' attitudes toward learning and education and to motivate them to study.

## REFERENCES

Anderson, Judith. "The Distribution of Chapter 1 Services: Which School Districts and Schools Serve Students in Chapter 1?" Paper presented at the Annual Meeting of the American Educational Research Association, San Francisco, 1992.

Anderson, Judith I.; Hollinger, Debra K.; and Conaty, Joseph. "Services and Staffing in Chapter 1 Public Schools." Paper presented at the Annual Meeting of the American Educational Research Association, San Francisco, 1992.

Commission on Chapter 1. *Making Schools Work for Children in Poverty.* Washington, D.C.: Council of Chief State School Officers, 1992.

Ingels, Steven J.; Scott, Leslie A.; Lindmark, Judith T.; Frankel, Martin R.; Myers, Sharon L.; and Wu, Shi-Chang. *National Education Longitudinal Study of 1988 First Follow-Up: Student Component Data File User's Manual.* Washington, D.C.: National Center for Education Statistics, U.S. Department of Education, 1992.

Peng, Samuel S., and Lee, Ralph M. "Measuring Student At-riskness by Demographic Characteristics." Paper presented at the Annual Meeting of the American Educational Research Association, San Francisco, 1992.

Peng, Samuel S.; Wang, Margaret C.; and Walberg, Herbert J. "Demographic Disparities of Inner-City Eighth Graders," *Urban Education* 26, no. 4 (1992): 441–459.

U.S. Bureau of the Census. "Money, Income, and Poverty in the United States: 1988." *Current Population Reports*, ser. P–60, no. 166. Washington, D.C.: Government Printing Office, 1989.

# 4

# Program Design and Assessment Strategies in Chapter 1

## *Thomas Timar*

### INTRODUCTION

The history of assessing federal compensatory education reflects the educational policy discourse of the past twenty-five years. Throughout the 1970s and until 1988, policy relating to Title I of the Elementary and Secondary Education Act—and after 1982, Chapter 1—focused principally on ensuring that federal education dollars reached their intended beneficiaries. By the mid-1980s, as attention shifted from access to excellence, policy reflected that change by focusing on student outcomes instead of educational processes. In this chapter, I examine past and current federal compensatory assessment practices and their impact on the organizational culture of schools and on the education of disadvantaged children. The chapter's major theme is how formal institutions of government shape relations between educational policy and practice. My purpose is to assess the effects of policy on the capacity of schools to deliver high-quality services to children who traditionally have benefited only marginally from schooling. How can federal policy shape the organizational capacity of schools in a manner that promotes the academic progress of the poorest, lowest-achieving students in the nation's public schools?

Current trends in national curriculum standards and student assessment make it likely that measures of student outcome will play a significant role in the evaluation of Chapter 1 programs. It is worth considering, however, the impact such high-stakes assessment strategies have on organizational behavior and student achievement. Are they more likely to distort organizational goals as schools turn their attention to appearing successful at the expense of real student achievement? Assessment of students' achievement over the past three decades has simply delivered a stream of bad news: federal and state compensatory programs have not had significant and sustained effects on achievement. Focusing evaluation on student outcomes alone, however, does not illuminate the opacity of institutional culture, the inchoate mass of organizational variables that shape the quality of instructional practices, which in turn determine student achievement. There are effective Chapter 1 programs and there are effective schools. Levin's accelerated schools, Comer's community schools, and Sizer's coalition of essential schools show that inner-city schools can be successful. However, schools like Levin's, Sizer's, and Comer's have become successful because they have built strong organizational cultures. Current assessment practices ignore this critical dimension of policy and practice. Hence, in this chapter I propose that evaluation should focus also on the streams of services to students, rather than simply on assessment of individual students. While student progress matters, for the present it should be regarded as secondary to the assessment of organizational variables. I consider here the advantages of evaluation that discerns the robustness of a process (for instance, the capacity to provide rich educational environments in mathematics and science to inner-city children) rather than simply reporting students' performance on norm-referenced tests. The intent is to move evaluation from instantaneous and often misleading snapshots of students' performance to a process that informs federal policymakers about their own ability to shape institutional competence and organizational capacity. Finally, I assess opportunities for creating a policy context that fosters the building of an institution's capacity to perform.

Current assessments of Chapter 1 programs, which focus on student outcomes, place the burden of proof on Chapter 1 to show that its programs have an impact on academic performance. Perhaps the burden should shift to schools to show how they use Chapter 1 resources to improve the achievement rates of low-income, low-achieving students. Evaluation should address the broader questions: What should schools that serve predominantly low-income, inner-city children look like? In what ways might such schools be different from other schools?

## THE EVOLUTION OF CHAPTER 1 ASSESSMENT

Though the ostensible goal of Title I was to help local education agencies provide programs that "contribute particularly to meeting the special educational needs of educationally deprived children," the genesis of the Elementary and Secondary Education Act (ESEA) was firmly rooted in the civil rights movement and Great Society antipoverty programs. The significance of Title I's origins is that education became part of a larger struggle for social, political, and economic equality. Consequently, the federal interest in education was framed by the language of rights and entitlement. Education became the centerpiece of social policy, integral to a national commitment to social justice through equal opportunity.

As legal scholars have pointed out, however, it is easier to announce rights than to implement them (Yudof, Kirp, and Levin, 1992). Because the moral and legal impetus for Title I came from the federal government's championing the rights of children who were inadequately served by local schools, a vast legal and regulatory enterprise developed to ensure that students would, indeed, be served. Draconian measures were necessary in some instances to force schools to use federal funds for the benefit of disadvantaged children, and as a result those regulations did not necessarily achieve the intended effects. On the one hand, federal regulators were able to ensure that eligible students were served. On the other hand, monitors had little control over program quality. Another effect of federal monitoring and compliance strategies was to undermine those educators who made good-faith efforts to serve those children. Every school was treated as a potential miscreant (Kirp and Jensen, 1986).

The underlying premise of Title I regulation implied that schools as organizations were unimportant. Title I service delivery was predicated on the assumption that local compliance with federal mandates was sufficient to secure educational results for precisely those students whom the schools had the most difficulty educating. Assessment and evaluation focused on compliance with procedural requirements that were often labyrinthine. In order to comply with federal regulations, compensatory students were segregated from others. The resulting separation between students identified as disadvantaged and low-achieving from the rest simply exacerbated the isolation of Title I students and services.

The metamorphosis of Title I into Chapter 1, during the early years of the Reagan administration, made little substantive difference in services. Policy debates over the Educational Consolidation and Improvement Act (ECIA) generally evaded issues of program quality, focusing instead on issues of governance and responsibility. In the spirit of program devolution, federal policy simply shifted responsibility for overseeing programs to state and local levels. Funding was cut, but many of the compliance and accountability provisions remained. The change from Title I to Chapter 1 had negligible, if any, impact on schools. Assessment and oversight of Chapter 1 continued past strategies for regulating and monitoring compliance.

## CHAPTER 1 AND SCHOOL IMPROVEMENT: THE HAWKINS-STAFFORD AMENDMENTS

Continued disaffection among policymakers prompted major programmatic revision of Chapter 1 in 1988. According to one policy analyst,

> On both sides of the aisle, both chambers of Congress, and both ends of Pennsylvania Avenue, a feeling existed, not always articulated, that after more than two decades, Chapter 1 should be doing more than helping children make modest gains; it should be helping to close the widening gap that remained between them and their more advantaged peers. [Kober, 1992, p. 14]

The Hawkins-Stafford Amendments addressed these concerns by making changes in service delivery as well as evaluation and assessment (Kober, 1992). Among the many changes initiated by the legislation, the most important are those concerning program coordination, schoolwide projects, accountability for school performance, and parental involvement (Herrington and Orland, 1992; Sinclair and Gutman, 1991; Millsap et al., 1992) The amendments mark a significant shift in Chapter 1 implementation and evaluation policy by emphasizing program effectiveness and accountability.

The putative glue that binds Chapter 1 program effectiveness to accountability are the amendments' school improvement provisions. Schools that fail to show adequate progress toward established goals must develop school improvement plans. In cases of pervasive and persistent failure to show student progress, the law compels district and state intervention to assist schools. It should be kept in mind, however, that school improvement, and student progress, generally, are relative terms. Congress assumed that students receiving compensatory aid would progress at a greater rate than students without aid. In other words, students in Chapter 1 must show greater learning gains than they presumably would have shown in the absence of compensatory aid. In technical terms, the minimum level of adequate school performance for Chapter 1 students was operationally defined as a normal curve equivalent (NCE) gain greater than zero. Schools are required to initiate school improvement activities if they show neither gain nor loss in basic or more advanced skills. Congress also urged districts to adopt local standards and measures of student progress that were not based on norm-referenced tests as means of measuring performance. Failing to show substantial progress in those areas, too, would initiate school improvement activities.

Data show that over the past two years almost 4,000 school districts (27 percent of all school districts with Chapter 1 programs) have had at least one school identified as in need of improvement. Over 10,000 schools have been identified as needing improvement (Millsap et al., 1992). Many of those schools, moreover, have a large number of poor students.

Another change in the implementation of Chapter 1 initiated by the Hawkins-Stafford Amendments allowed schools with very high concentrations of students in poverty (at least 75 percent of students in poverty) to use Chapter 1 funds schoolwide, rather than only for eligible students. Clearly, using funds to benefit all the children in a particular school eliminates excessive preoccupation with audit trails and other technical compliance issues that characterized prior Chapter 1 and Title I implementation. Moreover, schoolwide projects affirm the need to develop an organizational, rather than programmatic, response to the needs of low-achieving students. Its legislative origins are rooted in findings from research on effective schools that emphasize schoolwide goals and program integration. Recent data show that the number of schoolwide projects has grown since the implementation of the new provisions. In 1990–91, there were

1,362 schoolwide projects, about twice the number in the previous year. In spite of the increase, only 2.8 percent of all Chapter 1 districts currently operate schoolwide projects (Millsap et al., 1992).

Closely related to the press for greater inclusion of Chapter 1 within schools is the Hawkins-Stafford Amendments requirement that schools coordinate compensatory services with the regular curriculum. In responding to earlier criticisms of Chapter 1, Congress intended, also, that the program bolster student achievement in more advanced skills, thus making Chapter 1 into something more than just a remedial program. Through coordination and articulation with other programs, schools would take greater ownership in the program, rather than treating it as "someone else's problem."

Finally, the amendments required districts to involve parents in Chapter 1 programs. While the law did not bring back the Title I parent advisory councils, districts must develop written policies for involving parents in planning, designing, and implementing programs. Additionally, the law mandates that schools inform parents of the content and goals of their children's programs and how their children are progressing, support parents' efforts to work with their children, and annually assess parent involvement activities.

## THE HAWKINS-STAFFORD AMENDMENTS: POLICY AND PRACTICE

The Hawkins-Stafford Amendments signaled a dramatic shift in compensatory educational policy. While prior policy tried to link policy with instructional practice, it did so only by implication. Policymakers seemed to believe that a combination of procedural incentives and regulatory sanctions would produce higher levels of student achievement among the poorest, lowest-achieving students and that compensatory programs could improve students' achievement independently of the overall quality of schools. The revised law, on the other hand, attempted to make the connection between Chapter 1 policy and instructional practice an explicit one.

While the amendments pushed Chapter 1 in the right direction, various evaluations of the impact of the revised law suggest only modest effects in its capacity to shape practice and even more modest effects in its capacity to change organizational behavior. The question, of course, is why, in spite of good ideas and intentions, the relationship between federal policy and student achievement continues to elude policymakers. If the Hawkins-Stafford Amendments have not had the intended effect, why not? In this section of the chapter, I address key provisions of the amendments (program coordination, schoolwide projects, school performance accountability, and parental involvement), their implementation, and their impact on teaching practice.

One recent study of Chapter 1 in four large urban districts concludes that the reforms are marginal and incremental. They did not have a significant impact and did not cause schools to reevaluate the quality of service delivery (Herrington and Orland, 1992). On the contrary, researchers found that

> reforms were generally seen as creating an additional burden by increasing administrative reporting requirements at the classroom, school site, and district levels. In this sense, the federal objective of stimulating more critical scrutiny of the program's educational effectiveness had occurred only marginally, if at all. No realignments of policy, administrative structures or service delivery had occurred as a result of the reforms. [Millsap et al., 1992, p. 176]

In assessing the effects of Chapter 1, the study found that the various programmatic components made little difference in overall effectiveness. The overall educational quality of the district was a more important determinant of the quality of Chapter 1 programs. In other words, organizational variables eclipse programmatic variables. Consequently, when Chapter 1 implementation was embedded in broader school reform efforts, attention to program quality and effectiveness was considerably greater. Another study that assessed the impact of the amendments on Chapter 1 implementation also found very little difference in program quality and effectiveness. More important, the study concluded that there was no consistent relationship between instructional quality and Chapter 1 program features. Program variables like small-group or pull-out instruction, staffing, and the like are not related to program quality (Rowan and Guthrie, 1989).

The two studies suggest several policy conclusions. It is quite clear that Chapter 1 is not capable of overcoming school and district deficits in developing good educational programs for economically disadvantaged students. The effectiveness of Chapter 1 is contextual, shaped by the capacity and willingness of schools to engage issues of student performance at a higher level than simply trying to decide what to do with Chapter 1 students. Consistent with a well-documented body of research, instructional quality flows from organizational competence. Chapter 1 evaluation studies reify other research findings that there is no ideal configuration of service delivery that leads to effective outcomes (Rowan and Guthrie, 1989). This conclusion is affirmed also by the effects of different programs like Community Schools, the Coalition of Essential Schools, Foxfire, Accelerated Schools, and the Urban Math Collaborative. How students are grouped, whether they are taught predominantly by aides or by classroom teachers, and other such program characteristics do not determine program quality. The findings are troubling, since so much of Chapter 1 policy is premised on precisely those kinds of assumptions. A good deal of regulatory stringency was predicated on the belief that Chapter 1 could, in fact, overcome ineffectual schools and that there was a single, best way to deliver services. While a strong regulatory and compliance orientation guaranteed that money flowed to those students for whom it was intended, research suggests that this orientation did not contribute to program quality. The findings are important because they affirm the limited reach of Chapter 1 to shape instructional practice. At the same time, they argue for a more inclusive view of school improvement, one that embraces Chapter 1 services within the larger framework of organizational design and purpose.

As Chapter 1 attempted to make the jump from regulation to accountability, assessment and evaluation became the putative springboard to facilitate that leap. As a strategy for school improvement, this move has serious limitations. The Hawkins-Stafford Amendments make school improvement the linchpin for Chapter 1 service delivery, assessment, technical assistance, and accountability. Lack of academic progress among Chapter 1 students triggers school plans for achieving higher levels of achievement and, eventually, district and state technical support. The success of the school improvement component, however, is dependent on various factors. Chief among them is the instrument used to assess student progress. As noted earlier, the universal measure for assessing Chapter 1 program quality is the Normal Curve Equivalent (NCE) gain. It is used to measure student progress and identifies schools in need of program improvement. Obviously, the NCE becomes a high-stakes instrument for schools, since lack of gain is an indication of program failure that reflects negatively on schools.

Consequently, there is considerable controversy over the use of the NCE. According to one study, relying on NCE gains as the principal measure of program performance does not create incentives for schools to improve Chapter 1 programs (Slavin and Madden, 1992). One of the principal objections to NCE is that it creates precisely the wrong incentives for schools. Researchers agree that schools that are identified as in need of improvement (as noted earlier, there are over 10,000 such schools) do not see their designation as an opportunity to redesign instructional services; instead they regard the classification as bad news (Millsap et al., 1992; Slavin and Madden, 1992). Because of the perceived stigma that attends identification of schools in need of improvement, schools will avoid, through various stratagems, falling into that classification. The resulting behaviors, according to one study, "run counter to common sense and sound instructional practice" (Slavin and Madden, 1992, p. 370). The rewards to schools are actually greater to retain students at their present grade levels, thereby avoiding a zero or negative NCE gain.

Moreover, the high-stakes nature of the test encourages schools to teach to the test. While teaching to the test is defensible if the test is a reliable and valid measure of a school's curriculum, it is difficult to defend if the test is standardized, measuring only general skills and knowledge that are only vaguely related to the school's academic objectives. Consequently, the NCE creates an unhealthy tension in schools as teachers are forced, perhaps against their better judgment, to teach to a test that is not a valid measure of a school's curriculum.

Another shortcoming of NCE gain as a measure of program effectiveness is that norm-referenced tests—the most used measures of student eligibility for Chapter 1 services and NCE gain— measure student progress only relative to other students. The tests are not an absolute indicator of what students actually have learned or how well those students compare to students in other schools or other districts, nationally or internationally. If all students in a school do poorly, Chapter 1 students look good by comparison. Similarly, Chapter 1 students might show progress in certain areas that are not measured by the test. Indeed, a criticism of current testing practices is that there are no instructional objectives connected to Chapter 1 and no defined standards of accountability. The general idea is that Chapter 1 students should do "better," but what "better" means is unclear.

Perhaps the most serious flaw in the use of NCE is that those who live by it have little faith in its efficacy. One study argues that "if NCE gains are to be used as high-stakes indicators of program effectiveness, they must be stable, meaningful, and reliable indicators. Clearly this is not the case" (Slavin and Madden, 1992, p. 375). According to the recent interim evaluation of Chapter 1 implementation, nearly 75 percent of schools identified as needing improvement regarded the accuracy of the identification process as either "fair" or "poor." This is a critical finding, since "the nature of school improvement activities undertaken rests in large part on whether districts perceived that the identification process is accurate" (Millsap et al., 1992).

Doubts about the identification process are not without reason. Student scores tend to fluctuate from year to year, due entirely to statistical randomness and regression toward the mean. Since student assessment has little credibility as a valid measure of student progress, teachers and administrators disassociate assessment from any need to improve program services. Many schools are reluctant to initiate school improvement activities because they believe that the next testing cycle will show improvement simply on the basis of statistical fluctuation. And, indeed, in many instances they guess right. Use of the NCE gain, then, is a dicey proposition for schools. It encourages schools to take a very conservative, risk-aversive, strategy for school improvement. Since there is no consistent, reliable, and valid connection between schools' instructional practices and their student assessment practices, the logical strategy for schools is to put their energies into making test results look good, not on improving instructional services (Wilson, 1992; Slavin and Madden, 1992). Ironically, reliance on NCE gains as the principal measure of implementation effectiveness encourages behaviors in schools similar to those encouraged by the procedural, regulatory-compliance measure it sought to replace. While outcomes have replaced procedures, the effect on organizational behavior is still to displace school goals with narrow programmatic goals. The general effect is to continue the organizational fragmentation of schools that characterized Title I and Chapter 1 prior to 1988 and that the Hawkins-Stafford Amendments aimed to remedy.

While about 66 percent of identified schools plan improvement activities and about 40 percent actually initiate the activities, the activities tend to be modest. According to the interim study, "among the most common activities undertaken were staff development, increased parental involvement, changes in the

Chapter 1 instructional model (e.g., in-class vs. pull-out), and computer installation. A few districts focused on the identifying mechanism, and a few others undertook no activities" (Millsap et al., 1992, p. 2–3). In light of Rowan and Guthrie's findings that there is no consistent relationship among instructional models, program activities, and program effectiveness, the prevailing improvement strategies are not encouraging.

The paucity of improvement activities is perhaps less attributable to a lack of imagination or willingness on the part of schools than it is to their limited capacities. Schools and districts often lack the expertise to develop or fine tune sophisticated assessment instruments as alternative measures of student outcomes. Because they lack expertise, schools generally rely on standardized tests, developed by commercial test publishers. Test publishers, on the other hand, defend the validity of their tests and argue that schools expect tests to perform manifold purposes for which they are not particularly well suited (Kean, 1992). Among other uses, schools depend on standardized assessments for evaluation and placement, progress, program improvement and effectiveness, and accountability.

While assessment and evaluation figures prominently in Chapter 1 implementation, schools have little expertise and few resources to draw on. While the Hawkins-Stafford Amendments call on states to play an increasingly significant role in program improvement, the authors of the interim study on Chapter 1 concluded that

> despite the obvious dedication and competence of state Chapter 1 coordinators and their staffs, there are serious limitations to what they can do regarding local Chapter 1 programs. Based upon information obtained during visits to nine state agencies and some of the districts they serve, we must express concern about the capacity of the state education agencies' Chapter 1 offices to exercise programmatic leadership. Staff sizes are small, other responsibilities already involve major time commitments, and staff members are much more comfortable with regulatory and fiscal matters than with curriculum and instruction in their dealing with school districts. [Millsap et al., 1991, pp. ix–x]

Generally, interaction between state agencies and schools tends to revolve around fairly routine matters. The most common interaction was in the form of state workshops on preparation of applications (84 percent), questions about application (77 percent), minor adjustments such as arithmetic errors in the application (63 percent), and workshops dealing with improvement and accountability provisions (68 percent) (Millsap et al., 1992, p. 7-5). State resources generally force states into monitoring for technical compliance. There is little in the way of ongoing discussion between states and their local districts concerning program improvement.

According to the 1992 Interim Report on Chapter 1 (U. S. Department of Education, 1992), parent involvement has increased as schools have expanded parent involvement activities. However, in this area also, it is difficult to identify the relationship between parent involvement and Chapter 1 effectiveness. While some schools make an effort to inform parents about their children's progress and involve parents in planning activities, in other schools parent involvement is a pro forma activity that schools engage in for the mere sake of compliance (Millsap et al., 1992, ch. 4).

## CHAPTER 1 AND ORGANIZATIONAL COMPETENCE

After nearly thirty years of trial and error with federal compensatory programs, it is clear that policy can change various dimensions of schooling. While formal structures like governance, assessment, and finance are readily changed, teaching practices remain strongly resistant to external pressure (Cohen and Spillane, 1992; Meyer, 1986). While the law can compel certain behaviors, it can enforce only minimal standards. Law cannot compel teachers, for instance, to be more "caring" or more "professional." These are vague terms and not legally enforceable (see, for instance, Fuller, 1964). However, they are essential ingredients of a school culture, particularly one that serves the most difficult to teach and educationally deprived students. An ongoing dilemma for policymakers is between hierarchical and coordinate models of control. The bright side of coordinate control is local ingenuity, capacity, and innovation; its dark side is parochialism and evasion. The bright side of hierarchical control is the regular flow of authority, ease of implementation, and coordination; the dark side is bureaucratization, rule-mindedness, and rigidity. The challenge to policymakers is how to maximize the positive aspects of both coordinate and hierarchical models of control while avoiding the negative aspects. Hence, policymakers must look beyond the formal structures of law—the preeminent policy strategy of the past thirty years—as the principal instrument for policy change. This is not to suggest, of course, that formal legal structures should be abandoned, but to suggest instead that they compose only one element in a complex constellation of institutional variables.

New ways of thinking about the relationships between policy and instructional practice are needed as well as a new vocabulary to define those relationships. Though current Chapter 1 policy moves beyond procedural mandates, program improvement must go beyond just accountability and must devote much more attention and resources to building organizational capacity. While it is likely that assessment of student outcomes will continue, in some form, to play a central role in the evaluation of Chapter 1 effectiveness, it is important to connect that assessment to the schooling experiences of students. As research has shown, little is currently known about the connection between program variables and student outcomes. While particular program features do not uniformly predict student outcomes, some schools have better Chapter 1 programs than do others.

Assessment strategies that attempt to isolate the effects of Chapter 1 will continue to distort organizational behavior. The critical question for policymakers is, Can federal dollars strengthen the capacities of schools to provide rich educational environments for poor children? It may be possible that, given the present level of resources, schools are expected to achieve the unachievable. Schools are expected to show achievement gains for students who are among the nation's most disadvantaged. Moreover, schools are expected to do so with meager resources—approximately one hundred hours of instruction over the course of an academic year—and with little external assistance. Nor is current policy cognizant of the pervasive problems outside the schools. Poverty, crime, unemployment, and high mobility are among the problems that resist amelioration through school improvement. Clearly, federal efforts to improve the academic achievement of generally poor, mostly inner-city children must take a broader view.

Hence, the focus of federal programs needs to shift from designing compensatory and remedial programs for a variety of student needs to creating effective learning environments for all students, whether they are poor, learning disabled, handicapped, language deficient, or gifted. Neither entitlement nor accountability has been able to accomplish that objective. The alternative suggests two simultaneous policy directions. One strategy is to deemphasize the formal, structural mechanisms of policy implementation (e.g., procedural rules, accountability) and to emphasize instead the cultural dimensions of schooling. Rather than thinking of policy as a formal, structural process of "implementation," it might be more fruitful to think of policy as a process of "mediation." The two concepts suggest divergent ways of thinking about the relationship between policy and organizational behavior.

The concept of mediated change is anchored in the idea that schools comprise unique cultures that combine the professional norms and values of teachers and administrators with local social, political, and economic conditions. It is a melange of attitudes about teaching and learning, teacher and parent expectations for students, community values, individual and collective ideologies, and the like. Clearly, such values are not readily displaced or dislodged by policy. To the extent that federal or state policy goals are consonant with local culture, implementation may coincide with policymakers' intentions. Where policy and culture conflict, policy tends to be subverted, fudged, redirected, or ignored (Cuban, 1984; Pressman and Wildavsky, 1984; Wildavsky, 1979; Timar and Kirp, 1987). This does not mean that culture cannot be shaped or changed. Certainly the attitudes of school officials and teachers are subject to various influences. The organizations to which teachers and administrators belong play a role in their professional socialization. Teachers and administrators may also have strong allegiances to community as well as to church groups. Teachers, administrators, parents, and community leaders are also influenced by the media. The logical question, then, is, What is the nexus between the formal institutions of government and local culture? Government can give policies form, but only culture can give them substance. This leads to an alternative formulation of policy implementation—one that views policy not as a set of structured events that lead from definition to implementation, but rather as a process of mediating cultural norms and values that inform policy across different levels of government.

Traditional views of policy implementation mirror traditional views of student learning. However,

> research on student learning over the past decade has led to a new view of the student as a constructive participant in building his or her own understanding of subject matter. Learners do not just absorb new information, but rather, they construct their own interpretations and relate new information to their existing knowledge and

understandings. Thus, experts and novices are seen to differ not merely in the *amount* of their knowledge, but also in the *types* of conceptions and understandings that they bring to a problem and in the strategies and approaches that they use. [Wilson, 1992, pp. 124–125]

Constructivist views of learning suggest that learning is a process of reconstructing prior knowledge as individuals integrate new and different understandings of the world around them. According to this theory, learning is not, as has been traditionally supposed, a process of building blocks—piling skills upon skills and information upon information.

Similarly, I propose that policy implementation is also a process of reconstructing prior knowledge. Educational policies that aim at making qualitative improvements in education require individuals to reconstruct existing beliefs and attitudes about schooling and learning. Traditionally, policy aims to change formal control mechanisms—administrative structures and incentives—as a way of shaping behavior in schools. A current trend in educational policy (school decentralization, for instance) aims at school improvement by altering formal control and providing incentives to teachers, administrators, and students. The underlying premise is that existing administrative and incentive structures do not leverage the necessary changes to attune the nation's system of schooling to the demands placed on it. Policy is also predicated on the assumption that there is a correct mix of options and it is policymakers' task to find them.

A constructivist theory of policy, on the other hand, proposes a rather different approach. It argues that individuals filter external demands for change through their cultural and ideological orientations and reconstruct those demands according to their ideological predispositions. (See Kagan, 1991; Wildavsky, 1991; Thompson, Ellis, and Wildavsky, 1990.) Local responses to policy are as much, or perhaps even more, colored by individual conceptions of fairness, definitions of learning and knowledge, and adherence to a particular social order as they are by the immediate demands that policy makes of them. The critical nexus for policy and practice is how the formal processes of government influence teachers' and school officials' conceptions of what they do. School reform, particularly when targeted at improving instructional quality and effectiveness, requires individuals not just to do things differently, but to think differently about the things that they do.

A constructivist theory of policy implementation, moreover, is consonant with the concept of "mediated" policy. It is a more nuanced theory of school change and certainly one that is more difficult to embody than neatly packaged policies that aim at disparate pieces of the educational process. According to the constructivist view, changing educational practice necessitates qualitative changes in teachers' and administrators' conceptions of educational phenomena. For example, implementing California's mathematics and science curriculum frameworks requires individuals to reconstruct conceptually what they believe mathematics and science education comprise (Cohen and Ball, 1990a, 1990b).

The second policy strategy is to redefine conceptually both the target population for Chapter 1 and the nature of the services. Broadening the target population to include all students in a school is a logical extension of current policy that encourages schoolwide implementation. However, identifying Chapter 1 *schools* instead of Chapter 1 *children*, shifts the programmatic focus in significant and important ways and eliminates the more troubling aspects of current practice. Focusing attention on schools also eliminates problems associated with current assessment and identification procedures. The object of federal policy is, after all, to improve the competence of schools that serve predominantly poor, inner-city children. The question that anchors current Chapter 1 policy is: How can federal dollars be used to provide compensatory educational services to the lowest-achieving students? The policy question should be reformulated to ask instead: What combination of federal, state, and local resources is needed to build the organizational competence of schools that serve mostly poor children? (Brynelson, 1992).

While policy needs to shift focus from service delivery to organizational capacity building, it must also take into account the demography of the schools that Chapter 1 serves. Poverty, unemployment, crime, mobility, high rates of teen-age pregnancy, along with the well-known litany of urban problems cannot be divorced from educational concerns. Hence, Chapter 1 policy might be expanded to encompass social and health services as well as economic development. Compensatory education is bound to have little effect in places like South Central Los Angeles, Detroit, and the District of Columbia where schooling is clearly not the path to the good life. Consistent with this line of reasoning, then, Chapter 1 policy should not only define schools as the targets of policy, but also help schools define how they can best serve their students.

## MODELS FOR CHAPTER 1 PROGRAM DESIGN AND ASSESSMENT

Current Chapter 1 assessment strategies are clearly inadequate to do all that is required of them. They are used for multiple purposes—program eligibility, program assessment and evaluation, student progress, school improvement, state and federal accountability, national student assessment. Program eligibility, as suggested in the preceding discussion, should not be based on students' test scores. Funding should target schools, not students. Similarly, assessment for school accountability should be bifurcated from state and national assessment of student academic progress. The former must focus on whether Chapter 1 schools are effective: Do they provide rich learning experiences? How do they organize curriculum and teaching to maximize student achievement? How do they serve broader student needs? How do they build an organizational culture for learning? How do they extend that culture to their communities? These are certainly richer and more meaningful questions for purposes of assessment and more likely to yield more nuanced responses than those that standardized tests provide.

The logical question, then, is, What assessment strategies connect federal policy goals to schools? Are there ways in which assessment policies can shape instructional practices, which, in turn, are instrumental in achieving higher levels of educational achievement for economically and educationally disadvantaged students? Such a strategy would certainly broaden the evaluation context from its current, narrow focus on student outcomes to a broader, organizational focus. Assessment should address how schools have changed as a result of Chapter 1 support. It would be important to know, for instance, how schools are different as a result of parent and community collaboration; what impact Chapter 1 has had on the working environment of schools; and to what degree Chapter 1 has prompted schools to alter the content and organization of instruction, curriculum, and testing. Organizational assessment might prompt schools to take a closer look at how they use resources, how they organize themselves, and the like. In this form, assessment might provide more useful information to both policymakers and practitioners than it does presently. The principal virtue of organizational assessment is that it creates a structural link between policy and practice. It does so by making schools self-conscious about matters of organizational design and purpose.

An assessment model that integrates accountability, organizational capacity building, and school improvement is the accreditation model. It is also consistent with the concept of "mediating" policy, that is, shaping organizational cultures that promote the federal interest in the educational achievement of economically disadvantaged children. The accreditation model could be structured in a number of ways. It could be organized around Chapter 1 Technical Assistance Centers already in operation, for instance. Assessment task forces could be regional or statewide. Where this model has been tried, it has proved to be successful. The California Community Colleges have used a similar method to evaluate a state-funded program that requires far-reaching and complex organizational changes. (The program is the "matriculation" mandate enacted by the legislature in 1985. It requires the state's 107 community colleges to provide various services to students in an effort to improve retention and transfer rates.) Teams composed of community college faculty and administrators, state chancellor's office staff, and faculty from the University of California or the California State University system evaluate programs of the colleges every three years. Similarly, evaluation teams could be composed of staff from Chapter 1 schools as well as non-Chapter 1 schools, state education agencies, Chapter 1 Technical Assistance Centers, regional laboratories, and faculty from colleges and universities.

Accreditation strategies for school improvement differ from regulatory strategies in that they seek to legitimate oversight activities on the basis of shared values rather than formal, legal authority. The difference is critical and goes to the heart of policy debates regarding the nature of policy implementation. As noted earlier, regulatory strategies that depend heavily on monitoring and sanctions have limited capacity to reach beyond *minimum* standards, to reach into the inchoate mass of organizational culture. Demands for change that are legitimated on the basis of shared educational values and organizational objectives are much more prone to shape the interests, norms, and professional allegiance of individuals on whom organizational change hinges. How teachers think and feel about their students, the expectations they hold for them, and their level of commitment are defined by a complex mixture of psychological, organizational, and cultural factors. (See, for instance, Muir [1977] and Kagan [1978] on the relationship between organizational culture and the shaping of professional attitudes.) Accreditation, as an implementation strategy, is an effort to shape the norms and values that define organizational decision making.

Another characteristic of accreditation-like mechanisms for accountability and improvement is how implementation itself is regarded. Unlike regulatory strategies that regard implementation as a discrete act, accreditation strategies view implementation as an ongoing process. Implementation of Chapter 1, like school reform generally, is not a "yes" or "no" proposition. Policy change often necessitates changes that cut to the heart of organizations. Hence, implementation becomes a process of learning or, put another way, a process of integration versus aggregation (Berman, 1986; Majone, 1989; Lindblom, 1990). The key integrative processes seek the creation, identification, and implementation of shared preferences. They invoke the classic political activities of thought, discussion, debate, and education (March and Olsen, 1989). Aggregation, on the other hand, is not change oriented. The aggregative process aims to build consensus from existing preferences. Aggregative theories emphasize majoritarian rule, and the political and legal processes by which such majorities are created. While aggregative processes are successful in deciding presidential elections—where the process is not one of transforming the polity, but is about building consensus around a candidate—and fashioning political consensus for specific policies, they are insufficient to initiate institutional change precisely because the process is deliberately not transformative. Hence, majoritarian processes, while useful in consensual decision making, do not change organizational culture.

The virtue of an accreditation strategy is that it goes beyond assessment for accountability. Its purpose is to create a network that shares ideas and strategies and that, more important, provides a professional anchor for individuals working in Chapter 1 schools. Assessment of Chapter 1 schools would include measures of student progress on various dimensions, the quality and effectiveness of programs, and the like. Evaluation information would be used by the school being evaluated as well as by state and federal oversight agencies. California has a similar process of school assessment called "Program Quality Reviews." Recently, the state education agency has looked at ways of developing similar program reviews for Chapter 1. There are many ways to structure the evaluation model that is suggested here. What I propose is intended to be illustrative rather than definitive.

Testing for purposes of national assessment of educational achievement of students who are served by Chapter 1 schools should be separated from assessment for program effectiveness. As suggested earlier, the concomitant use of assessment distorts organizational behavior in ways that is counter to effective teaching practices. If national policymakers wish to know how well, say, inner-city students are performing academically, that information should be available through mechanisms like the National Assessment of Educational Progress (NAEP).

An additional consideration is the creation of a professional cadre of evaluators, similar to Her Majesty's Inspectorate of Schools in England. (New York state is experimenting with an inspectorate system [Rothman, 1992].) The British inspectorate has inspected educational provisions in England since 1839. Current policy requires the Senior Chief Inspector to produce an annual report summarizing and commenting on inspections carried out over an academic year. The report may focus from year to year on different dimensions of schools. One year, for instance, the report may concentrate on mathematics and science education, the following year on language arts and humanities, and yet another year on social studies and geography. Inspectors would be well-educated, highly qualified individuals who would evaluate schools for accountability as well as provide important information to them about program quality and effectiveness. It is important to note that Inspectors are not monitors; they do not enforce regulations or compliance. No doubt, the specter of a federal or state school inspectorate produces considerable anxiety among some policymakers and school personnel. Much of that anxiety results from some of the excesses and overzealousness of federal program compliance monitors during the 1970s when enforcement fever was at its height. However, the British system does not carry that kind of baggage and a similar evaluation system in this country need not. Such an inspectorate could be established at the state level, for instance, or could be connected with the regional laboratories. The key to an evaluation scheme built around an inspectorate is its autonomy and professional expertise.

It should be emphasized that the accreditation and inspectorate models serve somewhat different ends. The accreditation model is more likely to encourage and develop a community and culture of Chapter 1 schools. By its very nature, it favors technical assistance over accountability. On the other hand, the inspectorate weighs more heavily toward accountability and oversight. Ideally, the two systems complement one another.

The accreditation and inspectorate models satisfy the need to complete the circle of policy intent, instructional practice, and assessment. They do not speak to the broader social and economic issues that entangle educational policy. In order to address education in the broader context, federal policymakers may wish to consider disaggregating the monolithic approach that presently characterizes Chapter 1 policy into more targeted and nuanced policy strategies. For instance, it is obvious that the educational and social problems of destitute children in urban and rural areas are dissimilar. Yet, current policy treats them as though they were alike. The needs of inner-city schools, the resources that should be targeted to them, are not those of rural schools. And the socioeconomic and cultural context in which urban and rural schools operate is, again, quite different. Consequently, there should be a distinct Chapter 1 urban policy that is part of a larger urban strategy. And a similarly distinct strategy ought to be developed for rural schools.

The conceptual model that I propose embeds Chapter 1 policy into a broader framework for social policy and economic development. It draws on a similar model developed in France (Best, 1992). Through creation of "zones d' éducation prioritaire" (ZEPs) (education priority zones), the government targets a number of resources to certain areas of the country that contain children who are identified as "at risk." These are the children of people living in poverty, the unemployed, those from racial or ethnic minorities, those from one-parent families, and those who have poor mastery of the primary language. Such families, "marginalized from society, or in any case, by-passed by social advances," tend to be grouped together in areas that are described as "at risk." Educational and social problems are addressed through confluent policies (Best, 1992). Current policy is to select priority areas to receive resources (in the form of additional teaching positions and operating subsidies) for education. Many of these are also areas that receive priority assistance for urban renewal and social support for their populations. These areas are called "Développement social des quartiers" (DSQs).

In general, policy aims at the convergence of educational

policy (ZEPs) with urban and social policy (DSQs) and stronger partnerships between schools and local authorities (municipalities, general and regional councils, etc.). The goal of policy is to integrate all government-provided public services within an educational policy targeted to social problems.

It is important to note, however, that the convergence of educational and social policy is part of a larger urban effort that includes creation of a Ministry of Cities and a comprehensive city development policy that combines town planning as well as social and cultural development for disadvantaged urban areas. It is important to remember also that policy implementation in France is greatly facilitated through a hierarchically integrated government bureaucracy. While in the past such coordination has proved difficult in a highly fragmented governance system such as ours, conceptually the ZEP and DSQ model may nonetheless be useful for federal policymakers.

Problems of scale and diversity create a much more complex policy environment in the United States compared to France. But that fact argues more persuasively for the need to develop policy that is less monolithic in intent and design and better targeted to diverse educational and social problems. Such a policy approach as the one proposed here also militates for a very different approach to program evaluation and assessment. The French, under the aegis of the Inspecteur général, create assessment task forces—similar to the accreditation model described earlier—that provide detailed, comprehensive information about program quality and effectiveness. Program quality is measured by its capacity to shape the academic and social development of students. The instruments used to measure the success of this policy are not those used to measure, for national assessment purposes, the academic achievement of French students.

## CONCLUSION

The Hawkins-Stafford Amendments signaled an important change in Chapter 1 policy. And though the policy shift was conceptually a positive move toward consonance between program services and student performance, it has fallen short of policymakers' expectations. It perpetuates a number of difficulties that have attended the program since its inception as Title I. Policymakers have learned a good deal since 1965 about policy implementation. It is a more nuanced and difficult process than had been imagined. While rules and regulations are easily verified and monitored for compliance, it is quite another matter to change instructional practices and the schools' capacity to serve economically disadvantaged and educationally deprived children. Effecting institutional change that is both far-reaching and broad necessitates a fundamental reconceptualization of current policy. While the Hawkins-Stafford Amendments initiated that shift, a more dramatic change is needed.

The challenge to policymakers is to design programs and evaluation in a way that encourages organizational coherence and integration rather than fragmentation. Policy should create incentives and provide resources for schools to do things not just better, but differently. Accomplishing that requires policymakers to think differently also about the relations between policy and practice. How can policy most effectively mediate organizational change? Moreover, policy must focus on schools as the locus of change. Rather than asking how policy can change students, we should first ask how policy can change schools that serve diverse student needs.

# REFERENCES

Berman, Paul. "From Compliance to Learning: Implementing Legally Induced Reforms." In *School Days, Rule Days*, edited by David L. Kirp and Donald N. Jensen. Philadelphia: Falmer Press, 1986.

Best, Francine. *The Educational Priority Area (ZEP) Policy: A Response to the "Children-at-Risk" Problem. A Case Study of the Education Priority Area of Alencon-Perseigne.* Paris: Inspecteur general de l'Education Nationale, Education Priority Area Assessment Task Force, 1992.

Brynelson, W. "Comments Regarding CCSSO Working Paper on Hawkins-Stafford Reauthorization." Memorandum to Gail ImObersteg, July 6, 1982. Sacramento, Calif.: State Department of Education, 1992.

Cohen, David K., and Ball, Deborah, L. "Relations between Policy and Practice: A Commentary," *Educational Evaluation and Policy Analysis* 12 (1990a), 249–256.

Cohen, David K., and Ball, Deborah L. "Policy and Practice: An Overview," *Educational Evaluation and Policy Analysis* 12 (1990b), 347–353.

Cohen, David K., and Spillane, James P. "Policy and Practice: The Relations between Governance and Instruction." In *Review of Research in Education*, vol. 18, edited by Gerald Grant. Washington, D.C.: American Educational Research Association, 1992.

Cuban, Larry. "School Reform by Remote Control: SB 813 in California," *Phi Delta Kappan* 66 (November 1984): 213–215.

Fuller, Lon L. *The Morality of Law.* New Haven, Conn.: Yale University Press, 1964.

Herrington, Carolyn, and Orland, Martin E. "Politics and Federal Aid to Urban School Systems: The Case of Chapter 1." In *The Politics of Urban Education in the United States,* edited by James Cibulka, Rodney Reed, and Kenneth Wong. Philadelphia: Falmer Press, 1992.

Kagan, Robert A. *Regulatory Justice.* New York: Russell Sage, 1978.

Kagan, Robert A. "Adversarial Legalism and American Government," *Journal of Policy Analysis and Management* 10, no. 3 (1991): 369–406.

Kean, Michael. "ESEA Chapter 1 Reauthorization: Testimony before the Advisory Committee on Testing in Chapter 1." Monterey, Calif.: CTB Macmillan/ McGraw-Hill, 1992.

Kirp, David L., and Jensen, Donald N., eds. *School Days, Rule Days.* Philadelphia: Falmer Press, 1986.

Kober, Nancy. *The Role and Impact of Chapter 1, ESEA, Evaluation and Assessment Practices.* Washington, D.C.: Office of Technology Assessment, 1992.

Lindblom, Charles. *Inquiry and Change.* New Haven, Conn.: Yale University Press, 1990.

Majone, Giandomenico. *Evidence, Argument, and Persuasion in the Policy Process.* New Haven, Conn.: Yale University Press, 1989.

March, James G., and Olsen, Johan P. *Rediscovering Institutions: The Organizational Basis of Politics.* New York: Free Press, 1989.

Meyer, John. "Organizational Factors Affecting Legalization." In *School Days, Rule Days,* edited by David L. Kirp and Donald N. Jensen. Philadelphia: Falmer Press, 1986.

Millsap, Mary Ann, et al. *The Chapter 1 Implementation Study: Interim Report.* Washington, D.C.: Office of Policy and Planning, U. S. Department of Education, 1992.

Muir, William. *Police: Streetcorner Politicians.* Chicago: University of Chicago Press, 1977.

Pressman, Jeffrey, and Wildavsky, Aaron. *Implementation,* 3rd edition. Berkeley: University of California Press, 1984.

Rothman, Robert. "New York Embraces Old Idea from Britain in Developing New Way to Evaluate Schools," *Education Week,* 9 September 1992, p. 1.

Rowan, Brian, and Guthrie, Larry. *The Quality of Chapter 1 Instruction.* San Francisco, Calif.: Far West Laboratory, 1989.

Sinclair, Beth, and Gutman, Babette. *A Summary of State and Chapter 1 Participation and Achievement Information for 1988–89.* Washington, D.C.: Office of Policy and Planning, U. S. Department of Education, 1991.

Slavin, Robert, and Madden, Nancy. "Modifying Chapter 1 Program Improvement Guidelines to Reward Appropriate Practices," *Educational Evaluation and Policy Analysis* 13, no. 4 (1992): 369–379.

Thompson, Michael; Ellis, Richard; and Wildavsky, Aaron. *Cultural Theory.* Boulder, Colo.: Westview Press, 1990.

Timar, Thomas, and Kirp, David. "Educational Reform and Institutional Competence," *Harvard Educational Review* 57, no. 3 (1987): 308–330.

U. S. Department of Education. *National Assessment of the Chapter 1 Program: The Interim Report.* Washington, D.C.: U. S. Department of Education, 1992.

Wildavsky, Aaron. *Speaking Truth to Power.* Boston: Little, Brown and Co., 1979.

Wildavsky, Aaron. "A World of Difference: The Public Philosophies and Political Behaviors of Rival American Cultures." In *The New American Political System*, 2d edition, edited by Anthony King. Washington, D.C.: American Enterprise Institute, 1991.

Wilson, Mark. "Educational Leverage from a Political Necessity: Implications of New Perspectives on Student Assessment for Chapter 1 Evaluation," *Educational Evaluation and Policy Analysis* 14, no. 2 (1992): 123–144.

Yudof, Mark; Kirp, David; and Levin, Betsy. *Educational Policy and the Law*. St. Paul, Minn.: West Publishing, 1992.

# 5

# Compensatory Education in South Carolina: Lessons from the Past, Visions for the Future

## *Lorin W. Anderson and Leonard O. Pellicer*

For almost two decades, South Carolina has been a hotbed of educational legislation. Beginning with the Education Finance Act of 1977 and progressing through Target 2000: School Reform for the Next Decade Act (passed in 1989), the citizens of South Carolina have witnessed a succession of major pieces of legislation designed to overhaul public school education and help elevate the state from its perennial position at the bottom of the heap.

This chapter focuses specifically on the impact of this legislation on programs designed for economically disadvantaged, low-achieving students. We begin with an overview of the most significant educational legislation enacted during this period. Next, we proceed to a brief description of studies of compensatory programs and students that have been conducted over the past five years. The major findings of these studies are presented and discussed. Finally, we describe the conditions under which programs for economically disadvantaged, low-achieving students in South Carolina have been successful and conclude with a set of recommendations and implications for the future.

## SIGNIFICANT EDUCATIONAL LEGISLATION IN SOUTH CAROLINA

Four of the legislative acts passed since 1977 stand out because of their potential impact on programs for economically disadvantaged, low-achieving students. They are the Education Finance Act (EFA) of 1977, the Basic Skills Assessment Act (BSAA) of 1978, the Education Improvement Act (EIA) of 1984, and the Target 2000: School Reform for the Next Decade Act (Target 2000) of 1989.

### The Education Finance Act (1977)

The EFA was a landmark piece of legislation in South Carolina's drive to catch up with the rest of the nation in providing reasonable educational opportunity for all students. The EFA was engineered to reduce dramatically the educational discrepancies resulting from both racial segregation and disparities in wealth among the various school districts in South Carolina.

The purpose of the EFA can be summarized in three words: adequacy, equality, and accountability (South Carolina Department of Education [SCDE], 1992). This purpose was achieved by determining the financial resources required to provide a child a minimally acceptable education and then adjusting this "base student cost" incrementally to reflect more costly educational programs for children with special needs.

For example, a child in grades 4 through 8 in a regular classroom setting is considered to represent the base student cost (that is, the least expensive educational program to operate on a per-pupil basis) and is thereby assigned a weighting of 1.0 in the funding formula. In contrast, a child classified as hearing impaired is assigned a weighting of 2.57. That is, it is assumed that it costs approximately two and one-half times as much to educate a hearing handicapped child as a "typical" fourth-through eighth-grade student. A number of funding weightings (currently fourteen) were established in the EFA to reflect a broad range of special educational needs of children so that school districts would have the financial resources necessary to provide every child with a so-called defined minimal program.

The EFA also established a reasonable balance between the portion of funds to be paid by the state (approximately 70 percent) and the local school districts (approximately 30 percent) in support of the defined minimum program based on a school district's ability to pay. For each school district, an "index of tax-paying ability" is computed based on the taxable wealth of the district as a portion of the total taxable wealth of the state. The ninety-one school districts, collectively, provide approximately 30 percent of the total annual cost of the defined minimum program in the state. Districts with less taxable wealth pay proportionally smaller shares of their defined minimum program costs while the state pays proportionally more of the defined minimum program costs in these districts.

The Education Finance Act of 1977 was a giant step forward in providing some measure of equality of educational opportunity for all the children in South Carolina regardless of where they resided. However, the EFA focused on minimums rather than optimums and left much to be desired in providing a dynamic driving force for excellence, one that would successfully raise the educational level of the citizens of South Carolina relative to that of the citizens of other states.

## The Basic Skills Assessment Act of 1978

The Basic Skills Assessment Act (BSAA) followed closely on the heels of the Education Finance Act. Passed in 1978, the BSAA mandated rather strict accountability measures to assure that funds expended under the EFA were being used to achieve the desired results. The most significant provisions of the BSAA are as follows:

1. The State Board of Education was mandated to establish statewide educational objectives in the basic skills in all grades. Later the Act was amended to include only those grade levels at which students were to be tested.
2. Criterion-referenced tests in reading and mathematics were to be administered to students at the end of grades 1, 2, 3, 6, and 8. At grades 6 and 8, essay-type writing tests were to be administered. In addition, a readiness test was to be administered to students entering first grade. Minimum standards were to be established for each subject at each grade level. A diagnosis of learning needs was required for students who scored below the established minimum standards in order to provide instruction that could bring all students up to standards.
3. An achievement test designed to measure adult life skills was to be administered at the end of grade 11. The test

was to be field tested through the 1988–89 school year when the State Board of Education would use the baseline data to determine who should receive a high school diploma in South Carolina and what credentials should be awarded to those failing to attain minimum standards.

The Basic Skills Assessment Act proved relatively effective in raising the achievement levels in the basic skills for students in general. It also did a fairly good job of helping to identify students who needed remediation across the public school spectrum. However, the BSAA did not provide funds for the remedial programs that children failing to meet the minimum standards needed in order to improve their academic standing. State funding for remedial programs in South Carolina was provided six years later with the passage of the Education Improvement Act.

## The Education Improvement Act of 1984

In 1984, the Education Improvement Act (EIA) was passed. The EIA, a blockbuster omnibus education bill, was designed to enact a quality public school program for "current and future generations" of South Carolinians by

1. increasing the academic skill levels of students;
2. strengthening the teaching and testing of basic skills;
3. elevating the teaching profession;
4. improving leadership, management, and fiscal efficiency;
5. implementing quality controls and rewarding productivity;
6. creating more effective partnerships among schools, parents, community, and business; and
7. providing school buildings conducive to improved student learning (SCDE, 1992).

The EIA provided for an additional one cent state sales tax to fund the more than sixty new programs included in the legislation. Although the single largest dollar amount in the EIA was devoted to teacher salary increases in order to keep South Carolina teachers at the average for the Southeastern region of the United States, there was significant funding for a number of important academic program initiatives.

The EIA contained provisions to increase the number of units required for high school graduation and, for the first time, mandated a high school exit examination to ensure that students graduating from South Carolina high schools were functionally literate in reading, writing, and mathematics. The legislation further provided funding for advanced placement courses in the high schools, academically and artistically gifted and talented programs, an early childhood program (four-year-old kindergarten), an out-of-school child development program, and additional funding for adult education, both developmental and remedial.

Perhaps the most significant programmatic aspect of the EIA was the establishment of compensatory education programs and remedial education services for students who had not achieved the required standards in reading, writing, and mathematics on the state's basic skills assessment tests or the first-grade readiness tests. These programs and services were funded at more than $65 million during 1992–93, a figure that represented one-fourth of the total EIA funds (SCDE, 1992). The primary objective of compensatory and remedial education in South Carolina was to reduce the number of students who failed to meet the standards on the basic skills tests by enhancing the learning of those who scored below the standards at each grade level.

Funding priorities established in the EIA favor students in grades 1 through 6 who score at or below the 25th percentile, but all other students failing to meet the basic skills test standards are also served on a priority basis as funds permit. In fact, statutes mandate that all eligible students be served if a district is to receive full funding. One hundred percent of students in a higher-priority category must be served before school districts may use remaining funds to serve students in the next highest category and so on until all available funds are expended.

South Carolina's compensatory programs and remedial services operate side-by-side with Chapter 1 programs, the long-standing federally funded program for low-socioeconomic, low-achieving students. Chapter 1 funds expended in South Carolina during fiscal year 1991 were slightly more than $78 million (Statler, 1992) while funding for state compensatory and remedial education through the EIA totaled more than $65 million (MGT of America, 1992). The relatively equal level of funding for the two programs indicates the magnitude of the state's initiative in compensatory education and further hints at the possibility for difficulties arising from trying to implement two programs with similar goals of similar magnitude in ninety-one individual school districts.

## The Target 2000 Act of 1989

Target 2000 expanded several programs initiated in the Education Improvement Act of 1984 and added several new programs to better prepare South Carolina students for work and life in the twenty-first century (SCDE, 1992). The new programs were intended to reduce school dropouts, strengthen the parental role as teachers of preschool children, promote teaching and learning of higher-order thinking skills, improve the art education curriculum, provide certain schools with flexibility in meeting regulatory requirements, implement comprehensive approaches for improving student development, performance and attendance, and provide additional support for training principals and teachers.

The financial and programmatic impacts of Target 2000 were relatively minor in comparison to the EIA. The 1992–93 funding for Target 2000 was approximately $12 million as opposed to more than $250 million contained in the EIA (SCDE, 1992). More than anything, Target 2000 was a reaffirmation of the state's commitment to improve the quality of education available to its citizens and pull itself up by its educational bootstraps in order to stand side by side with its sister states.

## Summary of Educational Legislation

Taken together, the legislative initiatives outlined above have had a tremendous impact on the substance and quality of education in South Carolina. In general, the impact of educational reform in South Carolina has been rather dramatic, even if it has not quite measured up to the expectations of either the reform advocates or the equally vociferous, though fewer in number, reform detractors. Much of what was anticipated by lawmakers during the framing of the various pieces of legislation has become reality. Equally important, however, are the unanticipated results of the legislative mandates that have become just as real.

# STUDIES OF COMPENSATORY EDUCATION IN SOUTH CAROLINA

The systematic study of compensatory education programs in South Carolina actually began with the congressionally mandated National Assessment of Chapter 1 in 1984–85. South Carolina was one of six states in which data were collected in an attempt to describe compensatory education from the student's point of view (Rowan and Guthrie, 1989). In each state, teams of three to four researchers spent about a month in four preselected schools conducting interviews with the school staff, talking to students, and observing the instruction received by students.

At each school, eight students were observed for an entire school day, and two students were observed for an entire week. Structured observation forms were used to code the amount of time students were instructed in various subjects, the instructional formats used by the teachers, the sizes of the groups in which students received instruction, and the providers of instruction (e.g., teachers, aides, machines). In addition, narrative records provided information about the instructional materials being used, the content and skill levels of instructional tasks on which students worked, the nature of verbal interactions between teachers and students, and the engagement and success rates of students during instruction.

The results obtained in all six states were aggregated and several reports were prepared (Lee et al., 1986; Kennedy, Birman, and Demaline, 1987). Because of the purpose of the study and the aggregation of the data, results unique to South Carolina were unavailable.

Over the past three years, however, four studies of compensatory education in South Carolina  have been conducted. Two of these studies (Anderson et al., 1989; MGT of America, 1992) have been supported financially by the EIA Select Committee, a committee of state legislators and others whose primary responsibility is the oversight of the implementation of the Education Improvement Act. A third study (Anderson et al., 1992) was supported financially by the federal government, through its support of the Southeastern Regional Vision for Education (SERVE) laboratory. Finally, the fourth study (Nielsen, 1991, 1992) was conducted by staff members of the South Carolina Department of Education as part of their responsibility for monitoring compensatory education programs in the state.

Brief summaries of these studies are shown in Table 5-1. It is interesting to note that three of these studies relied on multiple sources of data: (1) national- and state-level standardized tests, (2) questionnaires and/or interviews, and (3) school and classroom observations. The exception was the Nielsen study, which relied on achievement-test data only. Furthermore, the samples in general were quite large, involving 120 schools in one case (Anderson et al., 1989) and over 28,000 students in another (Nielsen, 1991, 1992).

Table 5-1
## Summary of the Design of Major Studies of Compensatory Education in South Carolina

| Author(s)/Date | Summary of the Design of the Study |
| --- | --- |
| Anderson, Cook, Pellicer, Sears, and Spradling (1989) | A sample of 120 schools was selected based on (1) the grade levels housed in the schools and (2) the effectiveness of both the compensatory program and the total instructional program in the schools. Questionnaires were mailed to the principal of each selected school. Separate questionnaires were to be completed by the principal himself or herself, regular classroom teachers, compensatory and remedial teachers, and teachers' aides.<br><br>Based on the questionnaire data, a sample of twenty-four schools was selected for visits. During these visits, trained observers used structured observation forms to record what they saw and heard in four classes (two reading/language arts and two mathematics), and collected the instructional materials used in the classrooms as well as the assignments given to students. |
| Nielsen (1991, 1992) | Using statewide data, these studies reported on the numbers of students served in the state EIA Remedial and Compensatory Programs, changes in student test scores from 1983 through 1990, and the continuity of service (that is, the proportion of students enrolled in the programs both in 1989–90 and 1990–91).<br><br>In addition, the results of two longitudinal studies were reported. The first longitudinal study included all students who began first grade in 1984–85. The 1984–85 school year was the first year after the passage of the Education Improvement Act. The total number of students on which complete data for seven years were available exceeded 28,000. Approximately 13,000 of these students were enrolled in a compensatory program for one or more years.<br><br>The second longitudinal study included students who were enrolled in the sixth grade in 1984–85. This sample allowed the examination of student performance during their high school years. The total number of students on which complete data for seven |

years were available exceeded 24,000. Almost 13,000 of these students were enrolled in a compensatory or remedial program for one or more years.

MGT of America (1992)

Thirty-two schools in more than twenty school districts were identified on the basis of three criteria: (1) each school had to receive three consecutive School Incentive Awards (an indication of their overall effectiveness), (2) each school had to have among the highest achievement gains on standardized tests when compared to other schools of a similar grade configuration (e.g., K–6) who served a similar student population (e.g., large numbers of students who qualify for free- and reduced-price lunches), and (3) each school had to have a compensatory or remedial program in mathematics or reading for all three years. Questionnaires were sent to principals of these thirty-two schools and on-site visits were made to eight schools.

Anderson, Sears, Pellicer, Riddle, Gardner, and Harwell (1992)

This study employed a four-phase research design. In Phase I, twelve schools whose compensatory students had achieved unusually high achievement gains in both reading and mathematics were identified from reports provided by the South Carolina Department of Education. In Phase II, demographic data were collected on these schools. In Phase III, questionnaires designed to collect data on three major programmatic variables (the delivery model, the classroom organization, and the relationship of compensatory and regular classroom instruction) were sent to each school.

Based on the data collected in Phase III, four schools were selected for intensive study (Phase IV). Two-day visits were made to each of these schools. The focus of these visits was on four issues: program effectiveness, school culture, curriculum, and teaching. During each visit, a variety of people were interviewed (e.g., administrators, teachers, parents, and students) and observations were conducted in classrooms.

## MAJOR FINDINGS CONCERNING COMPENSATORY EDUCATION IN SOUTH CAROLINA

In combination, the four studies summarized in Table 5-1 have produced a series of consistent findings. In this section, three major findings will be highlighted and discussed. They concern the fragmentation of the school program, the instructional delivery of compensatory education, and the effectiveness of compensatory education programs in South Carolina.

### *The Fragmentation of the School Program*

Independent of their intended purpose, categorical programs clearly have encouraged differentiation among students and the placement of different types of students into different programs and, hence, classrooms. The characteristics used to select students for the various programs tend to differ from program to program. Poverty and achievement are used to identify Chapter 1 students, while achievement alone is sufficient to place students into the EIA compensatory and remedial programs. Biologically or chemically determined disabilities result in student placement in federally funded special education programs, while abilities, aptitudes, and special talents are used to place students in state-funded gifted and talented programs.

Anderson and colleagues (1989) asked principals to account for each student at selected grade levels. Specifically, principals were asked to indicate the number of students in each of the following categories: (1) EIA compensatory/remedial program only, (2) Chapter 1 program only, (3) both EIA compensatory/remedial and Chapter 1 programs, (4) the federal program for handicapped students, (5) the state-funded gifted and talented program, or (6) no special categorical program. The results by grade level are displayed in Table 5-2.

Using these data, Anderson and colleagues arrived at three primary conclusions. First, the percentage of students placed in categorical programs tended to increase from elementary school to secondary school. In elementary schools, approximately one-third of all children were enrolled in categorical programs. By middle school, this figure had increased to 55 percent. At the high school level, this figure had decreased somewhat to 48 percent, perhaps due to the number of students previously enrolled in categorical programs who had dropped out of school.

Table 5-2

**Percentages of Students Enrolled in Categorical Programs**

| Categorical Program | Second Grade | Seventh Grade | Eleventh Grade |
|---|---|---|---|
| EIA Compensatory/ Remedial Program | 15 | 30 | 38 |
| Chapter 1 Program | 10 | 8 | 2 |
| Both EIA Compensatory/ Remedial and Chapter 1 Programs | 4 | 5 | 1 |
| Federal Programs for Handicapped Students | 4 | 5 | 3 |
| State Gifted and Talented Programs | 2 | 8 | 4 |
| Enrolled in No Categorical Program | 66 | 45 | 52 |

Note: Adapted from Anderson and colleagues (1989), page 18.

Second, of the students enrolled in categorical programs, the vast majority were enrolled in either federal- or state-funded compensatory programs. This figure ranged from one-quarter of all students in elementary schools to almost 40 percent of all students in secondary schools. Cumulatively, the best available data suggest that slightly more than one-half of all South Carolina public school students are or have been enrolled in some type of compensatory or remedial program during their school career (Nielsen, 1992; Statler, 1992). In contrast, an average of 4 percent of the students were enrolled in federal programs for the handicapped, while an additional 4 to 5 percent were enrolled in state programs for the gifted and talented.

Third, the burden of funding for compensatory education shifts from the federal government to the state government as students move from elementary to middle to high schools. This conclusion is consistent with the findings of Advanced Technology, Inc. (1983), that most Chapter 1 funds are used at the elementary school level.

This fragmentation of the total school program leads to several predictable results. First, compensatory programs tended to function quite independently and autonomously within the schools; there tended to be a lack of coordination and curriculum integration (Anderson et al., 1989; MGT of America, 1992). Regular and compensatory teachers tended not to communicate on a regular basis in most schools; attitudes toward compensatory programs of regular and compensatory teachers were quite different (with compensatory teachers' attitudes more positive, as expected). Second, school administrators tended to know more about some programs than others. In general, their understanding of the compensatory programs operating in their schools was very limited (Anderson et al., 1989; MGT of America, 1992). This finding was particularly noteworthy given the large proportion of students in most schools enrolled in state- or federal-funded compensatory programs. Third, the effectiveness of the compensatory program tended to be related to the number of other categorical programs operating within the school. For example, Anderson and colleagues (1989) found EIA compensatory programs were less effective in schools that also housed Chapter 1 programs.

## The Instructional Delivery of Compensatory Education

The issue of instructional delivery is composed of two parts. One concerns the model used to deliver instruction (e.g., pull-out, in-class, computer laboratory); the other concerns the staff responsible for delivering the instruction. The studies conducted in South Carolina shed light on both of these issues.

With respect to the delivery model, there is evidence that different models are needed for reading and for mathematics. In reading, the alternate class or replacement model was superior to all others (Anderson et al., 1989; MGT of America, 1992). Implementation of this model requires that students be given compensatory instruction *in lieu* of regular classroom instruction. In mathematics, the floating aide or in-class model was superior to all others (MGT of America, 1992). Implementation of this model requires that instruction be delivered in the regular classroom with both regular classroom teachers and compensatory aides involved in the delivery.

In addition to those delivery models that seem to "work," much is to be learned from those that apparently do not work. The special class or traditional pull-out model was found to be the least effective in one study (Anderson et al., 1989) and was not mentioned at all in another (MGT of America, 1992). Apparently, "double dipping" students is not very effective. While several reasons for this lack of effectiveness can be offered, the reason most consistent with the other data is that the traditional pull-out model contributes to the fragmentation mentioned in the previous section. Implementation of this model virtually requires that students receive instruction from multiple teachers using multiple texts while being given multiple assignments. Furthermore, since two teachers are responsible for student learning "on paper," there is the possibility that no teacher actually assumes responsibility.

With respect to the effectiveness of computer laboratories, the evidence is clearly mixed. Anderson and colleagues (1989) found that computer laboratories were equally likely to be effective or ineffective. Similarly, MGT of America (1992) found that while principals attributed programmatic success to the use of computers, there was no evidence from the site visits that this was indeed the case.

These findings are consistent with the results of previous studies that technology alone has little effect on student learning and effectiveness (Clark, 1983). Rather, the effectiveness of technology depends on the way in which it is used and to what ends. In this regard, MGT of America (1992) suggested, based on their findings, that classroom teachers should be an integral part of computer-assisted instructional strategies.

The second component of instructional delivery is the staffing of the compensatory programs. In South Carolina, as is true nationwide (Anderson and Pellicer, 1990), one-half or more of the staff employed to work with students in compensatory programs are paraprofessionals such as teacher aides (Statler, 1992). While there is nothing inherently wrong with the use of paraprofessionals in compensatory programs, there is strong evidence that those currently employed in South Carolina are minimally qualified and receive no training (Reynolds, 1990). For example, fewer than 20 percent of teacher aides were college graduates. Moreover, fewer than 15 percent of the aides surveyed received any training in the teaching of remedial reading, writing, or mathematics, or in the teaching of low-achieving or underachieving students. Fewer than 6 percent had received training related to tutoring, diagnostic-prescriptive teaching, or the unique characteristics of "at-risk" students. In this regard, principals interviewed in the MGT of America (1992) study suggested that one of the keys to the effectiveness of the EIA compensatory program was "positive intervention with aides/tutors."

Finally, one must question the status or prestige associated with a program staffed largely by noncertified personnel. In this regard, the senior author of this chapter, Lorin Anderson, asked an audience of approximately five hundred educators whether paraprofessionals would be used to teach gifted and talented students. The answer was a resounding "no."

## The Effectiveness of Compensatory Education in South Carolina

The most compelling evidence concerning the effectiveness of compensatory education in South Carolina comes from reports issued by the South Carolina Department of Education (Nielsen, 1991, 1992). In order to examine this evidence properly, we must begin with an examination of who is served in the compensatory programs. According to the most recent evaluation report issued by the South Carolina Department of Education (Nielsen, 1992), approximately 40 percent of all black students and approximately one-sixth of all white students are currently enrolled in state-supported compensatory or remedial programs. In addition, almost three-fifths of the students enrolled in these programs are eligible for free or reduced-price lunches. Unfortunately, neither racial nor socioeconomic status data were presented in the most recent report on Chapter 1 programs issued by the Department (Statler, 1992).

By traditional effectiveness standards (that is, a normal curve equivalent [NCE] gain of 1 or more), the vast majority of compensatory programs are effective. With respect to Chapter 1, for example, Statler (1992) reports that the average gain of Chapter 1 students in reading across the state is approximately 5.1 NCEs, while the average gain of Chapter 1 students in mathematics is approximately 8.3 NCEs. With respect to the EIA compensatory and remedial programs, Nielsen (1992) reports that approximately 10 percent of the schools had gains in reading of less than 1.0 NCE, while only 8.2 percent had gains in mathematics of less than 1.0 NCE.

This apparent effectiveness, however, hides quite compelling evidence of program ineffectiveness. Almost one-third of elementary school students who were enrolled in EIA compensatory or remedial programs for one year were enrolled in these programs for the majority of their elementary school careers (Nielsen, 1992). For secondary school students, this figure is even larger. Almost one-half of the students who were enrolled in EIA compensatory or remedial programs for one year were enrolled in these programs for the majority of their secondary school careers (Nielsen, 1992).

Two other pieces of data question the effectiveness of the EIA compensatory and remedial programs. First, while 99 percent of students who had never been enrolled in the EIA compensatory program passed the South Carolina Exit Examination (SCEE) the first time it was administered, only 42 percent of those students who had participated in the compensatory program *for even one year* did so. To understand the significance of this finding, one must understand that students who do not pass the SCEE do not receive a high school diploma. Thus, the long-term effectiveness of the state-funded compensatory program is clearly called into question. Second, the effectiveness of the EIA compensatory program has decreased over the past two school years (Nielsen, 1992). That is, the average NCE gains have decreased over this time period.

Finally, Anderson and colleagues (1989) identified two factors related to program effectiveness. For elementary school students, the allocation and use of instructional time is positively related to student achievement. Specifically, students at this level appear to benefit if they are disrupted less, have more direct contact with teachers, and have more supervised seatwork. For secondary school students, on the other hand, program effectiveness is related to the difficulty and complexity of the assignments given to the students. In general, assignments given to these students are far less difficult than those given to their noncompensatory peers and far less difficult than compensatory students would need to receive in order to pass the tests that serve as "gatekeepers" to the regular school program and success at subsequent grade levels. Anderson and colleagues (1989) also suggested that while an increase in the difficulty of these assignments may cause an increase in the number of errors made by students, this increase is *positively* related to student achievement.

## ELEMENTS OF SUCCESSFUL COMPENSATORY EDUCATION PROGRAMS

In addition to the descriptive findings from the four major studies, a series of recommendations was offered by the authors of these studies. This section focuses on these recommendations. Specifically, two types of recommendations are included: (1) recommendations supported by the results of multiple studies and (2) recommendations emanating from a single study, if they are considered significant and are not contradicted by the results of another study.

It should be noted that a number of recommendations contained in the original studies are not discussed here because we judged them to be less important to program improvement than those discussed in this section. Furthermore, the 1992 study by Anderson and colleagues did not contain recommendations in the traditional sense but rather concluded with a discussion of "recurring themes" that were common in schools with successful compensatory programs. For purposes of discussion, these recurring themes have been incorporated into this section as if they had been written in the form of recommendations.

Table 5-3 contains twelve recommendations for improving compensatory education in South Carolina. By necessity, some of the recommendations may be worded differently from the way they were worded in the original studies. However, every attempt has been made to retain the essential meaning of each individual recommendation while, at the same time, combining recommendations from multiple studies in the interest of parsimony.

## *Recommendation 1. Meaningful and appropriate goals must be at the heart of an effective compensatory program.*

Of the four studies reviewed in this chapter, only the 1992 study by Anderson and colleagues addressed directly the relationship of goals to program effectiveness. The study found that in schools with highly successful compensatory programs, about half the time the goals for the compensatory education programs were set for the schools by the district administration. At the same time, however, in every instance additional program goals were set at the school level. These school-level goals typically were tied to improving the self-esteem of compensatory students coupled with improving students', staff's, and parents' attitudes toward the program. Regardless of their origin, program goals were well articulated and were understood and widely endorsed by all those involved in the implementation of successful compensatory programs.

Interestingly, the development of basic skills was not a goal frequently expressed by teachers and administrators working in successful compensatory programs. Rather, the central goal for those working in successful compensatory programs was to enable students to move back into the academic mainstream and to function academically and affectively at levels that ensured they would remain there. Perhaps as a consequence, teachers in

Table 5-3
**Recommendations Resulting from Major Studies of
Compensatory Education in South Carolina**

| | Anderson et al., 1989 | Neilsen, 1991, 1992 | MGT of America, 1992 | Anderson et al., 1992 |
|---|---|---|---|---|
| 1. Appropriate goals must be at the heart of an effective compensatory program. | | | | X |
| 2. The use of the normal curve equivalent (NCE) as a standard for program gain should not be the only criterion used in measuring program success. | X | X | X | X |
| 3. If normal curve equivalent gains are to be used as a measure of program success, then a higher standard than 1.0 NCE gain on average should be established. | | X | X | |
| 4. All students who qualify for services should be served based on level of need. | | | | X |
| 5. Strong leadership is essential to program success. | X | | X | X |
| 6. The most qualified instructional personnel should be assigned to the students with the greatest level of need. | | | X | X |
| 7. Personnel involved with the education of compensatory students should be provided ongoing training for improving the effectiveness of compensatory programs. | X | | X | X |
| 8. Every effort must be | | | | |

Table 5-3
**continued**

| Recommendations | Anderson et al., 1989 | Neilsen, 1991, 1992 | MGT of America, 1992 | Anderson et al., 1992 |
|---|---|---|---|---|
| made to instruct and test students on grade level to prevent them from falling further behind grade-level peers. | X | X | X | X |
| 9. Alternative methods of delivering program services to compensatory students should be identified and used. Barriers to program design flexibility on the part of school districts should be reduced or eliminated so far as possible. | X | X | | X |
| 10. Compensatory programs must be better integrated within the total school program. | X | | X | X |
| 11. Ways must be found to actively involve compensatory students in the learning process. | | | X | X |
| 12. Additional technical assistance in organizing and administering compensatory programs should be made available to all school districts through the Department of Education. | X | | X | |

successful programs generally set goals for themselves that were futuristic; that is, these goals referred to what their students would be *able to do* at certain points in time. Teachers in successful programs also set internal goals for themselves. In this way, they were able to maintain the level of effort required to ensure their students were successful. The results of the study by Anderson and colleagues (1992) make it clear that the establishment of meaningful goals is a driving force in forging successful compensatory programs.

*Recommendation 2. To the extent that normal curve equivalent (NCE) gains are used as a measure of program effectiveness, a standard higher than 1.0 NCE gain on average should be established.*

This recommendation is supported by two of the four studies. Interestingly, neither of the studies by Anderson and colleagues (1989, 1992) addressed NCE gains as measures of program success. In their 1992 study, Anderson and colleagues found that successful schools tended to ignore average NCE gains in favor of setting standards for program success that were directly tied to individual students (e.g., "every child will score at or above the 50th percentile"). It should be emphasized that successful compensatory programs in this study had no tolerance for student failure. The expectation was that every child could and would succeed.

MGT of America (1992) recommended an increase in the mean NCE gain used to judge program success from its present level of 1.0 to 3.0 by 1996. The Nielsen (1991, 1992) study, although recommending a raise in the standard used to determine program success, did not specify the level to which the standard should be raised.

*Recommendation 3. The use of the normal curve equivalent (NCE) as a standard for program effectiveness should not be the only criterion used in evaluating program success.*

All four studies supported this recommendation. Although NCE gains provide some indication of how students are progressing as a group academically, they provide no information that can be used to judge the achievement of other program goals such as growth in student self-esteem, the improvement of student attitudes about school, and increased parental and community involvement in children's education. What is needed in addition to measures of academic achievement is a more holistic assessment of compensatory programs including examinations of program goals in relationship to a school's culture, the nature of the academic requirements of the program, and a detailed analysis of the actual classroom teaching.

*Recommendation 4. All students who qualify for services should be provided services, although the extent of services provided should depend on the level of a student's need for the services.*

This recommendation is derived primarily from the 1992 study by Anderson and colleagues, which was the only study of the four to address this issue. In this particular study, all of the successful schools studied made every effort to serve as many students as possible. To accomplish this goal, a combination of models was used in a comprehensive schoolwide approach. For example, one school used an alternate class model to provide services to those students with the greatest need, a computer laboratory model to provide services to a second group of students with a more moderate level of need, and an after-school tutorial program for a third group of students who fell just below the standard on the state basic skills tests.

While on the surface it might appear that program effectiveness could be increased by concentrating all available resources on the most needy group of students, this may not be the case. Perhaps serving as many students as possible alters the school culture in such a way that helping each student succeed to his or her maximum potential becomes the predominant value. In such schools, the overall achievement levels reached by students in compensatory programs may be significantly enhanced.

*Recommendation 5. Strong building-level leadership is essential to program success.*

Three of the studies (Anderson et al., 1989; Anderson et al., 1992; MGT of America, 1992) supported this recommendation. Building-level leadership in schools with unusually effective programs shared at least two important characteristics. First, a strong principal was present who was viewed by the faculty as an instructional leader. Principals in these schools were viewed by their faculty as committed, competent, and hard working. They spent much of their time circulating throughout the school interacting with students and staff members while observing in classrooms. They encouraged teachers to work hard to meet the needs of the students who came to the school not ready to learn because of circumstances beyond their control. Therefore, in "thought, word, and deed," these principals were strong advocates of children enrolled in compensatory programs.

Second, in these successful programs, leadership was shared.

Principals felt secure is sharing power with their faculty through elaborate committee structures and advisory groups, and by relinquishing authority to lead teachers or faculty team leaders. While leadership was shared in different ways in different schools, the result was always that teachers and other staff members felt and exercised a responsibility for the well-being of the school, its programs, and its students.

### Recommendation 6. The most qualified instructional personnel should be assigned to the students with the greatest need.

The studies by MGT of America (1992) and Anderson and colleagues (1992) support this recommendation while the 1989 study by Anderson and colleagues alludes to the problems encountered when assigning less qualified instructional personnel to deal with children with serious learning problems. If less qualified personnel are assigned to these programs, sufficient training should be provided to them so that they are able to deal effectively with these students.

### Recommendation 7. All personnel involved in the education of compensatory students should be provided with ongoing training.

With the exception of the Nielsen (1991, 1992) study, all other studies support this recommendation. Children enrolled in compensatory programs have special needs that must be met if they are to be able to achieve the primary goal of compensatory education; most notably, these children need to be able to overcome the educational and economic disabilities that keep them from being able to perform successfully in the academic mainstream. Furthermore, these needs change over time.

Many, if not most, principals, teachers, and other staff members employed in schools today have not been trained specifically to understand or meet the needs of compensatory students. In fact, they are far more likely to be aware of the problems faced by special education students than by compensatory students.

Both school districts and state education authorities must assume increased responsibility for providing support to those who provide instruction to compensatory students. This support may be in the form of information concerning the strengths and weaknesses of these students or staff development programs aimed at providing the knowledge and skills professional educators require to effectively meet the needs of compensatory students.

*Recommendation 8. Every effort must be made to instruct and test students on grade level to prevent them from falling further behind their grade-level peers.*

This recommendation is unanimously endorsed by all four studies. For too long, it has been common practice in compensatory programs to instruct students at the level at which they appear to be functioning, rather than at the grade level where they are placed. When these students are administered standardized tests, however, they are tested on grade level. As a consequence, while students may be successful in their compensatory programs (i.e., they may earn passing or even superior marks), they ultimately fail to achieve scores on standardized tests that are high enough to enable them to exit the programs and return to and succeed in the academic mainstream.

When students who enter compensatory programs are functioning below grade level academically, the majority of instruction provided to such students must be on grade level. Any below-grade-level instruction that is given to these students must be directly related to on-grade-level instruction and presented at as rapid a pace as possible. If, at the end of a school year, students are having difficulty meeting the promotion standards, the placement of these students in multiage classes or bridging/transition classes should be favored over retaining students at the same grade level.

*Recommendation 9. Alternative methods of delivering program services to compensatory students should be identified and used. Barriers to flexibility in program design on the part of school districts should be reduced or eliminated so far as possible.*

This recommendation was supported in three of the four studies, the MGT of America (1992) study being the exception. The MGT researchers apparently felt that local school districts had both sufficient flexibility and the wherewithal to design programs to best meet the needs of compensatory students.

The other three studies emphasized the importance of looking at delivery systems that, while not currently used to a great extent, would provide services to students that were more effective than the traditional models that predominate both federal- and state-funded compensatory programs in South Carolina. It may be wise, for example, to provide the most needy students with before- or after-school programs or programs that take place during the summer to provide them with the additional time they need in order to catch up with their grade-level peers.

### Recommendation 10. Compensatory programs must be more completely integrated within the total school program.

This recommendation appears in all studies except the Nielsen study, which relied on achievement data only. Successful compensatory education programs cannot exist within a vacuum. In practice, the effectiveness of compensatory programs must be judged in relation to the effectiveness of all other programs operating in a school. In a state where the majority of students receive some type of compensatory education during their school careers, it seems unreasonable to assume that a school can be effective if the compensatory education program operating in the school is not.

As was shown in an earlier section of this chapter, however, the proliferation of educational legislation within the state has resulted in a fragmentation of the total educational programming in schools. There is little communication, sharing of resources, or agreement on either the academic goals or operating procedures among those given the responsibility for the success of the individual programs within a particular school.

Barriers to communication must be identified and removed. Teachers, principals, other staff members, and parents must talk about the needs of children and how those needs can best be met through effectively using all resources in the school, not just those earmarked for special populations. Important questions must be asked and the answers to these questions must be heard.

### Recommendation 11. Ways must be found to actively involve compensatory students in the learning process.

The MGT of America (1992) and the Anderson and colleagues (1992) studies lend empirical support to this recommendation. Active involvement of students in their own learning has been repeatedly shown to be a prerequisite to effective learning. Students cannot learn well unless they are totally involved in the learning process. As a consequence, effective teaching is notably student-centered. Student-centered teaching requires frequent interactions between students and teachers, a shared responsibility for student learning, and concern by teachers that students actually do learn what they are expected to learn. Student-centered teaching precludes a reliance on teacher talk, worksheets and other "drill and practice" exercises, and students working in isolation from the teacher and their classmates.

In Anderson and colleagues' study (1992), teachers in schools with successful compensatory programs knew their students well and were able to assess their individual strengths and weaknesses. They knew what would work with individual children and what would not. When their students talked (which was frequently), teachers listened attentively. The emphasis was on teaching strategies that kept children "on task" and involved in learning the entire time they were in a teacher's class. Very little seatwork of the "fill-in-the-blank" variety was noted. On the contrary, there was a great deal of discussion and frequent exchanges of opinion. Children were challenged to think, consider, and reconsider. This kind of active involvement in learning appears to be central to the successful learning of compensatory students.

*Recommendation 12. Additional technical assistance in organizing and administering compensatory programs should be made available to all school districts.*

Both the Anderson and colleagues (1989) and the MGT of America (1992) studies drew attention to the need for technical assistance to school districts attempting to meet the needs of compensatory students. While the South Carolina Department of Education appears to be the best equipped to meet this need, there are other potential sources of assistance available.

The University of South Carolina in collaboration with the Southeastern Vision for Education (SERVE) in Greensboro, North Carolina, is now in the third year of a research and development project designed to provide assistance to schools. Furthermore, a variety of programs have been developed to help schools meet the needs of these students. Examples include Success for All (Slavin et al., 1990), Jostens Learning (undated), Higher Order Thinking Skills (Pogrow, 1990), Reading Recovery (Pinnell, 1990), and Family Math/EQUALS (Kreinberg, 1989).

## IMPROVING THE QUALITY OF COMPENSATORY EDUCATION

There are several difficulties inherent in translating recommendations from research studies into practice. Two of the most problematic are as follows. First, recommendations from researchers traditionally have a "grocery list" quality to them. That is, the recommendations are simply listed with no coherent framework provided by the researchers so that practitioners can understand them. Second, recommendations typically focus on what should be done, with little help provided to practitioners as to how to do it.

In an attempt to overcome these difficulties, the South Carolina Educational Policy Center (1992) has developed both a conceptual framework for improving compensatory education and a process for using the framework in working with schools. In this closing section, we shall describe the framework and discuss the process.

## The Conceptual Framework

As can be seen in Figure 5-1, the conceptual framework contains four interrelated components: program effectiveness, school culture, curriculum, and teaching. Three critical issues are defined in each of these components. We believe that all twelve critical issues must be addressed in a consistent manner if improvement efforts are to succeed.

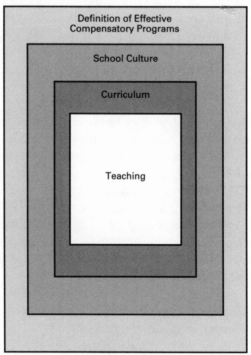

Figure 5-1
**Conceptual Framework for Improving Compensatory Education**

*Program effectiveness* refers to the criteria and standards that are used to judge the success of the program for those students the program is intended to serve. As a consequence, the following three critical issues are associated with program effectiveness.

1. *Goals.* What are the goals of the program?
2. *Standards.* What standards are used to judge the accomplishment of the program goals?
3. *Students served.* Which students are intended to be served by the program?

*School culture* refers to the priorities and status assigned to the program within the school. For example, the program may be seen as an integral part of the school or as a dumping ground for undesirable students. Similarly, the primary value of the program may be the additional money it brings into the school or the opportunity to truly serve those students in need. The following three critical issues are associated with school culture.

1. *Building-level leadership.* Who within the school provides leadership for the program?
2. *Staffing.* Who is responsible for providing quality instruction to the students in the program?
3. *Image.* How is the program perceived by parents and others outside the school?

*Curriculum* can be and has been defined in many different ways. Traditionally, curriculum encompasses goals and objectives, scope and sequence, textbooks and other instructional materials, and suggested learning experiences. In combination, these elements define "curriculum-on-paper." In contrast, the model focuses more on what may be termed "curriculum-in-action." While the intended curriculum is interesting, we believe that it is the curriculum experienced by students that directly affects their learning. Thus, the following three critical issues are associated with our definition of curriculum.

1. *Academic work.* What academic work (often referred to as assignments) is given to students?
2. *Opportunity to learn.* What opportunities are students given to acquire the knowledge, skills, and attitudes that are important for their future success?

3. *Curriculum integration.* What connections are made for students within the curriculum (e.g., connections across subject matters, connections across grade levels, connections across the various programs operating within the school)?

*Teaching* can be defined either as what teachers do or as the impact on students of what teachers do. As in the case of curriculum, we prefer the latter definition; thus the following three critical issues are associated with teaching.

1. *Student involvement.* What is being done or can be done to encourage or support the active involvement of students in the classroom and in their own learning?
2. *Student success.* What is being done or can be done to facilitate initial and sustained success for students in their efforts to learn?
3. *Effective teaching strategies.* What repertoire of teaching strategies do teachers possess or need to possess to be successful in reaching large numbers of students?

The conceptual framework shown in Figure 5-1 can be visualized as a series of increasingly smaller rectangles. This visual representation is intentional. We believe that the critical issues related to the components included as larger rectangles must be addressed and resolved before those associated with the components included as smaller rectangles. Stated somewhat differently, if the critical issues associated with the larger rectangles are problematic, then efforts to resolve those issues associated with the smaller rectangles are likely to be futile.

If, for example, program goals are not clear or if the standards for judging program effectiveness are weak, attempts to improve the school culture, the curriculum, or teaching will be in vain. Similarly, if the curriculum contains academic work that is far too easy or far too difficult for students or if students are denied the opportunity to learn what they need to learn in order to succeed in the future (both curriculum issues), then attempts to improve teaching will not pay off in any notable changes in student achievement and, hence, program effectiveness.

Finally, it is important to note that the conceptual framework includes a series of interrelated questions. Based on our years of research and practical experience, it appears that there are no universal answers to these questions. Stated somewhat differently, the answers to these questions appear to be context-specific. Since this is the case, it was necessary to develop a process that enabled practitioners to determine the answers to these questions and implement changes suggested by these answers to the best of their ability.

## The Implementation Process

The implementation process includes twelve steps, summarized in Table 5-4. Several comments on the implementation process are in order.

First, while all administrators, teachers, and other staff are kept informed (Steps 1 and 11), a smaller "working group" is directly involved in the implementation process. Second, implementation is clearly conceptualized as a rational process. For each critical issue, a set of options is identified. The advantages and disadvantages of each option are considered. Based on this consideration, a rational choice is expected. Third, many changes require outside assistance. Securing the necessary assistance is a responsibility of the change agent. Fourth, for change to occur, someone within the school (either an individual or a team) must be assigned and assume responsibility for overseeing the change. Finally, to ensure that changes within the conceptual framework are timely and consistent, a timetable must be established and followed to the extent possible.

## CONCLUSION

Despite the massive legislative initiatives that have been enacted since 1977, the quality of education provided to compensatory students in South Carolina leaves much to be desired. The plethora of categorical programs has led to the fragmentation of the total school program, concerns for appropriate delivery models and instructional staffing, and questions of program effectiveness. At the same time, the results of four systematic studies of compensatory education in the state have produced a series of reasonable recommendations. In order to implement these recommendations, the South Carolina Educational Policy Center in collaboration with the Southeast Regional Vision for Education (SERVE) Laboratory has developed a conceptual framework and related implementation process. The conceptual framework includes the critical

Table 5-4
## A Summary of the Implementation Process

1. Provide an overview of the conceptual framework and implementation process to all administrators, teachers, and other staff members.
2. Select a Program Improvement Team (PIT) of approximately 8 to 16 members. The PIT should consist of administrators, counselors, teachers (both regular and categorical), and paraprofessionals. The selection should occur through some combination of volunteerism, election, and appointment.
3. Engage members of the PIT in a series of team-building exercises. We have found that many administrators and teachers are not accustomed to working together in groups and making consensual decision. These exercises enable them to do so.
4. Have members of the PIT explore the options available for each of the twelve critical issues and the advantages and disadvantages associated with each option. The methods learned during the team-building exercises should be used to accomplish this task as well the next several tasks.
5. Based on the relative weights of the advantages and disadvantages for each option, have members of the PIT identify the most desirable option(s) for each critical issue.
6. Have members of the PIT explore the current status of each critical issue in their school. That is, what goals currently are in place? What academic work is currently given to students?
7. Have members of the PIT compare the most desirable option(s) with the current status for each critical issue and determine the changes that need to be made in order to substantially improve program quality. In general, two types of changes are needed. In the vernacular, the first change involves doing things not currently being done. The second change involves doing the same things better than they are currently being done.
8. Have members of the PIT examine the entire set of changes and "non-changes" in light of two criteria: *internal consistency* (that is, the extent to which all decisions fit together in a cohesive whole) and *financial feasibility* (that is, the extent to which the changes are affordable). If problems exist, the PIT must make the changes necessary to meet both criteria.
9. Have members of the PIT determine the assistance they would need to implement the suggested changes.
10. Have members of the PIT determine a person or persons who are responsible for ensuring that the suggested changes for each of the four components of the conceptual framework are implemented. One person or team should be assigned to each component. This person or these team members can be administrators or teachers in the school who are not members of the PIT. Also, some mechanism by which they report to the PIT should be established.
11. Report to all administrators, teachers, and other staff concerning the plans for program improvement (including the areas that will remain

Table 5-4
**continued**

---

the same, the areas in which changes are needed, a rationale for both
stability and change, and the identification of those who are
responsible for overseeing the changes) and secure the endorsement of
all involved in program improvement.
12. Once endorsement has been received, develop a timeline for
implementation of the school improvement efforts, which includes the
needed resources, the responsible parties, and the beginning and
ending date for each activity.

---

issues that must be addressed for substantial program improvement to take place, while the implementation process relies on administrators and teachers to make the decisions that will result in substantial program improvement. This combination of substance and process is needed if we are to learn from the mistakes of our past and create a truly productive learning environment for economically disadvantaged, low-achieving students.

## REFERENCES

Advanced Technology, Inc. *Local Operation of Title 1, ESEA 1976–1982: A Resource Book.* Reston, Va.: Advanced Technology, 1983.

Anderson, Lorin W.; Cook, Nancy; Pellicer, Leonard; Sears, James; and Spradling, Richard. *A Study of EIA-funded Remedial and Compensatory Programs in South Carolina.* Columbia: South Carolina Educational Policy Center, 1989.

Anderson, Lorin W., and Pellicer, Leonard O. "Synthesis of Research on Compensatory and Remedial Education," *Educational Leadership* 48, no. 1 (1990): 10–16.

Anderson, Lorin W.; Sears, James; Pellicer, Leonard; Riddle, Melba; Gardner, Carol; and Harwell, Diane. *A Study of Characteristics and Qualities of "High-flying" Compensatory Programs in South Carolina as Examined through the Framework of the SERVE Model for Effective Compensatory Programs.* Columbia: South Carolina Educational Policy Center, 1992.

Clark, Richard E. "Reconsidering Research on Learning from Media," *Review of Educational Research* 53 (1983): 445–459.

Jostens Learning. *Partnership for Success.* Torrance, Calif.: Jostens Learning, n.d.

Kennedy, Mary M.; Birman, Beatrice F.; and Demaline, Randy E. *The Effectiveness of Chapter 1 Services.* Washington, D.C.: Office of Educational Research and Improvement, U.S. Department of Education, 1987.

Kreinberg, Nancy. "Needed: An Agenda for Equity in Mathematics Education," *Peabody Journal of Education* 66 (1989): 127–146.

Lee, Ginny V.; Rowan, Brian; Allington, Richard A.; Anderson, Lorin W.; Bossert, Steven T.; Harnischfeger, Annegret; and Stallings, Jane A. *The Manage-*

*ment and Delivery of Instructional Services to Chapter 1 Students: Case Studies of Twelve Schools.* San Francisco, Calif.: Far West Laboratory for Educational Research and Development, 1986.

MGT of America. *An Evaluation of the Compensatory and Remedial Programs for the Educational Improvement Act Select Committee of the South Carolina General Assembly.* Tallahassee, Fla.: MGT of America, 1992.

Nielsen, Barbara S. *Evaluation of the 1989–90 EIA Remedial and Compensatory Program.* Columbia: South Carolina Department of Education, 1991.

Nielsen, Barbara S. *Evaluation of the 1990–91 EIA Remedial and Compensatory Program.* Columbia: South Carolina Department of Education, 1992.

Pinnell, Ginella S. "Success for Low Achievers through Reading Recovery," *Educational Leadership* 48, no. 1 (1990): 17–21.

Pogrow, Stanley. "Challenging At-risk Students: Findings from the HOTS Program," *Phi Delta Kappan* 71 (1990): 389–397.

Reynolds, Beth P. "A Comparative Study of the Relationship of Teacher Aides' Qualifications, Performance Responsibilities, and Interactions with Teachers to the Effectiveness of Selected Remedial and Compensatory Programs in South Carolina." Doctoral dissertation, University of South Carolina, Columbia, S.C., 1990.

Rowan, Brian, and Guthrie, Larry F. "The Quality of Chapter 1 Instruction: Results from a Study of Twenty-four Schools." In *Effective Programs for Students at Risk.* Boston: Allyn and Bacon, 1989.

Slavin, Robert E.; Madden, Nancy A.; Karweit, Nancy L.; Livermon, Barbara; and Dolan, Larry. "Success for All: First-year Outcomes of a Comprehensive Plan for Reforming Urban Education," *American Educational Research Journal* 27 (1990): 255–278.

South Carolina Department of Education. *1992–93 Funding Manual.* Columbia: South Carolina Department of Education, 1992.

South Carolina Educational Policy Center. *A Guide to Decision Making for the Improvement of Compensatory Education Programs.* Columbia: South Carolina Educational Policy Center, 1992.

Statler, Charles R. *ESEA, Chapter 1 Status Report, FY 1991.* Columbia: South Carolina Department of Education, 1992.

# 6

# Programs for Children with Limited English Proficiency: An Assessment of Present Practices

## *Aquiles Iglesias*

For many individuals, the function of bilingual education programs in the United States is to provide limited-English-proficient (LEP) students with the English skills necessary to assimilate into the mainstream of our society and to advance academically and socially. For others, bilingual education is seen as a mechanism that perpetuates cultural and linguistic differences that challenge a view of our country as a melting pot and creates social and political tension among groups. To a third group, bilingual education is a mechanism that empowers a large segment of our society and uses one of our country's greatest resources, linguistic diversity. These divergent views on the function of bilingual education, based on sociopolitical rather than

The research reported herein is supported in part by the Temple University Center for Research in Human Development and Education (CRHDE) and in part by the Office of Education Research and Improvement (OERI) of the U.S. Department of Education through a grant to the National Center on Education in the Inner Cities (CEIC) at Temple University. The opinions expressed do not necessarily reflect the position of the supporting agencies and no official endorsement should be inferred.

pedagogical reasons or research findings, undergird the controversy surrounding the programs funded under the Bilingual Education Act. Not surprisingly, the same sociopolitical forces that have guided the views of bilingual education have greatly influenced the type of research that has been conducted and the interpretation of findings.

How can a federal program serving such a small number of eligible students, with expenditures that are almost insignificant compared to other categorical programs, be surrounded by so much controversy? How can the integrity of the research in this area have been so greatly compromised by sociopolitical forces? Although no simple answers exist, our understanding of the value and efficacy of these programs will doubtless continue to be guided by sociopolitical forces rather than research, unless the facts and issues surrounding these programs are openly discussed. This chapter will contribute to the discussion by providing a historical perspective of bilingual education, a description of present practices, and the implications of present research findings for policy and practice.

## HISTORICAL PERSPECTIVE

Bilingualism and bilingual education are not new in the United States. From the colonization period until the nineteenth century, diverse linguistic groups coexisted. Although rarely valued or supported by our forefathers (Castellanos, 1983), the use of languages other than English was recognized by existing governments through various channels, including the publication of legal documents in a variety of languages. During the 1700s and 1800s, especially during the early 1800s, non-English and bilingual schools were accepted and common (Fishman, 1966; Kloss, 1971).

Fueled by the large migration of non-English-speaking, non-Northern Europeans during the late 1800s and early 1900s, exclusionary legislation eventually began to appear at the federal, state, and local levels. Bilingual programs were challenged during this period, as was the teaching of any language other than English. The anti-German sentiment that swept the country during World War I made speaking English the litmus test of national loyalty. Several states passed laws that forbade the teaching of any language other than English to children below high-school level (Crawford, 1989). Only a few isolated bilingual programs survived during this period of xenophobia. From the 1920s until the 1960s, bilingual education virtually disappeared from the United States.

Important changes were occurring simultaneously in the flow of new immigrants. The federal government established highly restrictive quotas designed to curb the influx of immigrant groups not already here in large numbers, particularly groups other than Anglo-Saxon and Nordic. These policies placed restrictions on immigrant groups that were considered unassimilable due to their language or culture.

The resurgence of bilingual education programs in the last thirty years evolved in response to the needs of an ever-increasing non-English-speaking population in the United States, the majority of which were recent immigrants. A national climate for greater tolerance of ethnic and linguistic minorities, coupled with a healthy economy that dampened opposition to immigration, provided the impetus for legislation, judicial decisions, and administrative regulations that redefined the federal government's role in the education of LEP students. Economic downturn and the government's more conservative agenda during the Reagan and Bush years further redefined existing programs. It is within this sociopolitical context that the evolution of bilingual education, in its present form, must be viewed.

## The New Immigrants

Historically, immigrant groups that have entered the United States have been absorbed in its society. For some groups, especially those that came to this country during the mid-nineteenth century, the process was relatively easy, since they were predominantly English speakers who were ethnically similar to the existing population. For others, especially those who migrated during the early 1900s, the process was somewhat more difficult due to differences in language and religion. Unlike the most recent immigrants, these two groups were able to succeed due to the existence of a manufacturing and agricultural base that could absorb uneducated and unskilled labor.

The latest major migration into this country began in the 1960s as a result of the Immigration and Naturalization Act of 1965 and a series of refugee acts passed by Congress during the last three decades. The newest immigrants, estimated to exceed 15 million, comprise three distinct groups: legal immigrants, refugees, and undocumented immigrants. The present pattern has diverged from a European orientation to a Third World one, with most immigrants arriving from Asia (34 percent) and Latin America (34 percent). The majority of these new immigrants are concentrated in ten states, with the greatest concentration in California (28 percent), New York (16 percent), Texas (9 percent), Florida (8 percent), Illinois (6 percent), and New Jersey (4 percent). One unique characteristic of this group, in addition to their non-European background, is their youth. Muller and Espenshade (1985) estimate that 60 percent of the new immigrants are between sixteen and forty-four years of age, the prime working and childbearing years. The path to social and economic integration into American society has been more difficult for this group of immigrants. Changes in the labor market have radically affected the available employment options, and individuals who are less likely to speak English are as a group disproportionately experiencing difficulty finding work.

The relatively young age and high fertility rate of the immigrant population is reflected in the number of LEP children enrolled in U.S. schools. In 1991, 6 percent of the public and private school population had a language background other than English, an increase of 14.3 percent from the 1989–90 figure. State and locally funded programs serve 1.6 million LEP students, while 1.7 million children are enrolled in federally funded programs. The bulk of the support for the education of LEP students stems from the Bilingual Education Act (Title VII of the 1968 Elementary and Secondary Education Act), but other laws also authorize federal programs to support bilingual education activity. Federal programs that provide language support for LEP students include Chapter I (Local Education Agency and Migrant Education Program), Indian Education, Emergency Immigrant Education, Bilingual Vocational Training, Adult Education, Special Education, and Head Start. Approximately 15 percent of the LEP population, or 300,000 students, are served by the Bilingual Education Act. Chapter I programs serve more LEP students than do Title VII programs, while the Emergency Immigrant Education programs serve approximately the same number of students as are served under Title VII.

## The Resurgence of Bilingual Education

The sudden influx of Cuban refugees into the Miami area in the 1960s was the impetus for a major revival of bilingual education in the United States. With support from the Ford Foundation, the Dade County School District initiated a dual-language program in which subjects were taught in the students' native language $(L_1)$ during half of the school day, and during the rest of the day the concepts were reintroduced in the students' second language $(L_2)$. Although innovative by U.S. standards, this form of education had been practiced for years in Cuba's bilingual schools. As a result of parents' familiarity with the program, the dual-language programs received highly favorable acceptance and support from the Cuban community. Seven years after this highly successful program was initiated, the first major bilingual education bill to be introduced in Congress, the Bilingual Education Act, was signed by President Johnson.

This Act, Title VII of the Elementary and Secondary Act of 1968, provided financial assistance to local educational agencies (LEAs) interested in implementing innovative programs designed to meet the special needs of children of limited English-speaking ability. LEAs wishing to help students with limited English proficiency were encouraged to apply for start-up funds. The method to be used for improving the education of LEP students was not specifically stated in this vague piece of legislation in order to satisfy those who saw the use of the child's mother tongue as a bridge to the acquisition of English and those who were interested in maintaining two languages. The initial funding of $7.5 million was not appropriated until 1970. The Act was reauthorized or continued in 1974, 1984, and 1988. Its current reauthorization expired on September 30, 1993, and will be considered, along with other sections of the Elementary and Secondary Education Act, in the 103rd Congress in 1994.

Since the inception of the Bilingual Education Act, planners have disagreed about the main goals and design of the program, issues that had been left vague in order to "permit both the ethnocentrists and cultural pluralists to see what they wanted in the Act" (Gaarder, 1970, p. 164). The first seventy-six programs funded were, according to Gaarder, assimilationist in focus, with little time and resources applied to the maintenance of the children's first language $(L_1)$. To a large extent, this early assimilationist perspective, which focused on language shift, was due to a lack of theoretical sophistication, a research base, practical know-how, and qualified personnel.

The 1974 Amendments to the Bilingual Education Act reflected a need for greater accountability and training of personnel. The Commissioner of Education was required to provide Congress with an assessment of the state of bilingual education, including educational needs of LEP students, activities, and costs. Funds were also earmarked for state education agencies, local education agencies, and institutions of higher education to receive training grants. Funds were also provided for the establishment of a network of centers focusing on assessment, dissemination, material development, and training.

The conservative social agenda of the 1980s led to demands for local flexibility that were reflected in the reauthorization of the Bilingual Education Act in the Education Amendments of 1984. Two new provisions were the inclusion of alternative instructional programs (4 to 10 percent of the overall funds), and a parental notification and consent provision. The alternative program provision allocated funds for LEAs to design programs in which the children's native language was not used in instruction. This provision was intended for LEAs with only a small number of LEP students with a common language, for those lacking qualified bilingual education personnel, and for those that had encountered difficulty establishing a bilingual education program. The amendments also required LEAs to inform parents or guardians of the LEP students of the reasons why their children were designated as needing bilingual education services. Further, parents had to be informed of the availability of alternative instructional programs, and had the right to decline enrollment of their children in bilingual or alternative programs and thus keep their children in mainstream classrooms. During the conservative 1980s, fiscal support for bilingual education dropped 47 percent, as compared to an overall drop of 8 percent for all educational programs (Lyons, 1990).

## Judicial and Executive Decisions

Prior to 1974, the judicial system's involvement in the education of LEP students was limited to voiding state laws that banned the use of languages other than English in school (Kloss, 1971). In the landmark case of *Lau v. Nichols* (1974), the Supreme Court decided unanimously that school districts must take affirmative actions to rectify the language deficiency that prevented language-minority students from effective participation in the educational program offered by the school district. This class-action suit was brought on behalf of non-English-speaking students of Chinese ancestry who alleged discrimination on the grounds that they were receiving instruction in English only, a language they could not understand. The plaintiffs claimed that the absence of any program to meet their needs violated the equal protection clause of the Fourteenth Amendment to the Constitution (an issue not dealt with by the Supreme Court) and Title VI of the 1964 Civil Rights Act: "No person in the United States shall, on the ground of race, color, or national origin, be excluded from participating in, be denied the benefits of, or be subject to discrimination under any program or activity receiving Federal financial assistance" (42 U.S.C 2000 d, 1970). In the decision, Justice William O. Douglas remarked, "There is no equality of treatment merely by providing students with the same facilities, textbooks, teachers, and curriculum; for students who do not understand English are effectively foreclosed from any meaningful education." Consistent with the courts' reluctance to interfere with the way local school districts implement educational policies, no specific remedies were provided. Although it did not expressly endorse bilingual education, the *Lau* decision supported the notion that federally funded schools have an obligation to eliminate language barriers, which effectively exclude LEP children from meaningful participation in instructional programs.

In the summer of 1975, the Department of Health, Education and Welfare's Office of Education and the Office of Civil Rights (OCR) jointly issued policy guidelines for school district compliance with Title VI of the Civil Rights Act. These guidelines, widely circulated but never published in the Federal Register, were referred to as the *Lau* Remedies. School districts with twenty or more students of the same language group who had been identified as having a primary or home language other than English were asked to develop compliance plans and submit them to OCR. Districts that did not meet the criteria of twenty or more language-minority students were still required to take affirmative steps, although they were not expected to be as comprehensive as those of the other districts. The *Lau* Remedies did not mandate a specific language of instruction, but rather conferred significant latitude to state and local educational agencies. The absence of federally mandated identification procedures for participation in

Title VI left the field open to state or local districts' definitions. Some states have laws, policies, regulations, or court decisions that establish a common statewide procedure to identify LEP students. Some states mandate or recommend a range of specific options on objective or subjective measures, while others have no policy and leave the decision to LEAs.

The *Lau* Remedies, never officially published and thus carrying no official weight, were challenged in the courts in 1978. In a court-approved consent decree, HEW agreed to replace the *Lau* Remedies with published compliance guidelines. In 1980, the newly created Department of Education published in the Federal Register a Notice of Proposed Rulemaking (NPRM) (45 Fed. Reg. 52,052) that provided objective specification for identification of language-minority students, assessment of English proficiency, provision of proper instructional services, and criteria governing exit from special instructional programs. Widespread criticism of the new standards forced then-Secretary of Education Shirley Hufstedler to suspend finalization of the standards. Her successor, Terrell Bell, formally withdrew the NPRM without issuing new standards. This withdrawal was interpreted by many as the elimination of both the legal mandate for bilingual education and federal support for bilingual education (Seidner and Seidner, 1982).

The *Lau* decision spurred several lawsuits (*Serna v. Portales Municipal Schools* [1974], *Aspira Inc. of New York Inc. v. Board of Education of the City of New York* [1974], *Rios v. Read* [1978], *United States v. Texas Education Agency* [1981]) that challenged the educational and legal adequacy of programs provided by some local school districts. The *Serna v. Portales* and *Aspira v. Board of Education* lawsuits resulted in court-mandated bilingual programs. In *Rios v. Read*, the courts argued that the mere existence of a program did not guarantee compliance, that quantity without documentation of quality was meaningless. The court's decision in the *United States v. Texas Education Agency* noted that a district's budget constraints were no excuse for failure to provide bilingual education.

Compliance with the *Lau* decision presently falls under the Equal Education Opportunity Act (EEOA), which was adopted by Congress just weeks after the Supreme Court's decision in the *Lau* case. EEOA mandated that educational agencies must take appropriate action to overcome language barriers that impede equal participation by the students in its instructional programs. Neither Congress nor the EEOA define what is meant by "appropriate action." This ambiguity led the courts, in *Castaneda v. Pickard* (1981), to develop a framework for determining whether or not an educational agency is fulfilling its EEOA responsibilities to language-minority students. The three-part test to measure compliance required that (1) the program be based on a sound educational theory or at least a legitimate educational strategy; (2) resources and personnel be available to transform theory into practice; and (3) the program achieve its intended goal of overcoming language barriers. The Fifth Circuit Court further stated that schools have the right to decide the sequence and manner in which schools implement their program, as long as the academic deficits incurred by participating in the language-remediation program are also addressed.

Legislative and judicial mandates have defined the legal obligations of educational institutions for the education of linguistic-minority students. These decisions have institutionalized, at least at the federal level, the notion that "equal" is not synonymous with "same," and that LEAs have a responsibility to guarantee a similar range of educational outcomes for all children, regardless of their linguistic background. The extent to which school districts have complied with this mandate and the methods used vary considerably across the country. Compliance with laws that address the rights of linguistic-minority populations, or any other civil rights law, requires cooperation from educational institutions and, if necessary, strict enforcement and sanctions. Despite numerous attacks from opponents and lax enforcement over the last twelve years, a variety of programs designed to meet the needs of linguistic-minority students presently exists throughout the country.

## PRESENT PRACTICES

### Students to Be Served

Information on the number of children likely to require special services is crucial to policy and program development. However, due to methodological issues and the constant influx of immigrants, few reliable estimates are available. Although existing studies probably underestimate the pool of LEP children, the implications of their findings are clear: substantial numbers of children would benefit from some type of specialized services.

The changing nature of U.S. immigration patterns makes

estimates of the LEP population obsolete almost immediately. For example, in 1990 over 1.5 million new immigrants were admitted to the United States. Many settled in linguistically isolated communities where a language other than English is spoken. The majority of these individuals came from countries in which Spanish is the dominant language and joined the 5 percent of the U.S. population who speak Spanish at home. Although many of these new immigrants will begin to acquire English almost immediately with little or no formal support mechanism, their children will require additional language support in order to perform adequately in our present educational system.

There have been several attempts by the federal government to estimate the number of people in need of these special services. Not surprisingly, the estimates obtained vary considerably depending on the method used. In the early 1980s, the Bureau of the Census surveyed a nationally representative sample of language-minority children. The sample included children who lived in households in which a language other than English was used substantially and who scored at or below the 20th percentile on a measure of language proficiency. Based on this sample, it was estimated that the LEP population between the ages of five and seventeen was between 1.2 and 1.7 million. More recent estimates, using state education agency (SEA) counts, puts the LEP population between ages five and seventeen at 2.2 million. These numbers should be viewed with caution, since considerable variation exists across and within states in the mechanism used to identify LEP children. In many states, LEAs have the option of selecting the assessment methods (teacher information or referral, parent information, home language survey, evaluation of student's record, assessment of achievement level, and language-assessment tests) and the cutoff points on an English-language proficiency test. As a result, a student who is LEP within one state or LEA might not meet other state or LEA criteria for identification and, hence, assistance.

Perhaps even more surprising is that the Bilingual Education Act, which was specifically established to serve these children, serves only 10 percent of them. Based on an SEA report that 85 percent of the LEP population are in programs specifically designed to meet their educational needs, it is highly probable that other federal, state, or local funds are being used to support these programs. Although very little data are available on these programs, it can be assumed that their main goal is to provide these students as quickly as possible with the skills necessary to function in an all-English classroom, and that little or no effort is made to maintain their native language.

## Identification and Assessment

Identification for program eligibility became the focal point of the *Lau* Remedies. Much emphasis was placed on the determination of the children's linguistic skills in English. The process seemed simple: decide which children did not have the necessary skills to function in an all-English classroom, and assign them to language-support programs. The threat of noncompliance with the Office of Civil Rights (OCR) made school districts turn to that office for guidelines on identification procedures and program design. In the absence of a research base, OCR developed a five-level system for characterizing schoolchildren's language patterns: (a) monolingual speaker of a language other than English, (b) predominantly speaks a language other than English, (c) bilingual (both languages spoken with equal ease), (d) predominantly speaks English, and (e) monolingual speaker of English. Children who fell into categories a or b were eligible for services. Although this framework gave rise to wide-scale language testing for the purpose of classifying students, the lack of specific national standards resulted in considerable variation in assessment procedures and tools used in the identification process. The tools used to identify communicative competence in English, rather than inherent differences in communicative skills across individuals, defined eligibility.

In an attempt to reach national consensus on the identification process, the Council of Chief State School Officers (CCSSO)(1992) recently recommended a process similar to that implemented by many school districts across the country. First, the CCSSO recommended that a screening for native-language background other than English be conducted within ten school days of registration. Second, the assessment instruments used for classifying, placing, and exiting students should cover all communicative competencies (reading, writing, speaking, and listening). In addition, the CCSSO suggested the use of stringent cutoff criteria that require a high level of English-language performance for classification as fully English proficient. Although the effort to bring consistency is laudable, there are several major problems with these recommendations.

Language screening, the first step in the process, tends to underidentify those children who need additional language support. The screening process relies heavily on parents' self-reports during registration, and parents who are unable to judge the English-proficiency level required to function adequately in the classroom (or who are skeptical and do not see the value of existing language-support programs) often report English as the home language. As a result, the children are placed in English-only classes where no language-support program is available. Although the process is sensitive to parents' needs and desires, it seems pedagogically inappropriate to place a LEP child in a regular program where assistance is limited or nonexistent. If the child is identified as coming from a home in which a language other than English is the dominant language, the CCSSO recommends that the child's English-language proficiency be assessed.

Even from the inception of this screening process, researchers (DeAvila and Duncan, 1979) questioned the validity of language-assessment procedures built on a divisible model of proficiency and with a heavy emphasis on the structural aspects of language. If language competence is defined as the knowledge of specific linguistic structures (such as wh-questions, tense and plural markers), then knowledge of those structures is measured. If, however, language competence is defined as communicative competence (Hymes, 1974), which includes more than linguistic competence, the measure will be broader in scope.

The present narrow linguistic definition of LEP contradicts our present understanding of the complex nature of communication, especially the sociolinguistic factors contributing to children's difficulty within the educational system. Cummins (1981, 1984) has argued that different communication skills are needed to function in context-embedded, face-to-face interactions (the type of skills generally assessed) and context-independent communication skills (those required for academic achievement). These skills develop at different times, with context-embedded language acquired faster than decontextualized language. The work of Au and Jordan (1981), Heath (1983), Iglesias (1985), Phillips (1982), and Rogoff (1990), among others, further suggests that minority children come to school with styles of communicating that differ from those necessary to succeed in the U.S. educational system. Although these differences in communicative styles play a crucial role in classroom performance, they are never assessed.

The CCSSO recommendation that assessment instruments used for classifying, placing, and exiting students should cover communicative competence in reading, writing, speaking, and listening is also problematic. Existing language-proficiency tests are, in general, discrete point tests that assume that sampling a limited number of key linguistic features is sufficient to provide a full picture of the child's language proficiency. This is a highly questionable assumption. Even if we used these tests to measure the student's English linguistic proficiency for reading, writing, speaking, and listening, we would have no information on the child's proficiency level in his or her native language. The lack of this information, which would be difficult to obtain for many of the languages spoken in the United States, ignores that a student's linguistic skills in his or her native language ($L_1$) transfer to the student's second language ($L_2$). For purposes of instruction, which is the main goal of any educational assessment, this information is crucial, since it would determine whether a particular skill needs to be learned or whether a new code (English) should be taught for an already learned skill.

The stringent cutoff criteria recommended by the CCSSO, requiring a high level of English-language performance for classification as fully proficient, would guarantee that students who are mainstreamed into English-only classes have the necessary skills to succeed. This recommendation, although easy to implement, has been objected to by many school districts throughout the country. These districts, especially those without a favorable attitude toward bilingual-education programs, argue that the somewhat lenient program-entry criteria and stringent exit criteria result in a disproportionately high number of children in these costly programs.

The broad categorization system presently used serves only to ascertain program eligibility. Like many other such programs, this broad categorization results in the placement of children in narrowly framed, socially isolated programs in which instruction has little relevance to the problems LEP children will encounter when entering an educational system that differs significantly from that which they have been socialized to enter. English-proficient children coming from the same cultural-linguistic community encounter the same problems and often are categorized to enter other narrowly framed, socially isolated programs that have little in common with the program developed for their LEP peers.

*The Programs*

Numerous language-support programs exist, many sharing outcome objectives but varying considerably in how they intend to achieve these goals. These programs contain explicit and implicit sets of values, which influence their direction. Explicitly, all programs are designed to increase the students' English skills, and in some programs their respective native languages. In addition, all programs transmit implicit sets of cultural norms that are consistent with the values, traditions, and expectations of the dominant groups in our society (Iglesias, 1985; Poole, 1992; Saville-Troike, 1979). The discrepancy between the cultural-linguistic norms the children bring from home and those expected in the schools (Au and Jordan, 1981; Heath, 1983; Lareau, 1989; Phillips, 1982) has the potential of becoming more of an impediment than the children's inability to speak the language of instruction. Thus, the greater the match between the LEP students' cultural-linguistic background and the program's curriculum and instructional approach, the greater the chance that a program will be successful regardless of language used for instruction. Despite the resounding evidence for the need to go beyond linguistic skills and to modify programs to accommodate children's cultural-linguistic background, instructional approaches and evaluation criteria reflect, for the most part, the narrow view of the problem as promulgated in the authorizing legislation.

A variety of program models focusing on linguistic skills have been implemented in order to guarantee that LEP students are offered equal access to and comparable outcomes from our educational system. Central to these programs is the goal of building English-language proficiency to a level at which children can compete equally with mainstream children. PL 100-297 established three different types of elementary and secondary bilingual programs: (a) transitional bilingual education, (b) developmental bilingual education, and (c) special instructional alternative programs. Transitional bilingual education is composed of structured English-language programs of instruction in which the child's native language is used solely with the intent of facilitating English-language competence. Developmental bilingual education includes full-time programs that teach English and one other language in a manner designed to develop competency in both. The most recently funded programs, special instructional alternative programs, are structured English programs that include special instructional services specifically designed to meet the particular linguistic and instructional needs of the children enrolled. These programs need not use the students' native language.

*Transitional Bilingual.* The main objective of transitional bilingual education is to employ each student's native language as a medium of instruction while he or she is being taught English. These programs combine structured English-language instruction with native-language instruction. They also tend to incorporate the students' cultural heritage into the curriculum. Classes may include up to 40 percent non-LEP students. Students in these programs are expected to attend mainstream classes in subjects such as art, music, and physical education. In fiscal year 1991, 488 transitional bilingual programs, at a cost of $75 million, were supported by the federal government.

The transitional bilingual approach acknowledges that the acquisition of English skills, especially decontextualized academic language, takes time and that competency in $L_1$ provides an important cognitive foundation for $L_2$ acquisition and academic learning in general. Acquisition of a second language takes two to seven years, two years to master the oral skills of a second language (what Cummins [1989] refers to as Basic Interpersonal Communication Skills), and about five to seven years to master academic language (Cummins' Cognitive Academic Language Proficiency). In addition, the gradual introduction of $L_2$ and the instruction in $L_1$ provides the student with the comprehensible input necessary for second-language acquisition (Krashen, 1985) while providing the academic content in a language the student understands. This content, acquired in the native language during this transitional period of instruction, is assumed to transfer to English as the student progresses through the program.

Two types of transitional bilingual programs have been identified, early exit and late exit. In the early-exit programs, Ramírez, Yuen, and Ramey (1991) found some initial instruction in the child's primary language, thirty to sixty minutes a day, usually limited to the introduction of initial reading skills. All other instruction was in English, and instruction in the primary language was quickly phased out. By grade 2, virtually all instruction was in English. Ramírez's findings are consistent with those of others (IDRA, 1985; Legaretta, 1977; Wong-Fillmore and Valadez, 1986) who have found that classes labeled as bilingual, particularly those in which languages are not separated by a time block, are conducted primarily in English. Wong-Fillmore and colleagues (1985) have argued that the amount of English used in the classroom is not as crucial a factor as how and for what purposes the two languages are used.

In contrast to their findings on early-exit programs, Ramírez and colleagues found that in late-exit programs students received a minimum of 40 percent of their instructional time in their first language. Students remained in the program until the sixth grade, regardless of whether they were reclassified as fully English proficient. Although not conclusive, their findings tend to suggest that late-exit students may be achieving better results than early-exit ones. There was not only continued growth across grade levels but also an acceleration in the rate of growth, compared to the deceleration in growth seen in the early-exit and test-norming populations. These findings are consistent with the Skutnabb-Kangas and Tuokomaa (1976) findings that immigrant students in Sweden who had five to six years of education in their native language were more likely to approach the norms of Swedish students when both were tested in Swedish.

The findings of Ramírez, Yuen, and Ramey (1991) also suggest other programmatic differences between early-exit and late-exit classrooms. Both sets of teachers had comparable English skills, but the late-exit teachers had superior language proficiency in the students' first language. Some early-exit teachers did not have sufficient proficiency in the students' native language to teach effectively in the non-English portion of the program.

The effectiveness of transitional bilingual education has been the focus of numerous studies. The most widely publicized of these studies (Baker and deKanter, 1983) suggests that the case for bilingual education is extremely weak. The wide dissemination of these findings had a major impact on policymakers at all levels of the government. In contrast to the findings of Baker and deKanter, the work of Troike (1978), Dulay and Burt (1978), and Willig (1985) supports the notion that bilingual education has a positive effect. Willig's meta-analysis of the studies reviewed by Baker and deKanter revealed a significant positive effect size that was found for all major academic subjects, whether the tests were administered in English or in other languages. Unfortunately, because the counterevidence to the Baker and deKanter study has not received as much attention from the media, it has not had much impact on policymakers.

*Developmental Bilingual Education Program.* Of the three types
of bilingual programs, Developmental Bilingual Education programs (DBEs) are least often funded by the federal government.
In fiscal year 1991, there were twenty-four projects at a cost of
$3.8 million. This is surprising, considering this is the type of
program most often advocated by leading researchers in the area
of bilingual education (Cummins, 1989; Krashen, 1985; Padilla
et al., 1991; Tikunoff, 1985; Wong-Fillmore and Valadez, 1986).
Also surprising is the lack of information on the implementation and evaluation of these programs.

The goal of DBEs is to help children achieve competence in
English and a second language. The instructional strategies used
are designed to acknowledge, respect, and build upon the language and culture of the home (García, 1991). The programs
encourage use of the native languages as a medium of instruction and maintenance of the primary culture. Classes should,
where possible, include an approximately equal number of native English speakers and LEP students whose native language is
the second language of instruction.

Unlike the transitional program, this program acknowledges
that the acquisition of $L_2$ is not hampered by maintenance of $L_1$
(McLaughlin, 1987; Cummins, 1984) and views bilingualism from
a resource perspective. Advocates of this program argue that there
is a cognitive advantage to being bilingual (Díaz, 1983). Students'
access to more than one code, and the realization that language
is an arbitrary tool that can be manipulated, leads to greater
metalinguistic awareness and cognitive flexibility. This cognitive
advantage is achieved only when children maintain their bilingualism. The longer that students participate in the program,
the greater the benefits.

The effectiveness of DBE programs has received very little
attention primarily due to their recency. However, Ramírez's findings that late-exit students continued accelerated growth suggest
that DBE programs would have results as good as, if not better
than, the late-exit programs. Support for DBE programs is not
based solely on their effectiveness. The concern that immigrants
will over time (usually by the second or third generation) completely lose their language (Veltman, 1988) has prompted some
advocates of developmental bilingual education (Pease-Alvarez
and Hakuta, 1992; Santiestevan, 1991; Wong-Fillmore, 1991) to
suggest that our main concern should shift from the acquisition
of English to the impact of language loss on families and our

society. DBE could be a mechanism to prevent language loss from occurring.

*Special Alternative Instructional Programs.* To allow local school districts more flexibility in selecting educational approaches to meet the needs of their particular LEP students, the federal government began funding special alternative programs in 1984; there were 201 programs, at a cost of $21.5 million, in fiscal year 1991. Although a variety of programs fall under this rubric, the major characteristic of these programs is that they do not use the students' $L_1$. In their ideal form, these programs are patterned after the highly successful Canadian immersion programs.

The overall goal of these immersion programs is for children to achieve competence in reading, writing, speaking, and listening in a second language; normal levels of development in all aspects of $L_1$; age-appropriate levels of academic achievement; and a positive attitude toward the home language and culture as well as the target language and culture. The immersion model is based on the highly supported notion that people learn a second language the same way they learn the first, in contexts where they are exposed to it in its natural form and socially motivated to use it. The earliest immersion program (Lambert and Tucker, 1972) consists of three phases: (1) a monolingual phase, (2) a bilingual phase, and (3) a maintenance phase. During the first phase, all curriculum instruction is provided in the second language. In the second phase, both languages are used for curriculum instruction. In the final phase, selected courses are taught in the second language in order to maintain and further promote development of the second language. Subsequent immersion programs have differed with respect to the grade in which $L_2$ is used as a major medium of curriculum instruction, the amount of instruction offered in $L_2$ (partial or full immersion), and the number of years in which $L_2$ is used as a major medium of instruction.

Immersion programs, the most advocated variety of alternative instruction, have been found as effective as early-exit transitional bilingual programs (Ramírez et al., 1991). No conclusive evidence exists for the relative advantage of immersion over late-exit programs. One advantage of immersion programs is that students arrive at a high level of competence in $L_1$ and $L_2$ without falling behind in the content areas. Critics have argued, however, that immersion programs, developed by and designed for members of the majority society, are not universally effective.

This is especially true when the participants are members of a minority population. Lambert (1984) argues that immersion programs were designed as additive programs in which English-dominant children were exposed to a second language. Their success (Campbell, 1984; Lambert and Tucker, 1972) has been attributed to the enrichment nature (additive bilingualism) of the program and the lack of expectation that children will achieve full, native-like proficiency (Hernández-Chávez, 1984).

The greatest concern of critics of alternative instructional programs is that funding them is an act of tacit approval by the federal government for non-bilingual programs, indirectly sending school districts the message that it is appropriate to have programs in which minority-language children are placed in classrooms in which the medium of instruction is not their first language and in which there are no provisions for non-English-speaking children—similar to the so-called submersion programs of yesteryear.

## Implications of Research Findings on Policy and Practice

The present policy of the U.S. Department of Education is that there is no single best method of instruction but that, if properly implemented, any of the three major approaches can be effective in addressing the needs of LEP students. There are major limitations to this "everything goes" policy, which appears to be a vague, sociopolitical statement reminiscent of the 1968 Bilingual Education Act. First, it is based on judicial and legislative mandates that narrowly frame the problems encountered by LEP students and are inconsistent with present research on the nature of the problem. Second, the policy ignores the research base that has developed over the last two decades to substantiate or dispute the effectiveness of various programs and instructional features. Finally, it continues to send mixed messages about our government's commitment to promoting students' attachment to their ethnic language and culture. The present policy appears to join two incompatible agendas, the more liberal agenda of the 1970s and the conservative agenda of the 1980s. Rather than taking a leadership role in establishing policy for this national issue, the federal government appears to have given its responsibility over to local school districts and, in the process, contributed much to the complexity of the problem.

The federal government's leadership role was clearly evident in the 1960s and early 1970s, when it implemented programs specifically targeted to reduce or eliminate the "cause" of educational, economic, and social problems. During this federal activist period, programs were based on the cause-effect model from which the multitude of federally funded programs for LEP students was developed. Implicit in the development of such programs is the notion that a child's inability to speak English was the sole cause of his or her academic problem. The simplistic cause-effect programs are, at best, naive and have resulted in a surfeit of disjointed federal programs. The issue is not just the effectiveness of these programs, since most programs can be effective if sufficient resources are allocated and the output measures are carefully selected, but whether the effectiveness and efficiency of the existing disjointed programs can be increased so that limited federal, state, and local resources can reach all children who would benefit from such programs.

Rather than fixing the existing nonfunctional system, it might arguably be more effective to redesign programs based on the existing, albeit limited, research base. This does not mean, however, that the existing programs should be eliminated without replacing them with a better system. To do so would be morally irresponsible. The course of action to be followed, based on multiple interdependent decisions, will determine future policy. A series of programmatic decisions needs to be addressed when charting this policy.

*Decision 1: What Is the Goal of the Program?* The main argument in *Lau v. Nichols* was that the plaintiffs were provided unequal opportunity by being required to attend classes in a language they did not understand. No specific remedy was urged by the plaintiff in that case or in subsequent cases argued before the courts. Although it was a landmark decision in that it established the rights of linguistic minorities to equal access to the educational system, it has directed us into seeking narrowly framed solutions to a problem that extends beyond the language spoken by the students. It has been argued (Tharp, 1989) that a main cause of the underachievement of many linguistic-minority students is also a main cause of underachievement in many majority-culture students: the failure of the educational system to teach students who do not come from school-motivated families with verbal-analytic cognitive emphases. If this is the main cause of the linguistic-minority students' problem, and it appears to be a significant cause, then the goal of programs should be to provide children with these skills. The focus then shifts from equal access and equal opportunity to compete for the benefits of the educational system, to ensuring that all students receive equal benefits from the system. School restructuring efforts, especially those dealing with instructional approach, will greatly improve the achievement of linguistic-minority students.

The issue of whether to develop or maintain the home language of linguistic-minority students is more a sociopolitical than an educational question. Clearly, knowing the home language does not interfere with the acquisition of English, and there are clear social and cognitive advantages of knowing more than one language. In addition to arguing the point from a cognitive and social advantage perspective, supporters of language maintenance have argued that the loss of the home language has detrimental effects on family functioning and the strength of our country. By contrast, some proponents of English-only have argued that language diversity creates social and political tension. Guy (1989) counters by saying that "language differences become politicized and divisive precisely when a dominant group tries to impose its language as an official requirement" (p. 12). The best alternative would be to provide the various program types in all communities, a highly costly proposition. In reality, the decision will continue to be based on local, sociopolitical forces rather than research.

*Decision 2: Should the Program Be Self-contained or Integrated Within the Existing School Structure?* Historically, programs designed for LEP students have been carried out in self-contained classrooms in which the students have little contact with non-LEP students or as part of a program in which students are pulled out of the regular classroom and given special instruction, usually English as a Second Language. Segregating these students was based on an eligibility issue (resources allocated for LEP students were to be used for LEP students only) and an economic one (how to maximize existing school resources to meet the needs of LEP students). The issue of eligibility is one that has become less important over the years, due to the federal government's encouragement to integrate LEP and non-LEP students in federally funded bilingual classrooms. However, economic constraints continue to encourage segregated classrooms. From an economic efficiency perspective, the grouping of all children needing a particular service is, in theory, best accomplished by concentrating all resources in particular classrooms. However, this segregation has resulted in service duplication, a more costly solution, and service fragmentation. As a result of this fragmentation, children have a more difficult time accessing the resources available to them within the existing system.

The full integration of LEP children into regular classrooms would require abolishment of eligibility criteria, provision of all services within the regular classroom, and a revision of staff roles and responsibilities. Eliminating the existing segregated program is a two-edged sword. On the one hand, continuing to segregate these students is not in their best interest, socially and academically. On the other, it is also to their disadvantage to be placed in regular classrooms in which no provisions are made to accommodate their needs.

*Decision 3: What Should Be the Goal of Students' Assessment?* Present assessment practices are limited to categorization. Assessment would be more effective if the findings could be used to assist teachers and other resource staff in guiding everyday instruction. The U.S. Department of Education's (1991) longitudinal evaluation of the effectiveness of services for language-minority students indicated that half the districts used only one entry criterion, and this criterion tended to be one of the least rigorous.

If the aim of assessing students is to link their needs with instruction, then an integrated diagnostic-prescriptive process is required in which each student's learning behavior and performance leads to the development of individualized learning plans (Wang, 1992). The assessment process must consider and value the abilities and experiences that students bring to the classroom. Rather than assessing students' deficits at a particular time, the assessment process should be an ongoing and interactive one in which professionals gather information on the students' strengths and needs.

*Decision 4: What Curriculum and Instructional Approaches Should Be Used?* The success of any particular program is dependent on the match between the students' instructional needs and the instructional approaches used. Evidence strongly suggests that the instructional approaches must take into consideration the students' natal culture and linguistic proficiency (Krashen, 1985; Tharp, 1989; Trueba, 1989; Wong-Fillmore, 1991). Also significant are cultural variations in the social structures most amenable to learning, in cognitive and communicative styles, and in the degree of motivation for academic achievement (Tharp, 1989). Students' proficiency in the language of instruction must be considered in order to ensure that students are receiving comprehensible messages. In addition, the communication environment of the classroom must guarantee that students have an opportunity to practice and develop their newly acquired linguistic skills.

*Decision 5: How Will the Effectiveness and Efficiency of Programs Be Assessed?* Most of the research literature on bilingual education has focused on program effectiveness. Major studies that have reviewed the literature on the effectiveness of bilingual education (Baker and deKanter, 1983; Dulay and Burt, 1978; Lam, 1992; Troike, 1978; Willig, 1985; Zappert and Cruz, 1977) have been hampered by the poor quality of evaluation efforts, resulting in a high rate of rejection of available findings. These methodological flaws (e.g., lack of specificity of program characteristics, inadequate sample size, no control for socioeconomic status) have precluded any conclusive statements about program effects.

Inadequate assessments are not limited to large-scale research studies. The lack of guidelines or standards for program compliance, the lack of knowledgeable evaluators, and nonsupportive and uncooperative school administrators have limited local efforts to strengthen programs and judge the effectiveness of instruction at the local level (Lam, 1992). Given the lack of federal leadership, it is not surprising that the CCSSO found inadequate and inconsistent information about retention, drop-out rates, and special education referrals of LEP students. Only thirty states collect statistics on the number of students retained in grade, only sixteen collect statistics on LEP students placed below grade level for their age, and thirty-two collect information on the number of LEP students who drop out while enrolled in a language-assistance program. Fewer than ten states have a mechanism for monitoring the academic status of LEP students after they are placed in English-only classes. At the local level, the information gained from program evaluations is rarely used for program improvement.

Using indicators that are consistent with program goals, evaluations must be designed to ascertain whether particular goals have been achieved. Some of these indicators might measure factors other than school success or degree of English proficiency.

The information gained from these evaluations must be used to plan and revise programs in subsequent years.

## The Challenge

Our challenge as educators is twofold. First, a mechanism must be developed to maintain the connection between the children and the social network that provides, and will continue to provide, support in overcoming the challenges these children will encounter throughout life. In many cases, members of their social networks who provide protection, advocacy, and a moral anchor speak a language other than English. At the same time, a mechanism must be provided to assist children in establishing new connections that will link them to the larger, English-speaking population. Restricting access to either one of the networks would be counterproductive to our mission—preparing children to become competent adults in our society.

## REFERENCES

*Aspira Inc. of New York v. Board of Education of the City of New York*, No. 72 Civ. 4002 MEF (S.D.N.Y. Sept. 20, 1974).

Au, Kathryn Hu-Pei, and Jordan, Cathie. "Teaching Reading to Hawaiian Children: Finding a Culturally Appropriate Solution." In *Culture and the Bilingual Classroom: Studies in Classroom Ethonography*, edited by Henry T. Trueba, Grace P. Guthrie, and Kathryn Hu-Pei Au, pp. 139–152. Rowley, Mass.: Newbury House, 1981.

Baker, Keith A., and deKanter, Adriana A. "Federal Policy and the Effectiveness of Bilingual Education." In *Bilingual Education: A Reappraisal of Federal Policy*, edited by Keith A. Baker and Adriana A. deKanter, pp. 33–86. Lexington, Mass.: Lexington Press, 1983.

Campbell, Russell N. "The Immersion Education Approach to Second Language Teaching." In *Studies on Immersion Education*, edited by the California State Department of Education, pp. 114–143. Sacramento: California State Department of Education, 1984.

Castellanos, Diego. *The Best of Two Worlds: Bilingual-Bicultural Education in the United States*. Trenton, N.J.: New Jersey Department of Education, 1983.

*Casteneda v. Pickard*, 648 F2d 989 (5th Cir. 1981).

Council of Chief State School Officers. *Summary of Recommendations and Policy Implications for Improving the Assessment and Monitoring of Students with Limited English Proficiency*. Washington, D.C.: Council of Chief State School Officers, 1992.

Crawford, James. *Bilingual Education: History, Politics, Theory, and Practice*. Trenton, N.J.: Crane Publishing, 1989.

Cummins, James. "The Role of Primary Language Development in Promoting Educational Success for Language Minority Students." In *Schooling and*

*Language Minority Students: A Theoretical Framework*, edited by the Office of Bilingual Bicultural Education, pp. 3–49. Los Angeles: California State University Evaluation, Dissemination and Assessment Center, 1981.

Cummins, James. *Bilingualism and Special Education*. San Diego, Calif.: College Hill Press, 1984.

Cummins, James. *Empowering Minority Students*. Sacramento: California Association for Bilingual Education, 1989.

DeAvila, Edward A., and Duncan, Sharon E. "A Few Thoughts about Language Assessment: The *Lau* Decision Reconsidered." In *Bilingual Multicultural Education and the Professional: From Theory to Practice*, edited by Henry T. Trueba and Carol Barnett-Mizrahi, pp. 441-453. Rowley, Mass.: Newbury House, 1979.

Díaz, Rafael M. "Thought and Two Languages: The Impact of Bilingualism on Cognitive Development." In *Review of Research in Education*, vol. 10, edited by Edmund W. Gordon, pp. 23–54. Washington, D.C.: American Educational Research Association, 1983.

Dulay, Heidi, and Burt, Marina K. *Why Bilingual Education? A Summary of Research Findings*. San Francisco, Calif.: Bloomsbury West, 1978.

Fishman, Joshua A. *Language Loyalty in the United States: The Maintenance and Perpetuation of Non-English Mother Tongues*. The Hague, Netherlands: Mouton de Gruyter, 1966.

Gaarder, A. Bruce. "The First Seventy-six Bilingual Education Projects." In *Report of the Twenty-first Annual Round Table Meeting on Languages and Linguistics: Bilingualism and Language Contact: Anthropological, Linguistic, Psychological, and Sociological Aspects*, edited by James E. Alatis, pp. 163–178. Georgetown University School of Languages and Linguistics Monograph Series, No. 23. Washington, D.C.: Georgetown University Press, 1970.

García, Eugene. *Education of Linguistically and Culturally Diverse Students: Effective Instructional Practices*. Santa Cruz, Calif.: National Center for Research on Cultural Diversity and Second Language Learning, 1991.

Guy, G. R. "International Perspective on Language Diversity and Language Rights," *Language Problems and Language Planning* 13 (1989): 45–53.

Heath, Shirley Brice. *Ways with Words: Language, Life, and Work in Communities and Classrooms*. Cambridge, UK: Cambridge University Press, 1983.

Hernández-Chavez, Eduardo. "The Inadequacy of English Immersion Education as an Educational Approach for Language Minority Students in the United States." In *Studies on Immersion Education*, edited by the California State Department of Education, pp. 144–183. Sacramento: California State Department of Education, 1984.

Hymes, Dell. *Foundations in Sociolinguistics: An Ethnographic Approach*. Philadelphia, Penn.: University of Pennsylvania Press, 1974.

IDRA (Intercultural Development and Research Associates). *The National Longitudinal Evaluation of Services for Language Minority Students*. San Antonio, Tex.: Intercultural Development and Research Associates, 1985.

Iglesias, Aquiles. "Cultural Conflict in the Classroom." In *School Discourse Problems*, edited by Danielle N. Ripich and Francesca Spinelli, pp. 79–96. San Diego, Calif.: College Hill Press, 1985.

Kloss, Heinz. *Laws and Legal Documents Relating to Problems of Bilingual Education in the United States*. Washington, D.C.: Center for Applied Linguistics, 1971.

Krashen, Steven. *The Input Hypothesis: Issues and Implementation.* White Plains, N.Y.: Longman, 1985.

Lam, Tony C. M. "Review of Practices and Problems in the Evaluation of Bilingual Education," *Review of Educational Research* 62, no. 2 (1992): 181–203.

Lambert, Wallace E. "An Overview of Issues in Immersion Education." In *Studies on Immersion Education,* edited by the California State Department of Education. Sacramento: California State Department of Education, 1984.

Lambert, Wallace E., and Tucker, Richard. *Bilingual Education of Children: The St. Lambert Experiment.* Rowley, Mass.: Newbury House, 1972.

Lareau, Annette. *Home Advantage: Social Class and Early Intervention in Elementary Education.* Philadelphia, Penn.: Falmer Press, 1989.

*Lau v. Nichols,* 94 S.Ct. 786, 1974.

Legaretta, Dorothy. "Language Choice in Bilingual Classrooms," *TESOL Quarterly* 11, no. 1 (1977): 9–16.

Lyons, James. "The Past and Future Directions of Federal Bilingual Education Policy," *Annals of the American Academy of Political and Social Science* 508 (1990): 66–80.

McLaughlin, Barry. *Theories of Second Language Learning.* London, UK: Arnold, 1987.

Muller, Thomas, and Espenshade, Thomas. *The Fourth Wave.* Washington, D.C.: Urban Institute Press, 1985.

Padilla, Amado M.; Lindholm, Kathryn J.; Chen, Andrew; Durán, Richard; Hakuta, Kenji; Lambert, Wallace E.; and Tucker, G. Richard. "The English-only Movement: Myth, Reality, and Implications for Psychology," *American Psychologist* 46, no. 2 (1991): 120–130.

Pease-Alvarez, Lucinda, and Hakuta, Kenji. "Enriching Our View of Bilingualism and Bilingual Education," *Educational Researcher* 21, no. 2 (1992): 4–19.

Phillips, Susan U. *The Invisible Culture: Communication in Classrooms on the Warm Springs Indian Reservation.* New York: Longman, 1982.

Poole, Deborah. "Language Socialization in the Second Language Classroom," *Language Learning* 42, no. 4 (1992): 593–616.

Ramírez, J. David; Yuen, Sandra D.; and Ramey, Dena R. *Longitudinal Study of Structured English Immersion Strategy, Early-exit and Late-exit Transitional Bilingual Education Programs for Language-minority Children.* Final Report to the U. S. Department of Education, Executive Summary. San Mateo, Calif.: Aguirre International, 1991.

*Rios v. Read,* 42 480 F. Supp. 14 (E.D.N.Y. 1978).

Rogoff, Barbara. *Apprenticeship in Thinking: Cognitive Development in Social Context.* New York: Oxford University Press, 1990.

Santiestevan, Cristina. *Use of Spanish Language in the United States: Trends, Challenges, and Opportunities.* Charleston, W.V.: ERIC Clearinghouse on Rural Education and Small Schools, 1991.

Saville-Troike, Muriel. "Culture, Language, and Education." In *Bilingual-Multicultural Education and the Professional: From Theory to Practice,* edited by Henry T. Trueba and Carol Barnett-Mizrahi. Rowley, Mass.: Newbury House, 1979.

Seidner, Stanley S., and Seidner, Maria M. *In the Wake of Conservative Reaction: An Analysis.* Bilingual Education Paper Series, vol. 6, no. 4. Los Angeles, Calif.: Evaluation, Dissemination, and Assessment Center, 1982.

*Serna v. Portales Municipal Schools,* 499 F2d 1147 (10th Cir. 1974).

Skutnabb-Kangas, Tove, and Tuokomaa, Pertti. *Teaching Migrant Children's Mother Tongue and Learning the Language of the Host Country in the Context of the Sociocultural Situation of the Migrant Family.* Helsinki, Finland: Finnish National Commission for UNESCO, 1976.

Tharp, Roland G. "Psychological Variables and Constants: Effects of Teaching and Learning in School," *American Psychologist* 44, no. 2 (1989): 349–359.

Tikunoff, William. *Applying Significant Instructional Features in the Bilingual Classroom.* Rosslyn, Va.: Inter-America Research Associates, 1985.

Troike, Rudolf C. *Research Evidence for the Effectiveness of Bilingual Education.* Rosslyn, Va.: National Clearinghouse for Bilingual Education, 1978.

Trueba, Henry T. *Raising Silent Voices: Educating the Linguistic Minorities for the 21st Century.* New York: Newbury House, 1989.

United States Department of Education. *The Condition of Bilingual Education in the Nation: A Report to the Congress and the President.* Washington, D.C.: U. S. Department of Education, 1991.

*United States v. Texas Education Agency,* No. 5281 Civ. A (U.S. Cir. 1981).

Veltman, Calvin. *Language Shift in the United States.* Berlin, Germany: Mouton de Gruyter, 1988.

Wang, Margaret C. *Adaptive Education Strategies: Building on Diversity.* Baltimore, Md.: Paul H. Brookes, 1992.

Willig, Ann C. "A Meta-analysis of Selected Studies on the Effectiveness of Bilingual Education," *Review of Educational Research* 55 (1985): 269–317.

Wong-Fillmore, Lily. "When Learning a Second Language Means Losing the First," *Early Childhood Research Quarterly* 6, no. 3 (1991): 232–247.

Wong-Fillmore, Lily; Ammon, Paul; McLaughlin, Barry; and Ammon, Mary Sue. *Learning English through Bilingual Education.* Washington, D.C.: National Institute of Education, 1985.

Wong-Fillmore, Lily, and Valadez, Concepción. "Teaching Bilingual Learners." In *Handbook of Research on Teaching,* 3rd ed., edited by Merlin C. Wittrock, pp. 648–685. New York: Macmillan, 1986.

Zappert, Laraine T., and Cruz, Roberto. *Bilingual Education: An Appraisal of Empirical Research.* Berkeley, Calif.: Bay Area Bilingual Education League/ Lau Center, Berkeley Unified School District, 1977.

# 7

# What Works and What Doesn't Work: The Case for an Inclusive System

## Margaret C. Wang, Maynard C. Reynolds, and Herbert J. Walberg

The increasing diversity of students in today's schools has led to much categorization and labeling and to a set of fragmented categorical programs. In principle, an inclusive school system should provide for the diverse needs of all students, including those requiring special, remedial, or compensatory education. In practice, however, a disjointed and separatist second system for special students has developed and continues to be the norm.

These separations take place under many names: special classes, special schools, resource rooms, suspensions, expulsions, ability grouping, transition classes, and "time-out" rooms. Demeaning labels such as "retarded" and "disturbed" are sometimes used to

The research reported herein is supported in part by the Temple University Center for Research in Human Development and Education (CRHDE) and in part by the Office of Educational Research and Improvement (OERI) of the U.S. Department of Education through a grant to the National Center on Education in the Inner Cities (CEIC) at Temple University. The opinions expressed do not necessarily reflect the position of the supporting agencies and no official endorsement should be inferred.

rationalize placement practices. Studies of these second-system programs generally place them on the "doesn't work" side of the dichotomy suggested by our title. In this chapter, we briefly describe the problem, review what "doesn't work," and then discuss "what works" in enhancing learning and making schools both inclusive and effective for *all* students.

## THE PROBLEM

Imagine this situation in a large elementary school.

The principal has proposed that all the specialists join with the general staff of the building to try a coordinated approach to serving children who have special needs. One out of five teachers in the building now works in categorical programs, mostly in separate classrooms. Part-time staff (e.g., a school psychologist, a social worker, a vision specialist, an English-as-a-Second-Language supervisor, most teachers' aides) also commonly serve in categorical programs.

A growing number of children are being referred to the principal's office. On a typical day, the principal may be confronted with a variety of problems to which categorical programs either do not or are not "allowed" to respond. They may include the following instances:

- A fourth-grade boy who is struggling unsuccessfully in academics and who runs away from the school
- A fifth grader who pridefully brings live ammunition to school to show to his classmates
- Several students who come to school only occasionally and refuse (or do not know how) to do assigned work
- A fifth-grade student who needs to go home regularly to feed her two-month-old baby
- A pregnant sixth-grade student for whom arrangements must be made for regular visits to the health clinic to ensure that proper prenatal care is provided
- A third-grade girl who is far behind her classmates in learning and inconsistent in taking her anticonvulsant medication

Teachers of primary grades report that many children who need intensive help in language and reading do not qualify for the learning disability (LD) program (designed for children showing a wide discrepancy between "ability" and "achievement") or the Chapter 1 program (limited to students who have a sufficient number of eligibility "points" according to an increasingly selective statewide eligibility system). The migrant education program is designed to serve only children whose parents have recently moved to secure agricultural employment. There are no provisions for serving poorly motivated children, those under stress from family problems, or those suffering neglect and abuse.

The local chapter of the Urban League has approached the school superintendent with complaints about the wide use of IQ tests and the frequent labeling of African-American children as retarded or emotionally disturbed. Finally, an upcoming visit by federal and state monitors has teachers upset about an abundance of paperwork they consider useless.

Many schools are better coordinated and under less stress than the one described above, but many are not; the latter find themselves in a losing battle with "disjointed incrementalism" (Reynolds and Wang, 1983, p. 191). This term refers to the launching of a series of narrowly framed programs one by one (each justified in its own time and way, but based on the false assumption that it will not affect the others). Each program has its own eligibility, accountability, funding, and advocacy systems, which results in a complex set of separate programs and a costly pupil allocation system or, simply put, excessive "proceduralism" (Gartner and Lipsky, 1987).

All too often, procedural requirements overshadow attention to educational substance and learning progress. And, too often, this "obsession with process has allowed us to ignore dramatic inequalities in substantial outcome" (Haney, 1991, p. 194). Regrettably, program monitoring often focuses more on what goes into filing cabinets than on what goes on in classrooms. Furthermore, this procedural emphasis stands in sharp contrast to new calls by policymakers for clear evidence of learning progress. Meeting these new, outcome-oriented expectations is a challenge to educators associated with categorical programs.

## THE STANDARD OF THE NATIONAL ACADEMY OF SCIENCES

How should we judge this highly segmented organization of school operations? When are special programs justified? One answer was provided by a panel of experts appointed in the early 1980s by the National Academy of Sciences (NAS). At the outset, the concerns of the NAS Panel were the racial and gender disparities in the placement of children in special education programs; the panel's attention shifted, however, to the quality of such programs. If programs had demonstrated clear and positive results in student learning, there would have been little concern for the high numbers of students assigned to them. But the panel ultimately found little value in the programs and classification schemes.

Referring to educable mental retardation (EMR), learning disability, and Chapter 1 programs, the panel reported: "We find no justification for the current categorization system that separates these three groups in the schools" (Heller, Holtzman, and Messick, 1982, p. 102). The panel added, "We can find little empirical justification for categorical labeling that discriminates mildly mentally retarded children from other children with academic difficulties" (p. 87). Further, "Similar instructional processes appear to be effective with EMR, learning disabled, and compensatory educational populations" (p. 102).

To address these deficiencies, the panel proposed the following standard for a school classification and placement system: "It is the responsibility of the placement team that labels and places a child in a special program to demonstrate that any differential label used is related to a distinctive prescription for educational practices ... that lead to improved outcomes" (p. 94). Adherence to this standard would have profound effects in the schools and in many related activities.

The NAS approach to classification focuses on instruction; it proposes educational classifications. In technical terms, the NAS panel proposed an Aptitude Treatment Interaction (ATI) standard for classification, that is, there must be evidence that, in considering alternative programs, some students have characteristics that make one alternative program desirable for them while other students profit more from different approaches. If this cannot be shown, then students should remain in regular classrooms.

## WHAT DOESN'T WORK

### Spurious Classification

In the past decade, several major studies and syntheses of research have shown that children in special education and other categorical programs, such as those under Chapter 1 and programs for migrant children, are being classified in dubious ways. Ysseldyke and colleagues (1983) reported that as many as 80 percent of all children could be classified as learning disabled by one or more of the procedures now in use in the nation's schools. Even if they were reliable or correct in some other limited way, many classifications are irrelevant to educational decisions. For example, there is no separate knowledge base for teaching reading to learning disabled students as opposed to Chapter 1 students.

In a research review directed primarily to Chapter 1 programs but with attention also to special education programs, Brophy (1986) concluded that there was no evidence of need for different kinds of instruction in these programs. He found only ordinal aptitude treatment interactions (ATIs), not disordinal ones, which suggests that students who fall behind in their learning often need *more*, but not necessarily different, instruction than other students. Haynes and Jenkins (1986) and their associates at the University of Washington have demonstrated in a series of studies that students in Chapter 1 and learning disabled (LD) programs show substantial overlap in characteristics. Furthermore, they actually tend to receive "less" instruction when assigned to these specially developed programs, even though the initial purpose was to provide extended and intensive instructional support (Allington and Johnston, 1986).

Thus, in the case of the two categories serving the largest numbers of students (Chapter 1 and LD), research does not show the distinctiveness required by the NAS standard. Our own summary of research, which involved scholars from across the nation and covered research in most areas of special education through the late 1980s, fully accords with the Brophy and NAS observations of no disordinal ATIs (Wang, Reynolds, and Walberg, 1987-1991). We do acknowledge, however, that students who are blind need uncommon approaches to instruction in reading and mobility, and that those who are deaf require specialized approaches to communication (i.e., some ATIs "work" and are necessary).

Moreover, recent reviews reveal a number of specific scientific and practical flaws in classifying students for special programs. First, procedures for classification and placement of children in special programs are often unreliable. A child may be classified as handicapped by one test or diagnostician and as nonhandicapped by another. Even a single diagnostician, working from an identical case record on two separate occasions, might produce two different diagnoses and classifications. These unreliable procedures lead to wide variations in rates of classification from state to state:

Discrepancies in state eligibility have resulted in large disparities among states in the percentages of students classified as educable mentally retarded (from 0.49 percent in Alaska to 4.14 percent in Alabama); learning disabled (from 0.83 percent in New York to 5.20 percent in Maryland); and emotionally disturbed (from 0.04 percent in Mississippi to 3.09 percent in Utah). [Morsink, Thomas, and Smith-Davis, 1987, p. 288]

Second, diagnostic procedures can be extremely time-consuming and costly, requiring the services of specially trained personnel; the time, energy, and other resources directed into diagnosis and classification are drawn away from instruction. A particularly acute problem is that much of school psychologists' time has been consumed in simple psychometrics just to make allocation decisions in categorical programs. As a result, a broader range of psychological services is largely undelivered in the schools. To the extent that diagnostic procedures are complicated by bureaucratic and legalistic procedures, they consume even more resources that could be channeled into direct educational services for children.

Third, some classifications cause needless labeling and stereotyping. Children are often treated differently simply because they have been labeled. For example, teachers and parents may have unwarranted lower expectations of children classified as retarded or learning disabled. In addition, children may lose self-confidence when they have been stigmatized by labels and removed from regular classes. Finally, Keogh (1988) notes that classifications depend, at least in part, on data that are unrelated to educational needs:

Decisions about special education classification are not only functions of child characteristics but also involve powerful organizational influences. Number of programs, availability of space, incentives for identification, range and kind of competing programs and services, number of professionals, and federal, state, and community pressures all affect classification decisions. [P. 237]

Such classifications fall far short of the NAS standard.

There appears to be a kind of hydraulic relationship across classification categories. A major court decision, for example, may cause a downturn in the use of one category and an upswing in another. Reschly (1987) pointed to a decline of 300,000 in the number of students classified as mentally retarded from 1976 to 1983, in contrast to an increase of over one million in the number classified as LD.

Concerns about classification, student placement, and quality of instruction in categorical programs are not new, nor are they confined to the field of special education. Several major systematic reviews of classification and placement procedures provide evidence that present methods are inadequate (Reynolds, Wang, and Walberg, 1987; Williams, Richmond, and Mason, 1986). Often they lead to expensive, segregative treatments that do not improve children's learning.

## The "Two-Step" Policy and Process

The difficulties in classification result largely from a "two-step" identification procedure. When a student has learning difficulties or behavior problems, it is common for the teacher to make a referral for placement into categorical programs. The referral leads into the two-step process.

***The First Step.*** The first step is to determine whether the child falls into a particular class of "entitled" students. Usually, this step is unrelated to educational needs, at least in any direct way. For a student to receive special education services, for example, it must first be determined that the student is handicapped. This usually involves classification of the student according to one of eight or nine different categories. This first step in categorical classification consumes an extraordinary amount of the time and resources of professional staff. Reschly (1987) writes: "The amount of time and energy now devoted to preplacement and reevaluations [in special education], which are dominated by determination of eligibility, represents [an] excessively costly and ineffective use of resources" (p. 51).

The categories are assumed (spuriously, in most cases) to be context-free; that is, it is assumed that the child could as well be studied in a hospital or psychological clinic as in the school and be labeled as, for example, "mentally retarded" or "emotionally disturbed". In migrant education, the first step in assessing a child's eligibility for special programs is a determination of parental work status.

The organization of categorical programs often follows the first-step classification approach. For example, special classes are organized for Chapter 1 students or for those labeled retarded, learning disabled, or emotionally disturbed. Similarly, teacher preparation and licensing often follow the same categorical bases, as do advocacy groups and as does much of the literature.

The prevailing first-step classification approaches generally "don't work" in the schools; they should be radically revised. Most of the categories assume an underlying taxonomy unsupported by any consensus in research or theory. The concept of mental retardation, for example, has been stretched to include the so-called "educable" or mild-range mentally retarded, and millions of children have been labeled mentally retarded based on tests lacking sufficient reliability or validity for decisions about instruction or school placement. Similarly, the mental illness label has been extended to relatively common behavior problems. To be sure, children with severe emotional and behavioral problems require special treatment, but typological classification concepts have been extended far beyond what scientific evidence would suggest is prudent. Unfortunately, these extended classification tendencies have grown substantially in recent decades.

It is true, of course, that policymakers may promote legislation in whatever categories they choose. For example, if they observe that many children in families of migrant workers show learning problems (i.e., the base or group rate for achievement is low), they may advance a program for children of this class. It remains for educators, however, to work with policymakers on how to address educators' legitimate concerns and then to organize programs without creating an incoherent school situation and assigning degrading labels to children. Indeed, there is important work to be done in the political arena to secure revisions in present "don't work" activities.

*The Second Step.* The second step involves an analysis of educational needs and the specific planning of an educational program and related services. A special placement is made only when the entitlement is clear from step-one and step-two results showing that there are "special" needs. Categorical funds tend to flow to the local school district as soon as the two-step process is complete. Significantly, the conditions triggering money flow are all on the input side. It matters not, as far as funding is concerned, whether the special program produces good outcomes.

We believe that the two-step process as described here is basically flawed; it should be changed to emphasize outcome data and to link funding patterns to learning outcomes and to policies concerning the "least restrictive environment" principle. We find the first step of categorizing children to be largely demeaning and unnecessary, and the use of "context-free" designations for categories of children to be mostly inappropriate as well. It is possible to design and operate school programs that attend to special problems of children by using only data that are relevant to instruction.

## WHAT WORKS: A KNOWLEDGE BASE ON EFFECTIVE PRACTICES

Much research has been conducted over the past half century on what yields better learning. This research deserves close attention by policymakers and educators as school programs are revised to serve children better. To summarize our conclusions, two policies are in order:

- For moderate learning improvements among children with special needs, avoid special placements. Instead, nearly all children with special needs should be integrated with "ordinary" children in regular classrooms.
- For extraordinary improvements for all children, employ educationally effective practices that focus directly on classrooms and homes, where learning takes place.

### A Synthesis of Studies of Effective Practices

Findings from a recently compiled, large-scale research synthesis on the influences of educational conditions, policies, and practices on academic learning suggest a consistently strong influence of proximal psychological variables (Wang, Haertel, and Walberg, 1993). By comparison, the "macro-level" policies (concerning administrative, financial, and organizational arrangements of states, districts, and schools) that have preoccupied reformers for the past decade show little relative influence.

Briefly, the synthesis focused on alterable variables, that is, conditions that can change in ways that enhance learning. Using a six-category conceptual framework of leading influences (Wang, Haertel, and Walberg, 1990), a total of 228 variables were identified as the basis for the synthesis study. Variables that are static or largely impervious to the influence of teachers, such as chronological age and socioeconomic status, were not considered, nor was literature in highly distinct fields such as education of students who are blind or deaf, treatment of major psychiatric disorders, therapy for speech disorders, or education of students with severe and profound disabilities. Table 7-1 identifies the six major categories of variables and further lists twenty-eight subcategories that are representative of the total pool of 228 variables.

The synthesis was composed of findings from three data sources: (a) content analyses of 179 authoritative reviews; (b) a compilation of effect sizes from 91 "meta-analysis" studies of learning effects; and (c) a survey of expert opinion on learning. More specifically, from the content analyses, some 10,000 detailed ratings were made of the strength of relationship between learning and each of the 228 variables as represented in the voluminous set of review articles and chapters. In addition, based on findings from the analysis reported in the 91 meta-analysis studies of the effect sizes, numerical summaries addressing the effects of the 228 variables were compiled. Expert opinions on influential variables of learning, the third data source, were based on ratings from a survey of the relative influences of the 228 variables. The survey respondents included educational researchers, school psychologists, state directors of Chapter 1 and special education, principals, and general and special education teachers.

Findings from these three data sources were in substantial agreement on the relative influences of the variables. The strong influence of proximal psychological variables, which directly affect learners in their classrooms and homes, is illustrated in Table 7-2. The table shows the relative influences on learning when the 228 variables are averaged into twenty-eight categories. The numbers are the equally weighted averages of the content ratings, the effect sizes, and the experts' ratings. They have been standardized to T-scores, which have a mean of 50 and a standard deviation of 10. Thus, effects above 55, for example, can be considered relatively high, and those below 45 can be considered low.

It is of interest to note that rankings of the relative influences of the variables derived from the survey ratings by respondents in the various professional roles (i.e., educational researchers, school psychologists, state directors of Chapter 1 and special education, principals, and general and special education teachers) were remarkably consistent. The median correlation among groups in their ratings of items was .88. The correlation of mean ratings by general and special education teachers, for example, was .95, the highest correlation observed. The lowest correlation

Table 7-1
## Six Major Categories and Twenty-eight Subcategories of Variables Influencing School Learning

| *Major Category/Subcategory* | *Illustrative Variable* |
|---|---|

Category I. Student Characteristics includes gender; academic history; and a variety of social, behavioral, motivational, cognitive, and affective characteristics.

| | |
|---|---|
| 1. Metacognitive Processes | Comprehension monitoring (planning; monitoring effectiveness of attempted actions and outcomes of actions; testing, revising, and evaluating learning strategies) |
| 2. Cognitive Processes | Level of specific academic knowledge in subject area |
| 3. Social and Behavioral Attributes | Positive, nondisruptive behavior |
| 4. Motivational and Affective Attributes | Attitude toward subject matter |
| 5. Psychomotor Skills | Psychomotor skills specific to subject matter |
| 6. Student Demographics | Gender and socioeconomic status |

Category II. Classroom Instruction and Climate includes classroom routines and practices, characteristics of instruction as delivered, classroom management, monitoring of student progress, quality and quantity of instruction provided, student/teacher interactions, and classroom atmosphere.

| | |
|---|---|
| 7. Classroom Management | Group alerting (teacher uses questioning/recitation strategies that maintain active participation by all students) |
| 8. Student and Teacher Social Interaction | Student responds positively to questions from teacher and other students |
| 9. Quantity of Instruction | Active engagement in learning |
| 10. Classroom Climate | Cohesiveness (class members are friends sharing common interests and values and emphasizing cooperative goals) |
| 11. Student and Teacher Academic Interaction | Frequent calls for extended, substantive oral and written response (not one-word answers) |

*continued on page 162*

## Table 7-1
## continued

| Major Category/Subcategory | Illustrative Variable |
| --- | --- |
| 12. Classroom Assessment | Use of assessment as a frequent, integral component of instruction |
| 13. Direct Instruction | Use of clear and organized direct instruction |
| 14. Classroom Implementation and Support | Establishing efficient classroom routines and communicating rules and procedures |

Category III. Out-of-School Contextual Variables includes community demographics, peer culture, parental support and involvement, and the amount of time students spend out of class on activities such as television viewing, leisure reading, and homework.

| | |
| --- | --- |
| 15. Home Environment/Parental Support | Parental involvement in ensuring completion of homework |
| 16. Peer Group | Level of peers' academic aspirations |
| 17. Community Influences | Socioeconomic level of community |
| 18. Out-of-Class Time | Student participation in clubs and extracurricular school activities |

Category IV. Program Design refers to the physical and organizational arrangements for instructional delivery, and includes strategies specified by the curriculum and characteristics of instructional materials.

| | |
| --- | --- |
| 19. Curriculum Design | Instructional materials employ advance organizers |
| 20. Program Demographics | Size of instructional group (whole class, small group, one-on-one instruction) |
| 21. Curriculum and Instruction | Alignment among goals, content, instruction, student assignments, and evaluation |

Category V. School Organization refers to culture, climate, policies, and practices, and includes demographics of the student body, whether the school is public or private, funding for categorical programs, school-level decision-making variables, and school-level policies and practices.

| | |
| --- | --- |
| 22. School Culture | Schoolwide emphasis on and recognition of academic achievement |
| 23. Teacher/Administrator Decision Making | Principal actively concerned with instructional program |

Table 7-1
**continued**

| Major Category/Subcategory | Illustrative Variable |
|---|---|
| 24. Parental Involvement Policy | Parental involvement in improvement and operation of instructional programs |
| 25. School Demographics | Size of school |
| 26. School Policies | Explicit schoolwide discipline policy |

Category VI. State and District Characteristics refers to governance and administration, state curriculum and textbook policies, testing and graduation requirements, teacher licensure, provisions in teacher contracts, and district-level administrative and fiscal variables.

| | |
|---|---|
| 27. State-Level Policies | Teacher licensure requirements |
| 28. District Demographics | School district size |

(.77) was between educational researchers and special education directors (Reynolds, Wang, and Walberg, 1992).

The consistency in what was considered influential in learning across the different professional groups further supports the validity of an inclusive approach to instructional effectiveness. What *every* student needs is powerful, state-of-the-art education programs based on what is known to work in the service of children. An illustration of this knowledge base is shown in Table 7-3. It lists the forty-five variables that received the highest average ratings (at or above 2.7 on a 3.0 scale) from the survey of expert opinions among educational professionals. Taken together, they form a considerable knowledge base on what works in enhancing student learning as judged by educational professionals. The variables and their influence rankings can serve as a basis for specifying the curriculum of teacher preparation programs (both preservice and in-service). They can also aid in arranging instruction in ways to achieve learning outcomes for all students, including those with special needs or otherwise considered at risk.

### Outcome Data on Special Programs

With respect to the second aspect of the NAS standard for special classifications and placements (the value of the programs), evidence on the effects of categorical programs is ambiguous at best. For example, in a prominent review of research on the

Table 7-2
**Relative Influences on Learning of Twenty-eight Subcategories of Variables**

| Subcategory of Variables | T-scores |
|---|---|
| Classroom management | 64.8 |
| Metacognitive processes | 63.0 |
| Cognitive processes | 61.3 |
| Home environment/parental support | 58.4 |
| Student/teacher social interaction | 56.7 |
| Social /behavioral attributes | 55.2 |
| Motivational/affective attributes | 54.8 |
| Peer group | 53.9 |
| Quantity of instruction | 53.7 |
| School culture | 53.3 |
| Classroom climate | 52.3 |
| Direct instruction | 52.1 |
| Curriculum design | 51.3 |
| Student/teacher academic interaction | 50.9 |
| Classroom assessment | 50.4 |
| Community influences | 49.0 |
| Psychomotor skills | 48.9 |
| Teacher/administrator decision making | 48.4 |
| Curriculum and instruction | 47.7 |
| Parental involvement policy | 45.8 |
| Classroom implementation/support | 45.7 |
| Student demographics | 44.8 |
| Out-of-class time | 44.3 |
| Program demographics | 42.8 |
| School demographics | 41.4 |
| State-level policies | 37.0 |
| School policies | 36.5 |
| District demographics | 32.9 |

effectiveness of programs for children classified as learning disabled, Keogh (1990) characterized the overall findings as "equivocal. . . . Based on the evidence to date, generalizations about effectivenes of these interventions for learning disabilities are limited" (p. 130).

Similarly, 180 studies of methods used with learning disabled students, such as perceptual motor training, showed essentially no effect (Kavale, 1987). In a broad review, it was found that "there is an absence of a conclusive body of evidence which confirms that special education services appreciably enhance the academic and/or social accomplishments of handicapped children beyond what can be expected without special education" (Semmel, Gottlieb, and Robinson, 1979, p. 267).

## Table 7-3
## Variables with Highest Mean Ratings from Experts for Having Potential to Enhance Students' Learning

| Variables | Mean Rating (from a 3.0 Scale) |
|---|---|
| **Category I: Student Characteristics** | **(2.1)** |
| Positive, nondisruptive behavior | 2.8 |
| Attitude toward school | 2.8 |
| Motivation for continual learning | 2.8 |
| Self-confidence | 2.8 |
| Level of reading comprehension ability | 2.8 |
| Self-regulatory, self-control strategies | 2.8 |
| Appropriate activity level | 2.7 |
| Cooperativeness with teacher | 2.7 |
| Attitude toward teachers | 2.7 |
| Attitude toward subject matter | 2.7 |
| Perseverance on learning tasks | 2.7 |
| Level of listening skills | 2.7 |
| Positive strategies for coping with failure | 2.7 |
| **Category II: Classroom Instruction and Climate Variables** | **(2.5)** |
| Teacher conveys enthusiasm about the content | 2.8 |
| Providing frequent feedback to students about their performance | 2.8 |
| Teaching for meaningful understanding | 2.8 |
| Time on task (amount of time students are actively engaged in learning) | 2.8 |
| Organization (class is well organized and planned) | 2.8 |
| Establishing efficient classroom routines and communication rules and procedures | 2.7 |
| Use of clear and organized direct instruction | 2.7 |
| Setting and maintaining clear expectations of content mastery | 2.7 |
| Corrective feedback in event of student error | 2.7 |
| Skills taught within the context of meaningful application | 2.7 |
| Good examples and analogies to concretize the abstract and familiarize the storage | 2.7 |
| Time spent in direct instruction on basic skills in reading | 2.7 |
| Time spent in direct instruction on basic skills in mathematics | 2.7 |
| Learner accountability (teacher maintains student awareness of learning goals and expectations) | 2.7 |
| Teacher "withitness" (teacher is continually aware of events and activities and minimizes disruptiveness by timely and nonconfrontational actions) | 2.7 |
| Teacher reacts appropriately to correct and incorrect answers | 2.7 |
| Teacher reinforces positive social interactions with students rejected by peers | 2.7 |
| Task difficulty (students are continually and appropriately challenged) | 2.7 |
| Low apathy (class members are concerned and interested in what goes on in the class) | 2.7 |

*continued on page 166*

Table 7-3
**continued**

| Variables | Mean Rating (from a 3.0 Scale) |
|---|---|
| **Category III: Out-of-School Contextual Variables** | **(2.3)** |
| Parental involvement in assuring regular school attendance | 2.8 |
| Parental interest in student's school work | 2.8 |
| Parental expectation for academic success | 2.8 |
| Educational environment | 2.7 |
| Parental involvement in assuring completion of homework | 2.7 |
| Parental application of appropriate, consistent discipline | 2.7 |
| Parental expression of attention to children | 2.7 |
| **Category IV: Program Design** | **(2.5)** |
| Clearly presented academic, social, and attitudinal program goals/outcomes | 2.7 |
| Availability of materials and activities for students with different abilities | 2.7 |
| **Category V: School Organization** | **(2.4)** |
| Teacher involvement in finding ways to increase academic performance | 2.8 |
| Teacher involvement in instructional decision making | 2.7 |
| Active collaboration between regular classroom teachers and special education teachers | 2.7 |
| Safe, orderly school climate | 2.7 |

Note: No variables under Category VI, State and District Characteristics, received a rating at or above 2.7. The mean rating of Category VI is 2.5.

Special education practitioners have so far failed to provide impressive data concerning the merits of their programs. For example, the so-called "efficacy studies" concerning special classes for students who are mentally retarded, which usually involved comparing measured educational outcomes for comparable students in special education and in regular classes, have yielded equivocal results (cf. Gartner and Lipsky, 1987). Furthermore, recent meta-analytic studies offer little more convincing evidence of positive outcomes of special education services that are provided in self-contained (segregated) special education programs (Wang and Baker, 1986).

Schools often contribute to children's learning problems. There is evidence of the so-called Matthew effects (Stanovitch, 1987): students who show limited progress in early phases of instruction in basic subjects, such as reading, tend to show progressive retardation over succeeding years. Data show that the "returning rate," that is, the number of students who are returned to regular classes after being placed in special education programs, has been embarrassingly low. Based on the findings from a nationwide study of special education in major cities, sponsored by the Council of the Great City Schools (Buttram and Kershner, 1988), the rate of student return to regular classes in the school districts that participated in the study for the particular year studied ranged from 0 to 8.8 percent. (These figures include students from kindergarten to twelfth grade.) This finding suggests that once students are placed in special education programs, they are unlikely to return to regular classrooms.

Broadly framed evaluation studies are, of course, very difficult to conduct with precision. It seems quite clear that many special education programs for distinctly and severely disabled students are beneficial. Indeed, in cases of severe disability, special education programs often represent the only opportunity available for education and are widely appreciated. Whether programs for mildly disabled pupils that involve separation from regular classes and schools are distinctly beneficial for such students is in doubt and a cause of widespread debate.

Recent evaluations suggest that pupils enrolled in Chapter 1 programs for economically disadvantaged children may show a slight acceleration in progress in basic skills such as reading and arithmetic (Carter, 1984; Slavin, Karweit, and Madden, 1989). In a recent study using the number of "days to learn" needed to reach various levels of achievement, there was no evidence of such acceleration; instead, compared with other pupils, pupils in categorical programs showed steadily decreasing rates of progress through the curriculum in reading and arithmetic (Reynolds et al., 1992). Several recent reports have suggested that such lack of effects of categorical programs such as Chapter 1 are the result of the programs being targeted too narrowly on basic skills and neglectful of the more complex elements of a modern school curriculum (Commission on Chapter 1, 1992).

## IMPLICATIONS FOR IMPROVING LEARNING

There is a new call for educators to give priority to outcomes over processes and results over procedures. The demand for improvement is not restricted to students with high, middle, or low levels of ability, nor to the categorical programs; the intent is to raise all students' achievement.

Clearly, local, state, and national leaders as well as the public want greater effectiveness from the nation's schools and reliable, tangible measures showing improved results. Policymakers have increasingly adopted results-oriented programs and evaluation methods. Whereas in the past they might have looked to spending or class size, which were thought to influence progress, policymakers have increasingly demanded the use of solid assessment procedures to demonstrate actual progress.

Many programs currently serving students identified as requiring "special" education and related services support (e.g., Chapter 1, special education, and other compensatory and remedial categorical programs) would profit from rigorous improvement efforts organized around principles identified as important for learning. Resources can be redirected to such efforts if we revise categorical approaches to instruction. Improvements on several other fronts that are both possible and necessary are briefly discussed in the following sections.

## The Merging of the Two Current Systems of Education

An inclusive approach to student diversity is justified by the high degree of agreement among special education and general classroom teachers about which variables or principles of instruction are most important in their work; research reviews and meta-analyses also support their views. This finding suggests a shared knowledge base on addressing the learning needs of all students, including those who require greater than usual instructional support. Furthermore, this knowledge—based on what works— suggests much overlap and potential merging in the preparation of special education and general classroom teachers in colleges and universities. Similarly, in-service education for special education and regular teachers can be carried out as a joint professional venture with emphasis on shared or common principles of pedagogy.

## Policy Revisions

On the policy front, we propose changes that support integrated forms of education for students who are currently segregated for service in the various special, remedial, and compensatory education programs. To this end, innovative approaches toward integrated forms of education for students should be encouraged and supported through policy revisions on a "waiver for performance" strategy. Under such a plan, local agencies might seek and be given waivers of existing rules and regulations when they advance ideas for integrated programs and offer to provide evidence of outcomes. Though flexible interpretation of existing rules and regulations may be somewhat facilitative, policy changes or waivers would more likely lead to systemic changes. It will be necessary, however, to ensure that when waiver strategies are used, no categorical funding losses occur for schools during their experimentation, and that they be authorized to combine funds now separated by categories.

Important steps in this movement have begun to take place, including: (1) the recommendations made by the Office of Special Education and Rehabilitative Services and by the Chapter 1 program of the Office of Compensatory Education Programs (Will and LeTendre, 1987); (2) the dialogue fueled by the joint position statement of the National Association of School Psychologists and the National Coalition of Advocates for Students (1986); (3) the recommendation by the Commission on Chapter 1 (1992) to provide coordinated in-class programs (in opposition to the predominant "pull-out" approach in implementing Chapter 1 programs) through legislation and an "openness" to innovation at the school level; and (4) the recommendations by the study group of the National Association of State Boards of Education (1992) that "state Boards should ensure that . . . students are not labeled . . . with a disability category in order to receive services" (p. 37).

In all of these changes, attention should be given to the features of instruction that work and are aspects of a totally inclusive school system. The responsibility for bringing about such changes falls not only on specialists but on all educators, parents, and members of the community who are in positions to be supportive. What we face is not a simple change. To be sure, progress has been made—nearly all children are in school, and the main obstacles remaining are details of arrangements within schools. Educators who concede to separate categorical programs sometimes do so with relief and will likely oppose the changes we urge. Some educators are comfortable in their present positions and feel threatened by change. But as emphasized by the special study group of the National Association of State Boards of Education (1992), it is time for broad revisions of categorical programs and for "emphasis . . . on improved instruction rather than the processes of classifying and labeling students" (p. 4).

## Teacher Education

In a period of rapid change in the structure of school programs, the institutions involved in preparing teachers face a difficult problem. They must prepare teachers who will be qualified for state certification and the realities of employment and who will also recognize the need for change. Ideally, changes in schools, colleges, and state licensing agencies should all take place at about the same time so that efforts in schools, teacher preparation institutions, and certification agencies are consistent and mutually reinforcing. In the wise words of the late Al Smith: "If you want to lead a parade, don't get more than two blocks ahead."

It is clearly necessary for universities to merge their programs in categorical areas and general education. Since there is no separate and distinct knowledge base for the teaching of any skill or subject to children in Chapter 1 programs or to those labeled learning disabled or educable mentally retarded, teacher preparation programs should be restructured to provide to prospective teachers a comprehensive program of "what works" in order to ensure desired educational outcomes for the increasingly diverse population of students to be served in today's schools.

Faculty in special education will be able to provide components in unified programs of teacher education where their expertise is particularly relevant, such as including working with parents and paraprofessionals; using strategies such as cooperative learning and direct instruction in one-on-one and small-group situations; and teaching social skills (Reynolds, 1991). Similarly, regular education faculty with different backgrounds or experience will be able to add valuable ideas and practices.

## A Scenario of an Inclusive Education System

Elsewhere we have considered what education might be like in the year 2000 if educators improved in several key areas (Wang, Walberg, and Reynolds, 1992). The following scenarios are not predictions but descriptions of programs and practices that could serve all students better, including those with special needs, in an inclusive education system.*

---

* This section on scenarios is adapted with permission of the publisher from Margaret C. Wang, Herbert J. Walberg, and Maynard C. Reynolds, "A Scenario for Better—Not Separate—Special Education," *Educational Leadership* 50, no. 2 (1992): 35-38.

*Instructional Teams.* In the year 2000, increasing numbers of special education teachers work directly with teams of teachers in various regular instructional environments. Regular education programs are far different from the one teacher/one class operations of the past. In general, through small groups or one-on-one teaching as part of the regular class operation, special education teachers provide instruction to students showing the least progress. They also help modify programs for those who learn most rapidly. They carry relatively heavy loads in pupil-assessment programs and in reporting to and collaborating with parents.

*Effective Instructional Strategies.* Students with special needs, along with all others, benefit in the year 2000 from the application of effective educational practices (none of which is fully implemented today). Few of the practices are new; they represent, in many instances, traditional—and even ancient—wisdom about effective education. For example, both regular and special-needs students benefit from increases in time spent in well-designed learning activities; parental involvement in the learning process; activities that are at suitable levels of substantive difficulty for individual learners; and constructive classroom and school climates. Furthermore, instruction for all students has the following features: instruction based on students' achievement needs; materials and procedures allowing students to proceed at their own pace; frequent assessment of progress; additional time available for students who need it; students taking responsibility for monitoring and guiding their own learning; and students helping one another and cooperating in achieving learning goals.

*Child Study and Classification.* Concerns about children with special needs focus mainly on the necessary modification of instructional programs. Children are not labeled, although programs may be. It is common, for example, for selected children in the primary grades to receive extended intensive reading instruction; others receive extended instruction in social skills. Children with particularly poor vision are taught to read by Braille methods. Again, while these adaptive programs may have labels, children will not. Planning for pupils is strictly based on students' instructional needs and is revised frequently.

*Monitoring of Students.* The school staff regularly monitors the progress of all students; for those showing most and least progress, there are intensive efforts to seek improvements. Students are identified by their progress toward important school goals and objectives, not labeled or classified in traditional special education style. High-achieving students are identified on the assumption that they also need adaptive school programs to continue learning at high rates.

*Meeting the Diverse Needs of Students.* Students formerly labeled learning disabled progress in regular classrooms through intensive tutoring, supplemented by working with computer equipment at home and school. Reasonably priced home terminals and modems allow each child to be "tutored" by a sophisticated computer in the afternoons, evenings, and summers. While it is possible to do much schoolwork at home, most students prefer to do the majority of their work in school because they want the companionship and stimulation of classmates and teachers.

*Coordinated Teacher Preparation.* Colleges and universities disband separate programs for preparation of regular teachers and most "special" teachers, such as those who serve learning disabled and educable mentally retarded children. University students who prepare for general teaching take courses that expand their resourcefulness as teachers of exceptional students. Most trainees are expected to be employed in regular classrooms, but also to act as team members with the teachers who work mainly with students needing extra help.

*School Coordination with Welfare and Health Agencies.* Schools are linked with their county departments of children's services, mental health, and social welfare. The school and county agencies agree to exchange information and create common procedures to determine eligibility for service. Counties place several professional workers at school sites to provide health services and coordinate welfare services. County and state officials grant the necessary waivers to facilitate a coordinated pattern of services both within the school and in the broader community.

*Coordination of Government Offices and Programs.* Federal and state officials heading categorical programs meet regularly to improve coordination of programs and to consider requests for waivers to permit coordination of programs at the school level. This results in more coherent programs in the schools, which thus serve all students more effectively. Schools are not penalized in any way for experimenting with programs. Members of Congress, updated on efforts to better coordinate programs, express readiness to support legislation that would provide more coherent programs for students with special needs and their families.

## CONCLUSION

Children are not "carved by nature" into the categories now used in schools. The fact that a subgroup of children can be classified by characteristics (such as economic disadvantage, parental occupation, ethnicity, disability, or even similar test scores) is irrelevant for educational purposes unless there is evidence that such classifications and placements will lead to better instruction and improved learning. We believe that educators have taken a basically flawed course in organizing an excess of categorical school programs. Accordingly, there is urgent need to reform the schools to break the cycle of reliance on categorical programs.

The needed revisions will be complex politically, economically, and professionally. Nonetheless, we must ask: Why continue the current approach to classification and placement of students requiring greater than usual support from educational and related services since it *is not working*? Should the field continue preparing psychologists to make distinctions in classification that lack demonstrated merit for improving student learning? Should universities continue to prepare teachers separately by category when research and practical experience consistently show that the distinctions are mere frostwork? Should we continue practices that promote disjointed programming that has not proven productive for students?

Many children currently being served in categorical programs, and many others not in these programs, have real learning problems that must be acknowledged and dealt with in a realistic fashion. But the manner in which we so often partition the children, teachers, and programs to deal with these problems is essentially flawed. Children who need to be served with the highest quality educational experience are too often labeled negatively and then set aside in educationally impoverished and unevaluated programs.

Are there well-tested ideas and practices that could be used as the basis for increased educational effectiveness? The answer is definitely yes. The state of the art far outpaces the state of actual practice in the schools. The scenario of practice in an inclusive education system, as described above, emerged from a broad review of research and current practice. But while the findings are impressive, much remains to be investigated, understood, and improved. The challenge is to improve current practices using the best of what we currently know as we continue to seek theoretical and practical advances that serve to promote learning for all children.

We believe that reframing the entire set of categorical programs is necessary, from legislative and regulatory levels to classrooms and individual students. These changes will not be easy, but we believe it is extremely important that schools put their programs together in a coherent fashion as well as reach out to parents and community and other service agencies to achieve broader improvements in the life situations and constructive learning opportunities of all children, particularly those whose present situations are most adverse.

## REFERENCES

Allington, Richard L., and Johnston, Peter. "The Coordination among Regular Classroom Reading Programs and Targeted Support Programs." In *Designs for Compensatory Education: Conference Proceedings and Papers*, edited by Barbara I. Williams, Peggy A. Richmond, and Beverly J. Mason, pp. VI-3-40. Washington, D.C.: Research and Evaluation Associates, 1986.

Brophy, Jere. "Research Linking Teacher Behavior to Student Achievement: Potential Implications for Instruction of Chapter 1 Students." In *Designs for Compensatory Education: Conference Proceedings and Papers*, edited by Barbara I. Williams, Peggy A. Richmond, and Beverly J. Mason, pp. 121-179. Washington, D.C.: Research and Evaluation Associates, 1986.

Buttram, Jane L., and Kershner, Keith. *Special Education in America's Cities: A Descriptive Study*. Washington, D.C.: Council of Great City Schools, 1988.

Carter, Launor F. "The Sustaining Effects Study of Compensatory and Elementary Education," *Educational Researcher* 21, no. 7 (1984): 4-13.

Commission on Chapter 1. *Making Schools Work for Children in Poverty*. Washington, D.C.: Council of Chief State School Officers, 1992.

Gartner, Alan, and Lipsky, Dorothy K. "Beyond Special Education: Toward a Quality System for All Students," *Harvard Educational Review* 57, no. 4 (1987): 367-395.

Haney, Craig. "The Fourteenth Amendment and Symbolic Legality: Let Them Eat Due Process," *Law and Human Behavior* 15 (1991): 183-204.

Haynes, Mariana C., and Jenkins, Joseph R. "Reading Instruction in Special Education Resource Rooms," *American Educational Research Journal* 23, no. 2 (1986): 161-190.

Heller, Kirby; Holtzman, Wayne; and Messick, Samuel. *Placing Children in Spe-*

*cial Education: A Strategy for Equity.* Washington, D.C.: National Academy of Science Press, 1982.

Kavale, Kenneth A. "Introduction: Effectiveness of Differential Programming in Serving Handicapped Students." In *Handbook of Special Education: Research and Practice,* Vol. 1, *Learner Characteristics and Adaptive Education,* edited by Margaret C. Wang, Maynard C. Reynolds, and Herbert J. Walberg, pp. 131–132. Oxford, England: Pergamon Press, 1987.

Keogh, Barbara K. "Learning Disabilities: Diversity in Search of Order." In *Handbook of Special Education: Research and Practice,* Vol. 2: *Mildly Handicapped Conditions,* edited by Margaret C. Wang, Maynard C. Reynolds, and Herbert J. Walberg, pp. 225–251. Oxford, England: Pergamon Press, 1988.

Keogh, Barbara K. "Learning Disability." In *Special Education: Research and Practice: Synthesis of Findings,* edited by Margaret C. Wang, Maynard C. Reynolds, and Herbert J. Walberg, pp. 119–142. Oxford, England: Pergamon Press, 1990.

Morsink, Catherine V.; Thomas, Carol C.; and Smith-Davis, Judy. "Noncategorical Special Education Programs: Process and Outcomes." In *Handbook of Special Education: Research and Practice.* Vol. 1: *Learner Characteristics and Adaptive Education,* edited by Margaret C. Wang, Maynard C. Reynolds, and Herbert J. Walberg, pp. 287–311. Oxford, England: Pergamon Press, 1987.

National Association of School Psychologists and National Coalition of Advocates for Students. *Position Statement: Advocacy for Appropriate Educational Services for All Children.* Boston, Mass.: National Association of School Psychologists and National Coalition of Advocates for Students, 1986.

National Association of State Boards of Education. *Winners All: A Call for Inclusive Schools.* Washington, D.C.: National Association of State Boards of Education, 1992.

Reschly, Daniel J. "Learning Characteristics of Mildly Handicapped Students: Implications for Classification, Placement, and Programming." In *Handbook of Special Education: Research and Practice.* Vol. 1: *Learner Characteristics and Adaptive Education,* edited by Margaret C. Wang, Maynard C. Reynolds, and Herbert J. Walberg, pp. 35–38. Oxford, England: Pergamon Press, 1987.

Reynolds, Maynard C. "Educating Teachers for Special Education Students." In *Handbook of Research on Teacher Education,* edited by W. Robert Houston, pp. 423–436. New York: Macmillan, 1991.

Reynolds, Maynard C.; Heistad, David; Peterson, JoAnne; and Dehli, Rosalie. "A Study of Days to Learn," *Remedial and Special Education* 13, no. 4 (1992): 20–26.

Reynolds, Maynard C., and Wang, Margaret C. "Restructuring 'Special' School Programs: A Position Paper," *Policy Studies Review* 2, no. 1 (1983): 189–212.

Reynolds, Maynard C.; Wang, Margaret C.; and Walberg, Herbert J. "The Necessary Restructuring of Special and Regular Education," *Exceptional Children* 53, no. 5 (1987): 391–398.

Reynolds, Maynard C.; Wang, Margaret C.; and Walberg, Herbert J. "The Knowledge Bases for Special and General Education," *Remedial and Special Education* 13, no. 5 (1992): 6–10.

Semmel, Melvin I.; Gottlieb, Jay; and Robinson, Nancy M. "Mainstreaming: Perspectives on Educating Handicapped Children in the Public Schools."

In *Review of Research in Education*, Vol. 7, edited by David Berliner. Washington, D.C.: American Educational Research Association, 1979.

Slavin, Robert F.; Karweit, Nancy L.; and Madden, Nancy A. *Effective Programs for Students at Risk*. Boston: Allyn and Bacon, 1989.

Stanovitch, Keith E. "Matthew Effects in Reading: Some Consequences of Individual Differences in the Acquisition of Literacy," *Reading Research Quarterly* 21 (1987): 360–407.

Wang, Margaret C., and Baker, Ed. T. "Mainstreaming Programs: Design Features and Effects," *Journal of Special Education* 19, no. 4 (1986): 503–521.

Wang, Margaret C.; Haertel, Geneva D.; and Walberg, Herbert J. "What Influences Learning? A Content Analysis of Review Literature," *Journal of Educational Research* 84, no. 1 (1990): 30–43.

Wang, Margaret C.; Haertel, Geneva D.; and Walberg, Herbert J. "Toward a Knowledge Base for School Learning," *Review of Educational Research* 63 (Fall 1993): 249–294.

Wang, Margaret C.; Reynolds, Maynard C.; and Walberg, Herbert J., eds. *Handbook of Special Education: Research and Practice*, Vols. 1–4. Oxford, England: Pergamon Press, 1987, 1988, 1989, 1991.

Wang, Margaret C.; Walberg, Herbert J.; and Reynolds, Maynard C. "A Scenario for Better—Not Separate—Special Education," *Educational Leadership* 50, no. 2 (1992): 35-38.

Will, Madeline C., and LeTendre, Mary Jean. *Joint Communique on Special, Compensatory, and Regular Education Program Coordination between OSERS and Compensatory Education Programs*. Washington, D.C.: U. S. Department of Education, OSERS, 1987.

Williams, Barbara I.; Richmond, Peggy A.; and Mason, Beverly J. *Designs for Compensatory Education: Conference Proceedings and Papers*. Washington, D.C.: Research and Evaluation Associates, 1986.

Ysseldyke, James; Thurlow, Martha; Graden, Janet; Wesson, Karen; Algozzine, Robert; and Deno, Stanley. "Generalizations from Five Years of Research on Assessment and Decision Making: The University of Minnesota Institute," *Exceptional Education Quarterly* 4, no. 1 (1983): 75–93.

# Section III
## THE FUTURE OF
## CATEGORICAL PROGRAMS

# 8

# From the Picket Fence to the Chain Link Fence: National Goals and Federal Aid to the Disadvantaged

## *Martin E. Orland*

Over the past two decades, federal categorical programs on behalf of disadvantaged children have been noteworthy for their stability amidst a fluid educational policy landscape. While scholars and policymakers have advocated, and in some instances implemented, reforms affecting the nature of schooling in important and fundamental ways, the basic normative model underlying the structure and delivery mechanisms for federal aid to pupils with special needs has remained constant and essentially unaffected by either the "Reagan Revolution" or other prominent policy reform movements in areas such as school restructuring, curriculum, and accountability. This model, which I label "picket fence federalism" after Wright's (1982) broad characterization of federal grant-in-aid structures, is based on federally defined legal provisions and implementation mechanisms designed to guarantee the delivery of supplementary education services to federally designated target groups. By their nature, such structures

The views expressed in this chapter are the author's and no endorsement by the National Education Goals Panel should be inferred. The author wishes to thank Ms. Leslie Lawrence for her assistance in preparing this paper.

encourage the institutional separation of categorical program services from more general school district policy and practice.

The purpose of this discussion is to argue that the picket fence model is beginning to crumble. For the first time, a general educational policy reform movement is likely to alter this central paradigm for providing federal services to the disadvantaged. These new reforms have been anchored by the process of setting and monitoring the six national education goals endorsed by the President and the nation's governors in early 1990. They embrace explicit and rigorous "world-class" standards of performance for *all* students, new forms of assessment aligned to these standards, and a "systemic" approach to education reform in which state and local education systems change disparate elements of educational policy in coherent and coordinated ways to produce higher-achieving students.

This new reform movement has already begun to alter the historic dialogue around federal categorical programs for the disadvantaged from debates over excellence versus equity, regulation versus bloc grants, and program separation versus integration to policy options that synthesize elements from these seemingly incompatible policy choices. The resulting federal categorical program structure is likely to evolve from the institutionally distinct "picket fence" model to one that explicitly recognizes the interdependence of federal assistance efforts and the broader education policies and school improvement initiatives. I label the new approach "chain link federalism."

I begin with an analysis of the origins and continuity of the picket fence model to support federal aid for disadvantaged students, focusing on the first and largest of these federal aid programs—ESEA Chapter 1. I then analyze the inherent limits of the picket fence approach for improving the quality of Chapter 1 instructional offerings. Next are described new models of reform that have been consistently advocated by a diverse set of national policy leaders and sustained by new agenda-setting bodies such as the National Education Goals Panel. Finally, I outline some of the specific changes in categorical program structure and service delivery that are now being proposed as a result of these recent reforms, reflecting the move from a picket fence to a chain link fence conceptualization of the federal role.

## CREATING THE "PICKET FENCE"

Wright (1982) invented the term "picket fence federalism" to characterize the way public services are delivered under categorical program arrangements. The fence "pickets" in this model represent the vertical (i.e., from the federal level down to the school building) categorical service delivery mechanisms for different programs (i.e., one "picket" for serving poor, low-achieving students, another for those with limited proficiency in English, another for students with disabilities, etc.).

The picket fence metaphor is meant to suggest that the shape and nature of federal categorical aid programs are determined much more by the provisions in federal legislation and regulations and in the actions of program administrators than by the policies and priorities of the locality where the services are being provided. As a result, the categorical programs may be quite distinct from, and bear little relationship to, other local services and programs. The strength of the vertical "pickets" in the model is attributable to a number of factors including the complexity of the specialized federal program rules and regulations, the perceived penalties for local administrators not complying with them, the shared values and longstanding personal relationships among federal, state, and local program administrators, and the traditionally strong support among client advocacy groups for the specialized services being provided.

The roots of the picket fence approach in support of poor, low-achieving children were largely laid down in the 1960s and early 1970s. They were created during an era of unprecedented concern and subsequent federal policy action to meet the needs of the poor, minorities, and other disadvantaged groups in all social policy arenas. In education, a special federal role was seen by its advocates as a way to compensate for historical inadequacies in services to these groups on the part of state and local governments (Bailey and Mosher, 1968). Such inadequacies, it was argued, were not happenstance but the result of systemic conditions. Because local school systems were typically dominated by the wealthy and politically powerful who catered to majoritarian interests (McConnell, 1966), pupils with special educational needs, such as children from minority groups and low-income families, were being denied equal educational opportunities. As Peterson subsequently argued (1981), local redistributive educational policies on behalf of these pupils would be counter to the economic self-interest of these communities, and thus unlikely to occur.

The response to this condition from those concerned about equal educational opportunity was to seek redress from higher levels of government. In Schattschneider's terms (1960), the locus of conflict over providing equitable educational services to students with special needs was expanded during the 1960s and early 1970s to the federal level. It was assumed (correctly) that dominant interests at the federal level would generally be more sympathetic to the policy demands of the disadvantaged than to state and local interests. Further, action at the federal level would impact the entire nation, not just some state and local jurisdictions.

In 1965, Congress passed the Chapter 1 program for disadvantaged students. (The program was known as ESEA Title I from 1965 to 1981.) Consistent with other social policies of the time, advocates for the disadvantaged intended that the program provide additional supplementary services to low-achieving children attending schools in poor communities (Bailey and Mosher, 1968). The strategy was to give categorical grants to local school districts through their state department of education. The local districts would identify disadvantaged pupils requiring extra services and design programs to address their needs.

However, virtually from the beginning state and local governments were not trusted to perform these tasks faithfully. As noted, federal compensatory programs like Chapter 1 emanated in the first place from a belief that because of nonsupportive state and local environments students with special educational needs were being systematically underserved. It was thus assumed that local communities would be inclined to use these funds for general purposes, rather than on behalf of the disadvantaged.

These fears were reinforced by critiques of early experiences with the implementation of Chapter 1 programs. In 1969, a program evaluation conducted by the NAACP Legal Defense Fund (Martin and McClure, 1969) revealed widespread diversions of funds from their intended beneficiaries. Instances of local districts using Chapter 1 monies to purchase school buses and swimming pools were documented as well as systematic efforts on the part of some school districts to allocate fewer state and local resources to Chapter 1 schools than to non-Chapter 1 schools. See Berke and Kirst (1972), Hughes (1972), McLaughlin (1976), and Murphy (1971) for other illustrations of problematic local implementation of Chapter 1 during this era.

The revelation of such program abuses throughout the early 1970s led to a significant tightening of the Chapter 1 legal framework. Local discretion was circumscribed by detailed procedures for identifying and selecting participating Chapter 1 schools and students and for documenting that services to these students supplemented, rather than replaced, their regular instruction. Similarly tight regulatory standards were also developed during this period for serving handicapped students under the Education for All Handicapped Children Act (Public Law 94-142) and students with limited English proficiency under ESEA Title VII, and to comply with the 1974 Supreme Court ruling in *Lau vs. Nichols.* These provisions included detailed specifications for how local administrators were to identify, categorize, and serve students with different handicapping conditions and English-language deficiencies.

During the 1970s, the federal government also backed up its legal framework for serving disadvantaged pupils by creating more elaborate administrative structures staffed by federal, state, and local program managers. Their purpose was to ensure that the rules and regulations were being carried out in accordance with the law. Program managers at all governmental levels tended to share a commitment on behalf of the special population groups they served. They also relied heavily on each other for the successful implementation of the regulatory framework. Federal administrators thus depended on state and local managers to monitor and implement the program rules and regulations, while local officials used the interpretation of these rules by state and federal program administrators (supported where necessary by monitoring and enforcement procedures) to help insulate their programs from general school district policies and practices (Farrar and Millsap, 1986).

Not surprisingly, advocates of special supplementary services to disadvantaged groups have historically fought to create and maintain "picket fence" arrangements for categorical service delivery. These have been viewed, for reasons highlighted earlier, as necessary to ensure that federal legislative intent is being faithfully adhered to. Indeed, evaluations of Chapter 1 since the advent of these structures have consistently shown that program services generally were reaching their intended beneficiaries. (See, for example, Kirst and Jung, 1982, and Birman et al., 1987.)

Over time, traditional "iron triangle" alliances (among equity-oriented interest groups, their supporters on congressional

authorizing and appropriations committees, and categorical program managers) served to solidify the support behind the picket
fence categorical program model for serving the educationally
disadvantaged. Occasional challenges to this model, chiefly in
the form of bloc grants permitting federal funds to be used to
serve the needs of the disadvantaged in locally determined ways,
have proven singularly unsuccessful in the Congress. Even President Reagan, at the height of his popularity and influence in
1981, was unable to get Congress to pass his proposal for consolidating Chapter 1 and aid for the handicapped into a single
bloc grant. The proposal was modified by the Republican-led
Senate Education Subcommittee and failed to be included in
the final budget reconciliation package. Support for the existing
categorical programs among interest groups and congressmen's
constituencies were specifically cited as critical factors in their
survival (*New York Times*, 11 July 1981, p. 1).

In the past decade, no proposals for fundamentally restructuring how federal categorical program services are delivered to
children with special needs have been seriously considered by
the Congress. Initial attempts by the Reagan administration to
permit parents of Chapter 1 children to trade in their federal
entitlement for a "voucher" that could be used to purchase services in public or private schools were easily defeated in the Congress. The last reauthorization of Chapter 1 in 1988 preserved
nearly all the program's key regulatory provisions. The
reauthorization bill enjoyed the support of the administration,
and was backed by virtually every major education constituency
group. It passed the Congress with only two dissenting votes.
Reauthorization legislation continuing the basic categorical program structures for the handicapped and for limited-English-proficient children emerged similarly unscathed during this decade.

## LIMITS OF THE PICKET FENCE MODEL

Despite the obvious political success recently enjoyed by the
picket fence model of federalism as applied to federal education programs for the disadvantaged, these programs have not
been immune from criticism. While Chapter 1 has succeeded in
providing additional educational services to educationally disadvantaged students, its effectiveness in closing the gap between
these students' achievement and that of their more advantaged

peers has been modest at best (Birman et al., 1987; U.S. Department of Education, 1992). Increasingly, scholars and policy analysts examining Chapter 1's educational effectiveness have questioned some of the instructional implications of the picket fence delivery model (Odden, 1987; Smith, 1987; Herrington and Orland, 1991; Timar 1992). As noted, the creation of an elaborate regulatory framework administered by teams of program specialists at the federal, state, and local levels protects the program from encroachment by other local programs and priorities. Such success, however, has its price. These same policies that protect local Chapter 1 programs from outside "intrusion" also encourage both program administrators and local system officials to ignore the most critical variable affecting services for these pupils: *the nature and quality of the pupils' overall school experiences.*

Picket fence approaches focus almost exclusively on the nature and effects of discrete categorical program "events." These events are largely independent of, and can even be antithetical to, the larger context in which schooling takes place. Accountability procedures ask questions like whether the right (i.e., legally prescribed) students are participating in the program, whether they are receiving the proper kind of help (i.e., help that is consistent with federal requirements), and whether they are benefiting from their participation (i.e., demonstrating achievement gains that are attributable to the program). But critical instructional questions regarding what happens to the student outside the periods when he or she is receiving the categorical service go unaddressed. These are not areas for program inspection and oversight, since such activities occur in places apart from those where categorical program events take place. They thus fall outside the responsibility of the categorical system.

When viewed in this way, it should come as no surprise that Chapter 1 has been the object of increasing criticism in recent years for providing a fragmented and uncoordinated instructional experience for participating children. Since the categorical picket fence is "event centered," there is little institutional incentive for either program or general district administrators to pay attention to conditions and activities falling outside it. Indeed, nearly all the incentives run in the opposite direction. Since accountability is centered on the categorical program event alone, it makes sense to create a separate administrative unit devoted solely to its operations, which then frequently leads to distinct Chapter 1 program offices with dedicated instructional personnel who report to program administrators rather than their school principal. Similarly, because administrators must document that only those eligible to participate in the program event are doing so, there is a preponderance of pull-out programs (in which Chapter 1 students receive program services outside of their regular class- rooms). And since the program is accountable only for achievement gains that are attributable to the event, administrators do not concern themselves with the impacts of the regular instructional program on Chapter 1 students' achievement. What is striking is that *none* of these administrative decisions is likely to be in the best educational interest of the Chapter 1 student. Each, how- ever, is consistent with the institutional incentive structure cre- ated by the picket fence model for delivery of categorical services.

Policymakers have for years been aware of critiques of in- structional aspects of Chapter 1, such as the absence of needed articulation between the categorical program and regular instruc- tional services, and an inordinate focus on pull-out instructional strategies and issues of regulatory compliance rather than pro- gram quality. They responded to these concerns with amend- ments to the legal framework in 1988 including requirements for increased program coordination between Chapter 1 and the regular instructional program, liberalizing the conditions in which Chapter 1 "schoolwide projects" would be permitted,* and re- quiring that schools failing to show gains in the achievement of their Chapter 1 students submit a plan for program improve- ment. However, because these reforms were grafted onto the traditional picket fence categorical program structure (Herrington and Orland, 1991), they have had at best only modest impacts on program services (see also, U.S. Department of Education, 1992). Concern remains unabated about the instructional qual- ity of Chapter 1 and, in particular, its weak links to overall local efforts on behalf of the educationally disadvantaged.

---

* In schoolwide projects, Chapter 1 serves an entire school rather than only designated low-achieving students within a school. By eliminating provisions for targeting individual students and being accountable for them, this reform has the potential for relating Chapter 1 more closely to the overall school instructional program. The 1988 amendments made it somewhat easier for districts with a very high incidence of poverty (75 percent or more of the students from families with poverty-level incomes) to choose this program service option.

## NEW MODELS OF REFORM

One of the reasons the picket fence model has endured is that despite its recognized shortcomings, no generally accepted alternative model of the federal role in meeting the needs of the educationally disadvantaged has emerged. There is strong evidence, however, that a new consensus is now beginning to form around ideas that directly challenge the picket fence paradigm. These ideas originated from the concerns of a diverse set of national policy leaders about the ability of our educational system to provide the necessary "human capital" to secure our economic well-being in the next century (see, for example, Committee for Economic Development, 1985; Council of Chief State School Officers, 1991; National Center for Education and the Economy, 1990; and National Governors' Association, 1987). In an era of increased global competition, it is argued, the knowledge and skills of our people are the most vital resource for determining our future standard of living. A world-class education system is therefore essential to provide the requisite knowledge and skills. Studies throughout the 1980s, however, including *A Nation at Risk* (National Commission on Excellence in Education, 1983) and comparisons of the performance of U.S. students in mathematics and science with that of students in other countries (Lapointe, Mead, and Phillips, 1988) strongly suggested that we did not possess such a system.

To correct this condition, national policy leaders agreed not only about the compelling need for fundamental reform in the educational system but also on some of the basic elements and directions that such reform should take. Among the reform components consistently advocated during the late 1980s were the following:

1. *Outcome-based accountability.* All public officials with education responsibilities should be regularly held accountable for the performance of their schools and students (Business Roundtable, 1991; National Governors' Association, 1986; U.S. Department of Education, 1988).
2. *Curriculum reform.* Curriculum frameworks must be modernized to reflect the content and skills that *all* students need to learn to ensure their own future success and that of the nation (Business Roundtable, 1991; Carnegie

Council on Adolescent Development, 1989; Committee for Economic Development, 1985).

3. *New forms of assessment.* Traditional multiple-choice norm-referenced exams should be replaced by more "authentic" performance-based evaluations of students' competencies and shortcomings (American Association for the Advancement of Science, 1988; Council of Chief State School Officers, 1990; National Research Council, 1989).

4. *Instruction for higher-order thinking.* Classroom instruction needs to place greater emphasis on higher-order reasoning and problem-solving skills for all students (American Association for the Advancement of Science, 1988; Council of Chief State School Officers, 1991; National Research Council, 1989).

5. *Restructured schools.* Principals and teachers should exercise greater control over their school policies and programs to allow for necessary changes in the organization of instruction and learning (Carnegie Council on Adolescent Development, 1989; Council of Chief State School Officers, 1989; National Governors' Association, 1989).

These reform ideas were given added impetus when the President and the nation's governors in February 1990 adopted six ambitious national education goals to be achieved by the year 2000 and when later that year a bipartisan National Education Goals Panel (NEGP) composed of governors, senior administration officials, and members of Congress was created. The function of the NEGP is to monitor national and state progress in reaching the six goals and to lead efforts for creating world-class national education standards and systems of educational assessment aligned to them (National Education Goals Panel, 1991).

In its brief history, the NEGP has helped to shape the national dialogue regarding the direction of educational change. It has embraced the notion of broad outcome-based accountability systems in education as reflected in its selection of performance indicators to profile progress in achieving each of the six goals. It has strongly advocated new outcome-based measurement systems where adequate indicators are currently lacking (such as the creation of an Early Childhood Assessment System to measure the status of children when entering kindergarten).

Most significantly, the Goals Panel has championed the idea of developing national education standards reflecting what all students should know and be able to do at designated grade levels, along with aligned systems of assessment to determine the degree to which students, schools, states, and the nation are meeting these standards. In 1991, the Panel created a National Council for Education Standards and Testing to report on the feasibility and desirability of such reforms (National Council for Education Standards and Testing, 1991). Based on a report of this Council, the Panel has advocated before the Congress the creation of a permanent body under the auspices of the Goals Panel to provide coordination, review, and oversight to new national standards and assessment systems.

The work of these national agenda-setting bodies is beginning to bear fruit. Following the lead of school districts in California, Delaware, Kentucky, and Vermont, school districts nationwide have begun to adopt these new policies on standards and assessment, and in the process have placed the special needs of disadvantaged groups into a broader context of systemic school reform. Increasingly, these districts are developing new curriculum frameworks that incorporate higher-order thinking skills for all students, designing new outcome-based accountability systems, aligning themselves with efforts such as the New Standards Project that will produce new performance-based student examinations in place of the traditional norm-referenced tests, and focusing on the school as the agent of reform through school-based management approaches.

## MOVING TO THE CHAIN LINK FENCE

The new reforms advocated by groups like the National Education Goals Panel and their advocates within the national education policy community represent the strongest challenge ever to the picket fence model of federal categorical service delivery for disadvantaged children. At least three underlying assumptions of the picket fence approach are fundamentally at odds with the direction of the national goals process and the new state and local reform policies emerging from recent national agenda-setting efforts:

- *Assumption 1. That the educational needs of the disadvantaged can be adequately addressed through supplementary basic skills remediation.* The Chapter 1 regulatory framework and related administrative oversight systems encourage the sorting of students by their apparent skill deficits and the delivery of separate remedial instruction to address identified basic skill deficiencies. The national goals process has consistently emphasized that *all students*, regardless of their educational and economic background, can and should master challenging content and complex thinking and problem-solving skills.

- *Assumption 2. That program oversight and accountability should focus on assuring that eligible students are being served legally (process accountability).* The picket fence approach focuses on regulatory compliance with detailed process requirements. The central objective of the system is to ensure that the right students are being served in a legally appropriate manner. The national goals process, by contrast, emphasizes outcome-based accountability models designed to ascertain whether all students are attaining higher-order skills consistent with ambitious national content standards.

- *Assumption 3. That federal aid programs for the disadvantaged should be administered and judged independently of the regular instructional program.* The picket fence model encourages the operation of an organizationally distinct Chapter 1 program that is both managed and evaluated separately from other programs and services. The national goals process, however, emphasizes systemic approaches to educational improvement (O'Day and Smith, 1992), in which policies in different policy and program areas (e.g., curriculum, teacher training, finance, accountability, assessment) are strategically aligned to support the acquisition of challenging content by all students.

National policy bodies are recognizing these basic incompatibilities between the picket fence approach and the new reform paradigm. The initial response has been to recommend wholesale changes in the Chapter 1 legal framework. While the specific federal legislative and administrative remedies proposed thus far vary, they share a revised concept of the federal role that places the needs of Chapter 1 students within a larger framework of overall educational service provision and improvement.

The new model for the federal role is akin to a chain link (rather than picket) fence because it assumes that *all* components of the service delivery system (like all links in the fence chain) must be both strong and connected in order for the education of disadvantaged children to be effective. Certain categories of students may have "special educational needs," but it is educationally dysfunctional when the curriculum, performance expectations, and remediation strategies for these students are separated from those of other students. Indeed, there is an inherent *interdependence* between effectively serving the needs of the disadvantaged and the nature and quality of general educational programs and services. The federal role should therefore foster, rather than inhibit, comprehensive strategies on behalf of disadvantaged students—strategies that are integrated components of a general strategy for educational improvement.

Among the major groups that have recently recommended fundamental changes to the Chapter 1 legal framework to implement this vision of a more integrated and comprehensive service delivery model (i.e., a chain link approach) are the College Board, the Council of Chief State School Officers, and the Independent Commission on Chapter 1. The findings and recommendations of the Independent Chapter 1 Commission are especially worthy of note because it was composed of traditional categorical program advocates, including representatives of the NAACP Legal Defense Fund, the Center for Law and Education, the National Coalition of Title I/Chapter 1 Parents, the National Education Association, and the American Federation of Teachers. In fact, some of the individuals and organizations represented on the Commission were instrumental in creating the Chapter 1 picket fence. The fact that they have begun to embrace a new model of federal intervention attests to the salience of the new reforms in providing a coherent alternative basis for structuring federal programs to educate the disadvantaged. Further, because the Commission's recommendations are coming from those seen by the Congress as sympathetic to the educational needs of the disadvantaged, it is likely that many of the changes being advocated will find their way into new legislation when Chapter 1 is reauthorized.

The Commission advocates a complete restructuring of Chapter 1 with "an entirely new framework [that is] fundamentally and profoundly different" (Commission on Chapter 1, 1992, p. 6). It specifically recommends that Chapter 1 schools be part of the national movement toward high standards for all students linked to new, more "authentic" assessment techniques. To accomplish this, it wants high content, performance, and system delivery standards for all children to form the basis for new Chapter 1 assessment

and accountability structures. To integrate Chapter 1 more fully
with ongoing instructional services, the Commission proposes that
all Chapter 1 students in eligible schools be considered "eligible"
for services, that the nature of such services be determined by
local school (rather than by central office) decisions, that it focus
on making the regular program as rich as possible (in contrast
to the traditional pull-out service model), and that there be substantial financial set-asides for professional and school development
to maximize the likelihood that the instructional strategies and
approaches are appropriate and effective. A congressionally mandated committee on Chapter 1 and a Federal Advisory Committee on Chapter 1 Testing have also proposed major changes to
the Chapter 1 law consistent with components of the new reform
model and the Independent Commission's recommendation.

Nor is Chapter 1 the only federal categorical program likely
to move from a picket fence to a chain link fence paradigm in
the foreseeable future. In October 1991, the National Association of State Boards of Education (1991) issued a report, *Special
Education: New Questions in an Era of Reform*, outlining a new service delivery strategy where special and general education services explicitly complement one another. The Center for Policy
Options in Special Education (1992) has recently published a
monograph describing restructuring options for serving students
with disabilities, including unified curriculum, outcome
expectations, and program administration structures for serving
general and special education students. And both the Council
for Exceptional Children (1992) and National Center for Educational Outcomes (1992) have urged that existing national data
collection systems be modified so that students with disabilities
are fully represented in assessment systems that are monitoring
progress in meeting the National Education Goals. There have
also been recent recommendations for relating the structure and
content of federal categorical programs for migrant children more
closely to general education programs and policies and to the
attainment of the National Education Goals (National Association of State Directors of Migrant Education, 1992).

## SUMMARY AND CONCLUSION

Paradigms in the federal policy arena (as elsewhere) reflect
"conventional wisdom" about social behavior. For years, it was

assumed by most national education policy leaders that states and local school districts were educational "backwaters" who could not be trusted to serve the needs of the disadvantaged. Picket fence federalism was the result.

Today, new models of education reform are emerging as a result of the work of agenda-setting bodies like the National Education Goals Panel, with states and school districts playing the lead role in their refinement and implementation. The reforms incorporate the needs of the disadvantaged into their more general policies and programs through such policies as new curricula content focusing on the attainment of higher-order thinking skills by all students, outcome-based accountability systems, new authentic assessments, and school restructuring.

These events have turned conventional wisdom completely around. Now the federal government is increasingly seen as the education "backwater," retaining an antiquated delivery model past its period of useful life. In particular, the fixation on categorical program "events" inherent in the picket fence model serves to fragment and isolate services to the disadvantaged, stifling more holistic approaches to both serving their needs and assessing their progress.

A new paradigm for federal assistance to disadvantaged groups is likely to emerge from this condition. I call the approach "chain link federalism" because it assumes the need to expressly recognize and address the interdependence of all elements serving the disadvantaged pupil, in order for federal intervention to be successful. While one can never be sure of the contours of pending federal legislation, the initial support for sweeping changes in Chapter 1 by its most traditional advocates—changes that attempt to fully integrate Chapter 1 within a framework of overall instructional reform—strongly suggests that the move from a picket fence to a chain link fence model will soon begin to take place.

Assuming it occurs, the transition from a picket fence to a chain link service delivery model will not be an easy one, and discernible improvements in the achievement of disadvantaged children should not be expected quickly. For one thing, most categorical and general district administrators are not used to working with each other in a coordinated fashion. Categorical administrators in particular are accustomed to working vertical fence "pickets," not horizontal "links." Most have been hired and trained to ensure regulatory "event" compliance, not to facilitate a coherent overall service delivery structure focusing on instructional content and quality. A commitment to retraining and professional development in the short run, and new administrative hiring and staffing structures in the longer run, will be critical if the chain link model is to fulfill its theoretical promise.

Despite these and other problems that are inevitable by-products of change in social programs, the move from a picket fence to a chain link service delivery model should be welcomed. Picket fence federalism is an inherently limited approach, protecting the ability of program participants to receive the assistance they are legally entitled to but, in the process, institutionalizing mediocre program services. There was a time when the need for such protection outweighed all other considerations. The fact that this time is likely past and that new, more productive service delivery arrangements can therefore be explored reflects a maturing intergovernmental service partnership that has considerable potential for benefiting disadvantaged children.

## REFERENCES

American Association for the Advancement of Science. *Science for All Americans: A Project 2061 Report on Literacy Goals in Science, Mathematics, and Technology.* Washington, D.C.: American Association for the Advancement of Science, 1988.

Bailey, Stephen K., and Mosher, Edith K. *ESEA: The Office of Education Administers a Law.* Syracuse, N.Y.: Syracuse University Press, 1968.

Berke, Joel S., and Kirst, Michael W. *Federal Aid in Education: Who Benefits? Who Governs?* Lexington, Mass.: Lexington Books, 1972.

Birman, Beatrice; Orland, Martin E.; Jung, Richard K.; Anson, Ronald J.; and Garcia, Gilbert N. *The Current Operation of the Chapter 1 Program.* Washington, D.C.: U. S. Department of Education, 1987.

Business Roundtable. *The Business Roundtable Participation Guide: A Primer for Business on Education.* Washington, D.C.: Business Roundtable, 1991.

Carnegie Council on Adolescent Development. *Turning Points: Preparing American Youth for the 21st Century.* New York: Carnegie Corporation of New York, 1989.

Center for Policy Options in Special Education. *Issues and Options in Restructuring Schools and Special Education Programs.* College Park, Md.: Center for Policy Options in Special Education, 1992.

Commission on Chapter 1. *Making Schools Work for Children in Poverty.* Washington, D.C.: Commission on Chapter 1, 1992.

Committee for Economic Development. *Investing in Our Children: Business and the Public Schools.* New York: Committee for Economic Development, 1985.

Council for Exceptional Children. *Statement of the Council for Exceptional Children to the Subcommittee on Elementary, Secondary, and Vocational Education of the United States House of Representatives with Respect to the Work of the Na-*

*tional Council on Education Standards and Testing.* Reston, Va.: Council for Exceptional Children, March 1992.

Council of Chief State School Officers. *Restructuring Schools: A Policy Statement of the Council of Chief State School Officers.* Washington, D.C.: Council of Chief State School Officers, 1989.

Council of Chief State School Officers. *Restructuring Learning for All Students: A Policy Statement by the Council of Chief State School Officers on Improved Teaching of Thinking.* Washington, D.C.: Council of Chief State School Officers, 1990.

Council of Chief State School Officers. *Higher Order Learning for All: A Report by the Council of Chief State School Officers on Restructuring Learning.* Washington, D.C.: 1991.

Farrar, Eleanor, and Millsap, Mary Ann. *State and Local Administration of the Chapter 1 Program.* Cambridge, Mass.: Abt Associates, 1986.

Herrington, Carolyn D., and Orland, Martin E. "Politics and Federal Aid to Urban School Systems: The Case of Chapter 1." In *The Politics of Urban Education in the United States,* edited by James G. Cibulka, Rodney J. Reed, and Kenneth K. Wong, pp. 167-179. Washington, D.C.: Falmer Press, 1991.

Hughes, John F. *Equal Opportunity: A New National Strategy.* Bloomington: Indiana University, 1972.

Kirst, Michael W., and Jung, Richard. "The Utility of a Longitudinal Approach in Assessing Implementation: A Thirteen-Year View of Title 1, ESEA." In *Studying Implementation: Methodological and Administrative Issues,* edited by Walter Williams, Richard F. Elmore, J. S. Hall, Richard Jung, Michael Kirst, Susan A. MacManus, B. Narver, Richard P. Nathan, and Robert K. Yin, pp. 119-148. Chatham, N.J.: Chatham Hosue, 1982.

Lapointe, Archie E.; Mead, Nancy A.; and Phillips, Gary W. *A World of Differences: An International Assessment of Mathematics and Science.* Princeton, N.J.: Center for the Assessment of Educational Progress, Educational Testing Service, 1988.

Martin, Ruby, and McClure, Phyllis. *Title I of ESEA: Is It Helping Poor Children?* Washington, D.C.: Washington Research Project of the Southern Center for Studies in Public Policy and the NAACP Legal Defense Fund, 1969.

McConnell, Grant. *Private Power and American Democracy.* New York: Knopf Publishing Co., 1966.

McLaughlin, Milbrey W. "Implementation of ESEA, Title I: A Problem of Compliance," *Teachers College Record* 77, no. 3 (1976): 398-415.

Murphy, Jerome I. "Title I ESEA: The Politics of Implementing Federal Education Reform," *Harvard Educational Review* 41 (February 1971): 35-63.

National Association of State Boards of Education. *Special Education: New Questions in an Era of Reform.* Alexandria, Va.: National Association of State Boards of Education, 1991.

National Association of State Directors of Migrant Education. *Rethinking Migrant Education: A Response to the National Educational Goals.* Washington, D.C.: National Association of State Directors of Migrant Education, 1992.

National Center on Education and the Economy. *America's Choice: High Skills or Low Wages.* Rochester, N.Y.: National Center on Education and the Economy, 1990.

National Center for Educational Outcomes. *Brief Reports on the National Educational*

*Goals and Students with Disabilities.* Minneapolis: College of Education, University of Minnesota, 1992.

National Commission on Excellence in Education. *A Nation at Risk.* Washington, D.C.: U. S. Department of Education, 1983.

National Council for Education Standards and Testing. *Raising Standards for American Education.* Washington, D.C.: National Council for Education Standards and Testing, 1991.

National Education Goals Panel. *The 1991 National Education Goals Report: Building a Nation of Learners.* Technical Report No. 91-09. Washington, D.C.: National Education Goals Panel, 1991.

National Governors' Association. *Time for Results: The Governors' 1991 Report on Education.* Washington, D.C.: National Governors' Association, 1986.

National Governors' Association. *Making America Work: Jobs, Growth, and Competitiveness.* Washington, D.C.: National Governors' Association, 1987.

National Governors' Association. *Results in Education, 1989.* Washington, D.C.: National Governors' Association, 1989.

National Research Council. *Everybody Counts: A Report to the Nation on the Future of Mathematics Education.* Washington, D.C.: National Academy Press, 1989.

*New York Times*, "Panels in Congress Limit Reagan Plan for Block Grants," 11 July 1981, p. 1.

O'Day, Jennifer A., and Smith, Marshall S. "Systemic Reform and Educational Opportunity." Unpublished manuscript, School of Education, Stanford University, 1992.

Odden, Allan. "How Fiscal Accountability and Program Quality Can Be Insured for Chapter 1." *In Policy Options for the Future of Compensatory Education: Conference Papers*, edited by Denis P. Doyle, Joan S. Michie, and Barbara I. Williams. Washington, D.C.: Research and Evaluation Associates, 1987.

Peterson, Paul. *City Limits.* Chicago: University of Chicago Press, 1981.

Schattschneider, E. E. *The Semisovereign People.* Hinsdale, Ill.: Dryden Press, 1960.

Smith, Marshall S. "Selecting Students and Services for Chapter 1." In *Policy Options for the Future of Compensatory Education: Conference Papers*, edited by Denis P. Doyle, Joan S. Michie, and Barbara I. Williams, pp. 109-134. Washington, D.C.: Research and Evaluation Associates, 1987.

Timar, Thomas. "Federal Educational Policy and Practices: Building Organizational Capacity through Chapter 1." Paper prepared for the Advisory Committee on Testing in Chapter 1. Riverside: University of California, 1992.

U. S. Department of Education. *Creating Responsible and Responsive Accountability Systems: Report of the OERI State Accountability Study Group.* Washington, D.C.: U. S. Department of Education, 1988.

U. S. Department of Education. *National Assessment of the Chapter 1 Program: The Interim Report.* Washington, D.C.: U. S. Department of Education, 1992.

Wright, Deil S. *Understanding Intergovernmental Relations*, 2d ed. Monterey, Calif.: Brooks/Cole Publishing Co., 1982.

# ———9———

# School-Linked Services and Chapter I: A New Approach to Improving Outcomes for Children

## *Michael W. Kirst, Julia E. Koppich, and Carolyn Kelley*

The general topic of integrated children's services has come to occupy an increasingly prominent place on the political and public policy agenda. The reason seems relatively straightforward: "Report cards" for children and families, whether examined from national, state, or local perspectives, reveal a steady decline in the life situations for many of this nation's young people.

A generation after President Lyndon Baines Johnson declared the nation's official War on Poverty, 20 percent of America's children remain poor. In fact, fully 40 percent of America's poor are children under the age of 18. Poverty in the United States knows no racial or geographic boundaries. But the problems attendant to it have a lasting impact on children's lives.

Large numbers of American children have inadequate health care, never see a dentist, and are left to care for themselves for long hours while their parents are at work. Many others encounter the juvenile justice system or come from abusive homes. The number of single parents has exploded dramatically since

This paper was prepared for the U.S. Department of Education Chapter 1 Reauthorization Study, November 1992.

Chapter I was initiated in 1965. And problems follow children into adulthood. Real wages for those with a high school education or less have declined precipitously in the last twenty-five years.

We believe that out-of-school influences, which consume more than 70 percent of children's lives, have a crucial effect on education and other life-enhancing or life-detracting outcomes for children. Moreover, a growing body of scholars, researchers, children's advocates, and social service providers have become convinced that education alone cannot overcome the *interrelated* problems of children and their families. Just as children's problems are not separate from the life situations of their families, the variety of challenges confronting large numbers of this nation's children on a daily basis cannot be separated one from another. They are intertwined and interconnected.

Many educators especially have come to realize that they cannot improve education without external support. They must form cohesive partnerships with other agencies and individuals outside the school's conventional purview. Moreover, those in education know that schools cannot become comprehensive social service providers by using only education funds and only school-related personnel. Finally, there is a growing recognition among educators and social service providers alike that the system currently in place for providing children's services is fundamentally flawed and in need of a complete overhaul.

We believe that Chapter I of the Elementary and Secondary Education Act can be a critical component of a new, potentially more effective system of school-linked services. Chapter I has an opportunity to play a particularly crucial role in schools in which 75 percent or more of the children are poor, and thus the entire school is eligible for Chapter I assistance.

In this paper, we will suggest how Chapter I can promote a system of school-linked services. We begin, however, by sketching the fundamentals and operational procedures of school-linked services. Then we will demonstrate how Chapter I, particularly the concepts embedded in schoolwide Chapter I activities, can be used to enhance a system of comprehensive school-linked services.

## THE OUTLINE OF A NEW SYSTEM OF
## SCHOOL-LINKED SERVICES

The concept underlying school-linked services (SLS) is a rather simple one: the school becomes the "hub," or focal point, of a broad range of child- and family-oriented social services. Schools do not assume primary responsibility for these additional services, but the school acts as the organizational touchpoint to make services available, accessible, meaningful, and appropriate for children and their families.

A working definition of school-linked services is:

> an interagency system linking schools and local public and private human service agencies with the support of business, higher education and other community resources. This system is designed to meet the interrelated educational, social, and psychological needs of children. SLS empowers parents to better tailor and consume public and private systems. [Kirst and Kelley, 1992, p. 9]

Advocates of school-linked services contend that the school provides the organizational context for the most sustained contact with most children. Nearly all young people attend school. Moreover, there is less stigma attached to attending school than there might be to making known the need for other social services. Schools, then, can provide an appropriate setting—some would argue the most appropriate setting—for integrating a range of services children need to succeed. (For a somewhat different perspective, see Chaskin and Richman [1992].)

In a system of school-linked services, services such as health care, counseling, and various forms of public financial assistance might actually be located at the school site, with professionals from social service agencies "outstationed" at the school. Alternatively, a case worker, familiar with a range of services, might be assigned to the school to work with children and their families, "brokering" an array of prospective service offerings.

SLS might be thought of as "one-stop shopping" for children's services. Under the current system, a typical situation for the consumer of children's services is that there are at least five agencies (welfare, children's protection, health, etc.) in five separate locations. Clients with limited resources have to travel, usually by bus, to reach all the offices where they might find services. School-linked services ease the burden on consumers of children's services by providing one convenient location, just as a Safeway supermarket provides a broad array of consumer products for its customers. But just putting services in one place is not sufficient if the existing services are inadequate, poorly designed, and badly executed. There must be attention to the quality, adequacy, and appropriateness of services, and how these services can be orchestrated to help children and families in a comprehensive, intensive, and effective manner.

Moreover, potentially effective programs share a few critical elements: a common belief that caring relations are crucial, and emphasis on coping strategies and provision of nonmonetary incentives to help youth value positive choices (Urban Institute, 1992, pp. 14–15). In addition, programs with the potential for success have a clear statement of the value or values motivating the program, adopt a family-centered orientation, display broad community involvement, find clear, consistent, and meaningful ways to include the education system, emphasize high-quality services, and carefully evaluate the needs of children and their families (Soler and Shauffer, 1993).

A system of school-linked services attempts to overcome the shortcomings and failures of the current system that aims to, but falls far short of, assisting poor children and their families. To be sure, there is a wealth of child- and family-oriented public policy and programs at the federal, state, and local levels. But a growing body of scholarly research points to the conclusion that conventional systems of assistance for children and families, which typically result in fractionated governance—multiple programs in multiple agencies—and unconnected funding streams—the classic categorical aid formulas—may be exacerbating rather than alleviating the problem of ensuring that services reach clients.

The current system of social service provision is plagued by a series of fundamental structural problems. The first of these is underservice. Too many children are slipping through the cracks in the social service system and receiving little or no assistance at all. The result is a highly inequitable system in which some children and families are able to avail themselves of service offerings and others are barely aware that help is possible.

The second problem with the current organization of social services for children and families is that, in general, it does not focus on prevention. Most governmental agencies, because of policy preference, fiscal constraints, or longstanding tradition, have adopted a triage approach to children's problems. They focus on acute cases rather than on prevention, and view problems as episodic rather than continuous. Consequently, service providers treat only the most severe and manifest problems, but pay little attention to preventing problems from developing in the first place.

Third, service provision is highly fragmented. The social service system generally is composed of a series of targeted programs with overlapping or conflicting eligibility requirements, and a complicated web of rules and regulations overseen by a bewildering array of seemingly autonomous bureaucracies. The state of California alone, for example, maintains 169 children- and youth-serving agencies overseen by 37 different state entities located in 7 different state departments. Social service agencies all too infrequently cooperate with one another or coordinate their efforts. Social workers rarely talk with mental health professionals who have little time to talk with school counselors who infrequently communicate with juvenile justice officials. Yet all of these professionals may be dealing with the same children and families.

Finally, the current system is unaccountable. Individual agencies focus on inputs rather than outcomes. And agencies pay scant attention to ways in which their systems impact on the total outcome, namely, the life prospects for children and families.

What is needed is exactly the reverse of the system that currently prevails. In other words, the system of services available to children and families needs to be reformulated so that it is comprehensive, continuous, integrated, equitable, and focused on outcomes (Schorr, 1988).

A viable SLS approach changes the underlying system of service provision. It is not a collection of projects added on to an unchanging base, but rather is reconstituted as a cohesive, integrated whole. Moreover, a well-developed SLS system pays attention to quality and outcomes. It is, in other words, accountable to its clients.

What might a school-linked services program look like in operation? First of all, the facility or set of facilities would be located on or near school grounds. (It is not essential that services be available at the school site—that the program be school-*based*—only that it have a direct connection to the school—that it be school-*linked*.)

The facility that houses a school-linked services operation might well be open from 6 A.M. to 6 P.M. to better serve the needs of working parents. The program itself might encompass the following components:

- Parent education and adult education programs funded by the local community college would be available at the school-linked services site.
- After-school recreation programs funded by various city government agencies would be available to participating children.
- A nurse practitioner who, unlike school nurses, can administer some medications and deal with some specific health problems, would be part of the school-linked services personnel.
- Mental health facilities, including counseling services, would be available to children and families.
- On-site assistance from the social welfare offices would be available to assist in solving family problems.
- Collaboration with various probation and job-training agencies would provide expanded opportunities for high-school-age students.
- School-based programs provided by agencies like Boys Clubs and the scouts would be expanded to become part of the comprehensive school-linked services effort.

## A DEMONSTRATION PROGRAM IN OPERATION

Some communities have launched interesting and innovative school-linked services efforts. One such community is San Diego, California. San Diego's program, called New Beginnings, is part of a national experimental school-linked services program, funded in part by the Annie E. Casey Foundation. New Beginnings is based in a single school, Hamilton Elementary School. What does this approach to school-linked services look like?

Hamilton Elementary School is part of the San Diego Unified School District, a K-12 unified district that currently educates more than 100,000 students. Hamilton is located in San Diego's inner-city area. It is, in other words, an urban school in an area of modest single family homes that have seen more prosperous times.

Hamilton is an old school. Among its "glitziest" features are the large gold letters on the outside of the building, which proclaim "Alexander Hamilton Elementary School." Otherwise, the outside of the building is nondescript institutional beige.

Inside, the floors of the school are "carpeted" in regulation brown linoleum. A visitor's eyes, however, are drawn immediately to a great set of murals decorating the hall walls.

Hamilton suffers from the deferred maintenance problems endemic to California schools. If one were to visit the school on a rainy day, it is likely one would see state-issued green metal wastebaskets positioned strategically in hallways and classrooms to catch the rain coming through holes in the roof.

Hamilton is the academic home to 1,300 students, grades kindergarten through 5. The school is on a year-round schedule, with students divided into four "tracks." Three tracks are in school at any given time.

Hamilton's student population is representative of the increasing heterogeneity of California's populace. The school's student body is 35 percent Hispanic, 25 percent Asian (Cambodians, Laotians, Hmong, and Vietnamese), 25 percent black, and 12 percent white.

Hamilton's students are not from well-to-do families. Many receive Aid to Families with Dependent Children (AFDC). Some children come to school hungry, some in ill health. Some of the students come from abusive homes. Many of the families are recent immigrants, and large numbers of the adults are unemployed. Many Hamilton children and parents do not speak English (twenty-one home languages are spoken at Hamilton).

One distinguishing feature of Hamilton Elementary School is its school-linked services program. Across the asphalt playground are two portable classrooms that house the New Beginnings Center, an interagency restructuring effort that represents the cooperation of the school district, the San Diego Children's Hospital, the San Diego Department of Social Services, the county Probation Authority, the City Housing Commission, and the San Diego Community College District. New Beginnings is meant to offer Hamilton students and their families a range of social services, all available on the school grounds.

Much study and planning preceded the initiation of New Beginnings. A preliminary analysis and feasibility study revealed that 60 percent of Hamilton families were involved with one or more of the participating social service agencies. Moreover, this same study revealed that $10 million was being spent on social services and out-of-classroom supports to families with children in the Hamilton attendance area. Some of these funds were being spent on duplicated services.

The New Beginnings Center officially opened in September 1991. The entire effort is designed to provide a continuum of services to children and families through three interlinked tiers.

Tier 1 is the school. Teachers serve as the primary resource for referrals and a source of on-going information and feedback about the effectiveness of services provided at the Center.

Tier 2 is the Center itself. It houses retrained staff from the participating agencies. Eight staff members, or "family service advocates," come from the ranks of educators, social workers, and health care practitioners. The advocates themselves are counselors, social workers, and a nurse practitioner.

New Beginning's Tier 3 is composed of an extended team of agency staff located in their "home" agencies. They meet regularly with Center staff for training and consultation.

What activities actually take place at the Center? What functions does the Center perform? First, all Hamilton School registration is handled at the Center. All students—whether they need social service assistance or not—report to the Center for registration. No stigma is attached to a child's initial appearance at the Center. Thus, Center staff are able to assess "hidden" needs of children and families. Family assessment is part of the school registration process. Center staff endeavor to determine the complement of services children and their families might need.

The Center itself provides immunizations and physical examinations for children, mental health services, and assistance in determining eligibility for various public assistance programs. (Health service offerings are in the process of being expanded through a new partnership with the University of California at San Diego Health Alliance.) The San Diego Community College District offers English-as-a-second-language and parenting classes.

New Beginnings represents a clear example of an effort to blend services for children and families in one location. The arrangement makes it possible, even necessary, for different professionals who deal with children to work as a team on behalf of each child and his or her family rather than, as often happens, as advocates for their particular services and programs. New Beginnings thus has potentially far-reaching consequences for the organization of social services for children and families.

## FUNDING SCHOOL-LINKED SERVICES

Of course, an SLS program must have funding. One important key to school-linked services is "stream diversion," which allows the system to be largely financially self-sustaining. Stream diversion does not rely on vast infusions of new funding, but taps existing funding streams and deposits them into one "pool."

It is thus not surprising that more creative and flexible use of federal program dollars is a recurrent theme in the financial strategies for school-linked services. The bulk of federal revenues derive from four major programs: Medicaid; Early and Periodic Screening, Diagnosis, and Treatment Service (EPSDT); Title IV E—Jobs Program; and Title IV F—Child Welfare Assistance and Family Support Act of 1988.

- *Medicaid.* Medicaid, created in 1965 through Title XIX of the Social Security Act, is a state-administered program to provide health services to the poor. Medicaid coverage and eligibility vary widely among states, and states have wide latitude in determining both Medicaid eligibility and benefits. States choosing to offer a Medicaid program must provide particular mandated services and may provide up to thirty-one optional services. One option is to expand a category known as "rehabilitation services." States could, in effect, develop a new category of rehabilitation services to be furnished by local school districts for Medicaid-eligible low-income children. Under this optional rehabilitation services classification, local school districts could become eligible Medicaid providers. The school district could then bill the state, which, in turn, bills the federal government.
- *EPSDT.* All states participating in Medicaid must provide Early and Periodic Screening, Diagnosis, and Treatment (EPSDT) that targets children and stresses prevention. EPSDT is designed to detect, diagnose, and fully treat children's health needs. EPSDT could be used to finance special education screening services, case management services and outreach, screening, and health prevention. Services provided under EPSDT are not required for Medicaid-eligible adults, so costs can be limited to children.
- *Title IV E.* Title IV E of the Social Security Act primarily reimburses states for foster care maintenance, but in 1980 was expanded to include efforts to prevent placement and restore families. Title IV E requires state matching of between 50 percent and 75 percent, depending on the state's wealth. Eligible services could be provided on school grounds.
- *Family Support Act.* The Family Support Act of 1988 (FSA) is designed to help AFDC parents obtain skills and training

needed to avoid long-term welfare support. Adult education programs on school grounds could be federally reim-
bursed and involve child care at the school. AFDC-eligible
teen parents could be covered for case management and
other school-based supportive services. FSA funds have a
matching rate of between 50 and 72 percent.

In short, several current federal social services programs could
be used to provide the bulk of funding for school-linked social
services. To tap these sources entails understanding their program requirements, creative design of school-linked services to
meet those requirements, and new school planning, record keep-
ing, and documentation to comply with federal billing and accountability standards. (See Kirst [1992] for a more complete
treatment of this topic.)

## THE HISTORY OF CHAPTER I AND SLS:
## A FAILED OPPORTUNITY

In 1965 and the immediate years thereafter, Title I (now Chapter I) was a major supplier of health and social services to eligible students. The first field review of Title I revealed that social
and health services were a prominent component of Title I programs, especially in the Southeast.

From an impoverished corner of Missouri, where an estimated
50 percent of the people were on relief, a case analyst reported:

> Every Title I dollar was really being spent for things like glasses, or
> for potatoes to feed the kids. A lot of people were working for noth-
> ing in the programs so that the dollars could be saved for the kids.
> A nurse told me that one out of three referrals in the summer pro-
> gram was having difficulty learning because of some physical condi-
> tion. Either they couldn't see the books they were supposed to be
> reading, or they couldn't properly hear the teacher. Some of the
> kids had gotten as far as the fifth grade without ever seeing right.
> I'd walk into a class and see kids asleep ten minutes after they got to
> school. They were tired simply from being hungry. There's some-
> thing wrong when a twelve-year-old kid has to fall asleep in the middle
> of the morning. I've had a lot of contact with city poverty, but this
> opened my eyes to something new! [National Advisory Council on
> the Education of Disadvantaged Children, 1965]

A similar report came from a researcher who analyzed a Title I program in a small town in South Carolina, where 94 percent of the school enrollment fell under the line of Title I eligibility, a family income level of $2,000:

> This program ended up almost entirely on the visceral level of feeding, clothing, equipping two schools with cafeterias where there were none before, and contracting with physicians, dentists, and nurses. It would have been a welfare program pure and simple, except that they still found their way clear to establish school libraries and bring them up to the State minimum requirement. There's one thing about a small Southern town like this. These people know—they're excruciatingly aware of—their big needs. They don't have to have a survey. They'll say, "The people over in that section are starving to death. The ones in this section won't come to school in the winter if they don't have clothes." So they threw all their money where they knew they needed it the most. Some people may say that this wasn't an educational program, but I don't have a word to say in criticism of what they did. You'd think it was all very depressing, yet all through the people there I found an excitement. They seemed to be bouncing with joy in their chairs, saying, "Somebody is really helping us get out of our bloody mess." [National Advisory Council on the Education of Disadvantaged Children, 1965, p. 38]

While these efforts were helpful, there was an inevitable limit to how much of conventional social service assistance the schools could provide. The old Title I model was school based, school funded, and school implemented. It represented no collaboration with or linkage to other services. Rather, the school attempted to "do it all." Moreover, there were hostile relationships between the War on Poverty, through the Office of Economic Opportunity (OEO), and educators. Thus, any natural collaboration that might have occurred was constrained by unsettled interagency relationships. The 1965 Chapter I field review reported:

> On the whole, local cooperation between Title I educators and Community Action Programs seldom goes beyond the formal requirement that local CAP central administrators affix a signature to Title I school plans. The 1965 National Advisory Council on Disadvantaged Children urged greater mutual involvement of school officials on the one hand and parents and neighborhood antipoverty groups on the other, in the planning and implementation of a concerted attack designed to change the total environment of the disadvantaged child. [National Advisory Council on the Education of Disadvantaged Children, 1965, p. 15]

As federal resources became more restrictive, Title I regulations discouraged the use of funds for social services. In 1970-71, local education agencies (LEAs) were required to obtain a sign-off and check with other agencies before schools could offer health or other social services. Schools, for their part, discouraged the use of Chapter I for health because sign-offs were time-consuming and relationships between agencies were distant. The concept of collaboration was largely unexplored. School boards, the governing arm of school districts, maintained scant contact with other children's service agencies.

The Chapter I check-off language was eliminated in 1976, but still there was no statutory or governmental impetus to link services. School-linked services became much like many other potential changes in Chapter I—feasible but rarely thought about and hardly ever implemented.

Current law provides authority for school-linked services and the use of Chapter I to provide social services. If LEAs complete a needs assessment that demonstrates the highest priority "impediments to learning" are health, social services, preschool education, and the like, then Chapter I funds can be used to provide these (Lobasco, 1992). A local district evaluation must show that this use of funds is helping in educational attainment.

But few schools understand school-linked services or even contemplate a potential role for Chapter I in initiating, implementing, and maintaining a system of SLS. Chapter I Technical Assistance Centers are not focused on and are rarely equipped to implement SLS. Schoolwide authority is a good conceptual complement to SLS, but not used for this purpose. Schoolwide projects, permissible in schools in which at least 75 percent of the students live below the poverty level, may use Chapter I funds throughout the school rather than targeting funds to selected students. As of 1991 there were 1,712 schoolwide projects in 520 LEAs in 42 states. The number of schoolwide projects increased after passage of the Hawkins-Stafford Amendments, since the requirement for matching funds was eliminated. Most schoolwide projects focus on reducing class size and implementing effective schools models. But there are about 6,000 schools eligible to adopt this approach.

We believe that a combination of schoolwide eligibility with SLS is the most promising way to proceed. Schoolwide projects avoid the issue of students who are not eligible for Chapter I receiving social services. Moreover, schoolwide services view the

instructional programs so that teachers know how family conditions affect students' performance in school. Unless teachers are invested in this system change—unless they "own" it—it becomes just another project grafted onto a host of seemingly autonomous, and endless, projects. Restructuring that is viewed strictly as a curriculum project of school-site decentralization has nothing to do with linking to services beyond the schools. Teachers must know how and when to refer students to a collaborative center and have regular channels for feedback from the center about how to reorient their instructional and disciplinary practices. Teachers need to have frequent conferences with center staff and to welcome their class parents who use center services.

• Developing a new system of accountability for interagency collaborations. Agencies need to track the joint outcomes of their combined services and determine the effectiveness of those services. A new data-collection system could be created in which some of the agencies are required to share forms and formats. An early step is to decide how employees from several agencies can be relocated near school grounds, and incentive systems established so that these relocated employees are encouraged to collaborate.

Chapter I could fund all or part of the start-up activities listed above.

In addition, Chapter I could also be used for some of the costs of building a merged management information system, and a common intake and assessment system. Under the current arrangement, families with multiple problems must tell their life story to an array of different bureaucracies. The broader focus of children rather than schooling outcomes could be financed in part by Chapter I evaluation money. The strategy should *not* be to shift all of these infrastructure costs to Chapter I, but some components might be financed by Chapter I funds.

Finally, Chapter I funds could also be used for staff development that enhances interprofessional work across several children's services agencies.

### System Implementation

Chapter I funds could also be crucial during the initial implementation phase, and could be used for the following initial implementation activities:

- Central offices need to appoint middle managers who provide liaison between school sites and district offices. Much of the management will be "groping along," but site administrators need someone to clarify and reinterpret central office policies.
- An early problem in some LEAs is how to retrofit existing school facilities for multiple children's services.
- Principals are crucial for organizing teacher involvement and assuring school personnel of the success of such programs.

One of the first steps in implementing a system of school-linked services involves developing or securing venture capital, or "glue money." Glue money cements the system together for start-up planning, for building information systems, for creating commitment among the line workers, and for planning for financing. Chapter I could be the glue money in a system of SLS.

### Operational Funding

SLS requires some coordination staff to supervise the "line workers" who have been redeployed from health, social service, juvenile justice, and other agencies to the school site. In some local contexts, Chapter I might be an appropriate source for coordination money. Other sources, including United Way or shared funding by several agencies, also might be appropriate.

## THE COMPREHENSIVE HEALTH READINESS STRATEGY

Martin Gherry of the Department of Health and Human Services and Jack McDonald of the U.S. Department of Education have proposed a comprehensive health readiness strategy based on Chapter I schoolwide areas. (This strategy would require the Secretary of the Department of Health and Human Services (HHS) to waive various Medicaid requirements.) This approach could provide major fiscal support for health and related services in schoolwide attendance areas, particularly in urban regions. Current Chapter I schoolwide projects are 50 percent urban, 24 percent rural, 12 percent small towns, and 87 percent suburban (Gherry and McDonald, 1992).

Under Gherry and McDonald's comprehensive health readiness strategy, a state would be permitted to declare any school attendance area that meets Chapter I criteria for schoolwide projects a "universal health readiness service area" or UHRSA. Within such an UHRSA, all school-age *and* younger children would be provided a comprehensive package of preventive and acute health care services, consistent with the requirements of the Early and Periodic Screening, Diagnosis, and Treatment (EPSDT) program and *without regard to the eligibility of an individual child* under the Medicaid program. The choice of a coordinated care mechanism for structuring the provision of these services would be left to state and local determination. Options would include direct services provided by Community Health Centers, Even Start programs, or other public agencies, and contracted services provided by a health maintenance organization (HMO) or other private coordinated care provider.

Consistent with EPSDT regulations for program design, the comprehensive health readiness strategy would include a comprehensive "case management" component that would permit states to fund an important new vehicle for coordinating a wide range of children's and family services and for improving the prevention of child abuse and neglect. The choice of structure for providing this service would again be left to state and local discretion and could be separated from or integrated with the responsibility for providing health care services. The financing of this entire comprehensive health readiness strategy would be drawn from joint federal/state capitated payments, principally under the Medicaid-EPSDT program.

## Administration

The comprehensive health readiness strategy would be jointly administered by the Chapter I program in the Office of Elementary and Secondary Education of the U.S. Department of Education and the Medicaid Bureau of the Health Care Financing Administration of the U.S. Department of Health and Human Services. A single consolidated application would permit states to request, simultaneously, designation for Chapter I schoolwide services and as a universal health-readiness service area (through the approval of a Medicaid waiver). Applications would be handled by both agencies at a central office level and on an expedited (no more than sixty days) review basis.

## Preparation and Planning

To assist states in developing comprehensive health-readiness applications and to plan for long-term learning-readiness systems change, grants jointly funded by HHS, the Department of Education, and interested foundations would be awarded to support state planning and capacity building over a twelve- to eighteen-month period. The major focus of this effort would be the formulation of plans based on school attendance areas, for ensuring learning assistance. At a minimum, these plans would address the provision and coordination of preschool and elementary education, child care, health care, nutritional support, parenting, adult literacy, and counseling services to all children and families residing in the attendance area.

The capitated funding strategy proposed by Gherry and McDonald could save between 18 and 23 percent of the total cost of Medicaid because of the elimination of individual and third-party billing requirements. But the federal share requires a state and local match of between 20 and 50 percent, depending on the wealth of the state. The match, however, might come from state and local funds that are freed up from the federal Medicaid assumption of current school health and special education costs. This strategy is called "refinancing" and uses matching dollars, local money that is newly eligible for federal reimbursement.

Another financing strategy could be "hooked" funding so that students flow easily from Chapter I to other related or reinforcing programs. For example, in some localities, foster children automatically qualify when they leave school to move to a local job-training program. All children in a schoolwide project school site could be part of an SLS project using some Chapter I money. Or Chapter I could pay for the second half of a full-day Headstart Program. Children in Chapter I schoolwide project schools would automatically qualify for health services under Gherry and McDonald's proposal.

## BARRIERS TO SCHOOL-LINKED SERVICES

Those who embrace the concept of school-linked services recognize its complexity. They, too, raise substantive questions about institutional challenges and real, or popularly perceived, barriers to an integrated-services approach. Issues to be confronted include the following:

- Funding—Services generally are funded categorically, making collaboration complicated, if not problematic.
- Space—Finding adequate and accessible space for a range of services can be a tricky matter, especially in overcrowded urban schools.
- Confidentiality—Providers raise concerns about sharing potentially stigmatizing information about clients, particularly minors.
- Governance—Who is in charge of a coordinated services effort? If one agency assumes primary governance responsibility, will the other participating agencies consider themselves full partners? If no agency takes the lead, then where does responsibility for service delivery rest?
- Staff training—Problems begin with splintered professional preparation on the university campus. Educators attend schools of education; social workers attend schools of social welfare; health professionals receive their professional preparation in schools of medicine or public health; juvenile justice workers are trained in criminology schools; county executives go to public administration schools; and so on. Interprofessional contact is rare; cross-professional education rarer still. As an example, recently a foundation in California gave a grant to a large university in the state to allow faculty members and students from the education school to "meet" their counterparts in the school of social welfare. They had coexisted in isolation from one another for forty years.

  Initial professional preparation is followed by involvement in isolated professional networks that rarely interact and have no staff development across professions. Since the professionals do not know one another, it is difficult to overcome, for example, informal legal conventions regarding the confidentiality of a child's records. It is not uncommon for five different agencies to be assisting the same child and family and not be aware of one another's involvement. Some children's records need to be confidential, but parents will often waive these rights. The information systems of the various children's agencies, however, are not linked or cross-referenced (Gardner, 1989).

The concerns raised, both by critics and by integrated service advocates, are real, yet so are the problems. Educators find
themselves increasingly handicapped as they attempt to create a
climate for educational success for students who, in ever larger
numbers, come to school ill-equipped to focus on academics.

## CURRENT FEDERAL PROPOSALS FOR SLS

Several federal-level proposals designed programmatically to
"match" Chapter I and school-linked services are circulating in the
policy environment. In this section, we review a selection of them.

### *Recommendations of the Independent Chapter I Commission*

The recommendations of the Independent Commission on
Chapter I (1992) suggest that health and social services be addressed at both the state and local levels. Governors would be
required to identify barriers to learning, develop plans to eliminate these barriers, and prepare an annual report on progress
toward eliminating health and social impediments to learning.

The key sections of the Commission draft relate to the local-
level reports to state education agencies concerning barriers to
learning from factors external to the schools such as poor health
and housing. LEAs would be required to assess "the extent to
which locally based collaborative efforts among education, health
and social service providers might facilitate increased access [to]
and effective delivery of services." In preparing these reports,
each LEA would be required to consult with other children's
and services agencies. The draft recommends the following statutory language: "LEAs may use Chapter I funds to pay professional and other staff salaries, and other expenses incurred in
carrying out the purposes of this section including ... integration and coordination of services with other local, state, or federal providers (Independent Commission on Chapter I, 1992).

This type of authority for using Chapter I for SLS needs to
be embedded in the broader vision and concepts analyzed in
the prior sections of this chapter. Requiring SEAs and LEAs to
analyze the interrelated problems of children may be merely an
exercise in paper shuffling if there is no impetus for interagency
collaboration. Collaboration starts in cities with agreements from
officials at the top of the social service system, such as school
superintendents, mayors (or their representatives), and directors

of social services agencies. Chapter I coordinators will not be able to initiate this kind of high-level dialogue or stimulate much without an analytical plan.

Even more of an impediment is that very few Chapter I coordinators know anything about how to devise a system of school-linked services. In at least one large city, for example, a school superintendent who wanted to use Chapter I for SLS was advised by his Chapter I coordinator that this was not an allowable expenditure. This kind of advice is correct if the district attempts to hire health and social service personnel for all schools, but, as previously suggested in this paper, Chapter I funds could be used for SLS in schoolwide projects.

Should this approach be adopted, Chapter I coordinators, who may lack enthusiasm for the change, will require intensive staff development in order to grasp the potential of collaboration and make it come alive. They must be reassured that SLS does not use school funds for social services—does not supplant, but only supplements—but rather is a convergence at the school site of many funding streams from numerous public or private agencies.

## Comprehensive Services for Children and Youth Act

The Comprehensive Services for Children and Youth Act (S1133) was introduced in 1991 in the U.S. Senate. The Act includes new monies that would provide many of the same types of services as could be provided with Chapter I funds in schoolwide eligible schools as described above. Although no action was taken on the bill in the legislative session just ended, the authors (Senators Edward Kennedy and Bill Bradley) intend to continue to pursue this type of legislation in the 1993 congressional session. The bill incorporated ideas introduced earlier in the session in the Link Up for Learning Act (S619) as well as ideas from the National School Board Association's school-linked services legislative proposal.

The Act would have provided $50 million in 1992 (and $75 million in 1993) in demonstration grants ($100,000 to $500,000 each) or planning grants ($50,000 in the first year) to sites linking schools with nonprofit and public-sector service providers. The federal share of the grant would be 80 percent, with local collaboratives providing 20 percent in cash or in kind. Funds could be used for renting space, coordinating services, integrating databases, integrating administrative structures, and developing networks, as well as for needs assessment and case planning and management by interagency teams of providers.

Eligible projects would be those that serve students enrolled in schools participating in schoolwide projects under Chapter I and the families of such students, or students enrolled in the most economically disadvantaged schools in the LEA, or out-of-school at-risk students, or a combination of the above groups. The bill also includes language amending the Hawkins Human Services Reauthorization Act of 1990 to identify and eliminate regulations that impede coordination and collaboration of services.

## Models for Improving the Quality of Low-Income, Urban, and Minority Schools

Several models have been developed by educational researchers and policymakers over the past three decades to address the special needs and problems of low-income, urban, and minority schools, the prime recipients of Chapter I funds and services. Among these are the Comer Model, Accelerated Schools, Effective Schools, and School-Based Management. Each program, in its own way, envisions the *school* as the unit of analysis. Each is predicated on a specific outcome orientation. Although each defines the educational problem slightly differently, the models all recognize the importance of focusing school resources on improving student learning. With this as a goal, each model attempts to create an environment in which teachers, staff, parents, and communities can work together to eliminate barriers to learning.

In theory, none of these models specifically requires an emphasis on school-linked coordinated services. However, SLS is entirely consistent with, and may actually enhance the potential benefits of, each of these models by eliminating barriers to learning by improving access to health and social services that can enable children and families to focus on learning, rather than on basic survival. In addition, a system of school-linked services contemplates services being provided by health and social service agency personnel, enabling teachers and other school personnel to focus on delivering quality education to students.

## CONCLUSION

In this chapter, we have illustrated how a system of school-linked services might enhance a reauthorized and revised

Chapter I. Specifically, we have endeavored to describe ways in which earmarked portions of Chapter I funds might break with the traditional categorical program orientation and instead become dollars that link a range of programs needed by those students who are the principal targets of Chapter I efforts.

We would conclude this chapter with some summary observations, suggestions, and caveats. First, it is important to remember that the problems of children cannot be separated from the problems of their families. Treating the "whole child" entails paying substantial attention to the home situation of the child.

Second, ESEA was seen (at least by some of its proponents twenty-five years ago) as an education-based solution to poverty. It was not that. Similarly, a system of school-linked services should not be viewed as a new "savior" program, this year's panacea for children in need. It is not that any more than ESEA was education's cure for poverty. School-linked services is a potentially useful and effective approach to coordinating education and social services for children—but it is not a panacea.

Third, in the early days of Chapter I (then Title I), regulations reigned supreme. Many regulations—the governmental impulse to require fund recipients to create a clear audit trail—have now been relaxed. We should take a lesson from this experience and guard against the bureaucratic temptation to overregulate and structure too tightly a system of school-linked services partially financed by Chapter I. A successful school-linked services effort is about professional discretion and cooperation, fiscal flexibility, and public accountability. Too many rules are likely to hobble such a program.

Finally, we restate at the end of this chapter what we stated at the beginning. A system of school-linked services must be comprehensive, continuous, and outcome-oriented. It should reflect an integrative rather than an additive approach to service provision. Toward this end, the measure of "success" of Chapter I funds devoted to school-linked services might well not be whether Chapter I retains its fiscal identity, but whether it serves as the fiscal "bridge" to link together a variety of existing programs.

## REFERENCES

Abt Associates. *The Chapter I Implementation Study.* Washington, D.C.: U. S. Department of Education, 1992.

Chaskin, Robert J., and Richman, Harold A. "Concerns about School-linked

Services: Institution-based versus Community-based Models." In *The Future of Children*. Menlo Park, Calif.: David and Lucile Packard Foundation, 1992.

Gardner, Sid. "Failure by Fragmentation," *California Tomorrow* (Fall 1989): 17–25.

Gherry, Martin, and McDonald, Jack. "Comprehensive Health Readiness." Paper presented to the CSSO Institute, St. Louis, Mo., July 1992.

Independent Commission on Chapter I. *Making Schools Work for Children in Poverty*. Washington, D.C.: Council of Chief State School Officers, 1992.

Kirst, Michael W. "Financing School-linked Services." University of Southern California Policy Brief no. 7. Los Angeles: University of Southern California, 1992.

Kirst, Michael W., and Kelley, Carolyn. *Changing the System for Children's Services*. Washington, D.C.: Council of Chief State School Officers, 1992.

Lobasco, William. (Chapter I administration, U.S. Department of Education). Interview, 1992.

National Advisory Council on the Education of Disadvantaged Children. *Education for Children of Poverty*. Washington, D.C.: U. S. Government Printing Office, 1965.

Policy Studies Associates. *State Administration of the Amended Chapter I*. Washington, D.C.: Policy Studies Associates, 1992.

Schorr, Elizabeth. *Within Our Reach*. New York: Doubleday, 1988.

Soler, Mark, and Shauffer, Carole. "Fighting Fragmentation: Coordination of Services for Children and Families," *Education and Urban Society* 25, no. 2 (1993): 129–140.

Urban Institute. *Confronting the Urban Crisis*. Washington, D.C.: Urban Institute, 1992.

# —— 10 ——

# Looking Ahead: Integrating Urban Policies to Meet Educational Demands

## Lisbeth B. Schorr

I assume I was asked to conclude the 1993 series of Joyce Lectures on urban education not despite my coming from another world but because of it. That world is the one outside the schools, the world that keeps encroaching on the classroom and on teachers and administrators in ways that threaten to make their already heavy burdens quite unsupportable. For the past several years, I have been trying to bridge the worlds of education and community services. As part of the National Alliance for School Restructuring, I have had the opportunity to work at the intersect between health services, social services, family and community supports, and schools. And for the last decade, I have been trying to understand the ingredients of programs and institutions that actually succeed in changing life outcomes for

This chapter is based on a lecture given May 21, 1993, at the University of Chicago under the sponsorship of the Department of Education and the Harris Graduate School of Public Policy Studies. The lecture was one of the presentations in the 1993 Joyce Lecture Series on "Urban Educational Reform: Federal, State, and Local Initiatives," a series made possible by a grant from The Joyce Foundation.

disadvantaged children. This work has led me to adopt three basic premises.

*First, if all children are to succeed at school, whole communities must take responsibility for supporting families as they nurture their children and for helping to assure each child's school success.* School success must become the goal of every system, not just of the schools.

The boy that comes to school red-eyed and bruised, the girl who tells the teacher of having witnessed her uncle's murder: these children cannot be ignored by their teachers. But neither can the teachers be expected to take sole responsibility for these children's troubles while attending to their own responsibilities for teaching and learning. Teachers need to be able to mobilize reliable help. That is why whole communities must take responsibility for helping to assure a child's school success.

*Second, the partnership between schools and parents and community agencies must be experienced by schools and school personnel as part of the solution, not as one more burden they are being asked to bear.*

*Third, improving outcomes for children means going beyond forging better linkages and coordination between schools and human services.* Linking up with services that are of mediocre quality, that are not provided with respect, flexibility, a family and community focus, and attention to relationships, will not improve outcomes for children. The challenge is a much larger one. To support universal school success, communities must be prepared to bring about changes in the nature and quality of services and supports.

I will next examine the context for these three premises. For a number of years now, the concern about America's domestic welfare has been steadily growing. The business community has been worrying about the shrinking pool of youngsters with the skills needed in today's high-tech economy. All Americans worry that current rates of failure in school—and of alienation, drug dependency, unmarried teenage childbearing, and violent crime—are becoming a threat to the very future of our society. All Americans worry that more and more children are growing up lacking the supports they need to become functioning adults. A front-page story in *The New York Times* quoted the director of an adolescent clinic in Oakland, California, as saying, "I don't like picking up bodies, but I do like the fact that it has gotten so dramatic, so out of hand, so embarrassing to this country, that it can no longer be ignored."

But until very recently, that rising concern has not been matched by an increased urgency in the search for solutions.

Quite the opposite. We have been in the midst of a crisis of confidence about whether American institutions, particularly governmental institutions, can be made to work to solve our most serious problems. Pervasive cynicism may be more of a threat than a shortage of public funds. Columnist William Raspberry had it right when he wrote: "You don't have to be mean-spirited to walk away from social problems. All it takes is the certainty that nothing can be done to solve them."

We certainly have had a decade of being bombarded with messages that nothing can be done, and even the most optimistic lose sleep wondering what, indeed, can be done to strengthen beleaguered families and to re-create a sense of community in America in the face of the dramatic social, demographic, and economic forces of the last twenty years that have radically transformed American life. We know we cannot turn back the clock. Families are smaller and more isolated, more children live with only their mothers, more mothers find they must work outside the home to make ends meet, industry has abandoned the cities, and the incomes of young families with children have plummeted— by one third, just between 1973 and 1990.

During the first half of this century, when there was an expanding demand for unskilled labor, moving out of poverty did not require the degree of skill and competence it does now. The routes out of poverty then were plentiful; a child's failure in school did not result in his or her economic failure as an adult. There was something to drop out *to*. But today, those jobs that require more brawn than school learning—that used to bring young people, with or without high school diplomas, with or without skills, into the labor market as soon as they left school— are now gone. They are in Hong Kong and Korea, and they are not coming back. The days when you could support a family without having skills taught in school are over. How ironic it is that just as what was required to be a productive adult had become vastly more demanding, the ability of the family and the community to help children succeed at school and to become productive adults had been eroding.

Today there are fewer informal institutions to buffer children from the effects of rising family stress, whether the family is stuck in the inner city or trying to make it in the suburbs. There are fewer supports when family struggles for economic security, whether on the assembly line or on the fast corporate track, leave parents so exhausted and so isolated that their comfort comes from alcohol and not from family outings, when coping energies are so used up by the marketplace that children feel abandoned and alone, and seek their consolation from equally unrooted peers and empty forays into the worlds of alcohol, drugs, and unprotected sex.

What this all adds up to we know well. At the same time that the schools are asked to educate all children to a much higher level of competence than ever before, they are faced with children who see little reason to work hard in order to learn, and who bring an overwhelming array of urgent unmet needs into the classroom. That means the old ways will no longer work. But there is very little agreement about who is supposed to do what to change things.

Overwhelmed school people feel that everyone expects them to do everything—if not to fix things directly, then at least to coordinate everything. They worry that they are expected to do work they were never trained for, whether it is diagnosing and treating family dysfunction or performing miracles of service coordination. They worry about whether they will have to become some diluted form of social worker, and whether their expanded roles will take a toll on their commitment to learning and teaching. I want to reassure school teachers and administrators that their perceptions that they cannot do it all, and that they cannot do any of it without good help, are valid.

Obviously, there are no easy answers. But there are answers, and some of the answers come out of what we have learned over the last decade about a vast variety of interventions that work. Considerable effort has gone in recent years toward identifying successful interventions, especially those targeted at children at risk. I began my own search for programs that work in the early 1980s, in response to the growing belief that nothing could really be done in the face of rising rates of disaster among the nation's young. I searched out programs that had in fact succeeded in changing outcomes among disadvantaged children. What I found was that all over this country there were programs and institutions that had shown the cycle of disadvantage can be broken, that life trajectories can be changed.

I found a sturdy body of research showing that the best predictors of what I called rotten outcomes—school dropout, teenage childbearing, adolescent violence, and long-term welfare dependence—occur early, and include trouble at school as early as third grade. And of course third-grade troubles, in turn, have much earlier antecedents. Among the risk factors that predict later trouble, in addition to poverty, are being born unwanted or to a teenage mother; being born at low birthweight; lack of bonds with a caring and protective adult early in life; untreated childhood health problems, and failure to develop minimal coping, language, and reasoning skills before school entry.

What is important about these risk factors is that every one of them has been successfully attacked by interventions we know how to provide. We *now know* that children who are born into poverty and disadvantage need not end up in poverty and disadvantage. It is now absolutely clear that the contention that in the world of social programs and education reform "nothing works" is in fact a canard. It is a myth that cannot be maintained in the face of the evidence now at hand. There are successful interventions that operate through the health system, through schools and preschools, through school-based clinics and youth service centers, through social services, child care, and family supports.

As I began to examine successes in many different domains, I got a surprise. Although I had set out simply to make the point that there are programs that work, I stumbled across a more important finding: programs that work have common attributes, and these attributes differentiate programs that have been successful in changing long-term outcomes from those that do not.

The good news, then, is not only *that* there are programs that work, but that we now also know a lot about *how* and *why* they work. Four of the most important commonalities I found among effective interventions are the following:

*1. Successful programs are comprehensive, intensive, flexible, and responsive.* Families that are already overwhelmed are not asked to negotiate their way through a maze of fragmented and distant services, each with its own eligibility determinations, waiting times, and application forms.

Successful programs encourage active collaboration across professional and bureaucratic boundaries. Staffs in these programs have extensive repertoires and wide community networks. They seem to be forever willing to "push the boundaries of their job description," to take on an "extended role" in the lives of the children and families they work with. Many of these programs provide their staffs with a pool of flexible funds, which they can use at their discretion to help a family buy a washing machine or a wheel chair, or get the car repaired. Sister Mary Paul, who runs a family service program in Brooklyn, says that no one in her program ever says, "This may be what you need, but helping you get it is not part of my job or outside our jurisdiction."

The flexibility of these programs often extends to where and when their help is available. They respond to the needs of families at times and places that make sense to the family, often at home, at school, or in neigborhood centers and at odd hours, rather than in distant offices once a week on Wednesday afternoons.

2. *Successful programs deal with children as parts of families, and with families as parts of neigborhoods and communities.* Successful programs know that strong families are the key to healthy children, and that healthy communities strengthen families. Most successful programs have deep roots in the community. They are not imposed from without or "parachuted" in, but are carefully integrated with specific local community needs and strengths, so that local communities have a genuine sense of ownership.

Successful programs work not alone with one generation, but with two—and often three. They nurture parents so that they can better nurture their children. They work with parents in a relentless problem-solving mode.

3. *Staff in successful programs have the time, skills, and support to build relationships of trust and respect with children and families.* They work in settings that allow them to develop meaningful personal relationships over time, and to provide services respectfully, ungrudgingly, and in partnership with parents and communities.

None of the programs that succeed is "lean and mean." That does not mean that "anything goes." Successful youth centers know that clear rules and certain discipline provide the security and predictability that is often missing in the lives of many young people today. It does mean that these programs are able to establish a climate that is warm, welcoming, and supportive.

Psychiatrist James Comer points out that relationship issues are particularly important among low-income people who have given up on helping systems. The quality and continuity of relationships and support are what make many other activities effective. Home visitors say it is respectful, trusting relationships that make parent education work. Case managers find that families known to an alphabet soup of agencies remain unhelped until someone finally is there long enough and close enough and persevering enough to forge the kind of authentic relationship that helps to turn lives around.

The quality of the staff is clearly central to the quality of the

program, and the ability of the staff to develop trusting and lasting relationships is the most important part of all.

Smallness of scale at the point of service delivery seems also
to be crucial. Large schools, large classes, massive outpatient clinics,
and large case loads vastly complicate the job of personalizing
interventions to respond to individual and family needs.

4. *Successful programs have a long-term, preventive orientation and
continue to evolve over time.* The people responsible for these programs have no illusion that they can implement the perfect model
program. They manage by groping along, they learn as they go,
and allow their programs to continually evolve to maintain their
responsiveness to individual, family, and community needs over time.

Successful programs operate in an organizational culture that
is outcome-oriented rather than rule-bound. Their approach is
long-term, inclusive, preventive, and empowering. They combine
a highly flexible mode of operation with a clearly articulated
sense of mission.

These attributes of success are not counterintuitive or surprising. What *is* surprising is that while these attributes are supported by theory, a convergent body of research, and front-line
experience in many different disciplines, they turn out to be so
at odds with the systems within which most programs must function.

As William Morrill of the National Center for Service Integration points out, yesterday's well-intentioned discrete program,
designed to resolve a particular problem for a particular target
group, has become part of today's morass of efforts that are fragmented, inflexible, narrow, crisis-oriented, and provider-driven,
that do not match family needs, and that do least well for the
families in the greatest trouble.

Within large public systems, effective programs remain the
exception and not the rule because most systems contain incentives that undermine precisely the elements that are the hall-
marks of effectiveness. After all, comprehensiveness, intensiveness,
flexibility, front-line worker discretion, a family and community
focus, and an emphasis on prevention and on continuing relationships of mutual trust are all undermined by categorical funding
and traditional rule making, and by how professionals are trained,
standards are set, and accountability is maintained.

Marc Tucker of the National Center for Education and the
Economy says, "When you find an individual school that works,
it is almost always because it is running against the grain. You
find a teacher or a principal who really does not give a damn

about the system. They are willing to ignore or subvert every rule in the book in order to get the job done for the kids." The situation is the same in health and mental health and in family support and social services. The process of making essential services coherently available at the local level has become so onerous that only a St. Francis of Assisi who is also a Machiavelli *and* a CPA can succeed.

Must it be ever thus, or can we bring about the kind of fundamental change that we now know is needed so that the rules *support,* rather than *subvert,* good practice? Can we engage in the kind of strategic thinking, experimentation, and risk-taking that would get us beyond the isolated models that deal with only pieces of what needs doing? While many communities and some states are taking giant steps toward the kind of cross-systems reforms that are needed, to my knowledge no American state or city or neighborhood is yet at the point of having put in place the entire continuum of services and supports that would lead to universal school readiness and school success.

Some see a conflict between those who contend that "we know what works and we can act on it" and those who believe that we cannot act until we "reinvent government." The evidence suggests that these are not conflicting positions. It is because of what we know about what works on a small scale and in special circumstances, that we must now reinvent our major institutions to extend the benefits of what works to much larger numbers.

Because we have to think and act much more strategically than we have in the past, I suggest six strategies that could help bring about the kind of systemic change that promises to turn around the escalating rates of rotten outcomes we see all around us.

*First, we must seize new opportunities to apply new knowledge about the earliest antecedents of school failure and other damaging outcomes.*

Despite recent attempts to discredit it, Head Start is known to be virtually unique among community-based programs that operate nationwide in its comprehensiveness, in its rootedness in local communities, and in its achievements. Head Start has shown that when three- and four-year-olds are systematically helped to think, reason, and speak clearly, when they are provided hot meals and health care, when families and communities become partners in children's learning, children achieve higher rates of school success and are in less trouble when they become adolescents. They are less likely to drop out, become pregnant, or be arrested. That is why the full funding of Head Start has such wide support.

But now the nation has become committed to school success for all. Now more and more mothers of young children need to be free to enter the work force. Now we know that the fundamental building blocks of school learning are forged in infancy, long before children reach what we used to think of as the Head Start age. For these reasons, full funding of Head Start will no longer be enough. To reflect new realities and new research, Head Start and other similar programs must be enriched and expanded—downward, sideways, and upward. Downward expansion from preschool to prebirth could support beleaguered families not for one year but for the whole five years of their children's development during the preschool period. Sideways expansion could assure that programs will be of excellent quality and available full day and full year. Upward expansion would assure not only that the children are ready for school but also that the schools are ready for the children. I visualize the expanded Head Starts of the Clinton era as including all the elements for which cost-effectiveness and long-term benefits have now been established: prenatal care, home visits, immunizations, parent support, and developmentally sound child care.

*Second, we need new kinds of training and professional development to enrich the skills of those who are at the front lines of reformed schools and services.*

Reformed, responsive community services and supports can be provided only by professionals with skills and mindsets that differ from today's norm, and differ from those traditionally taught in settings that prepare social workers, health and mental health professionals, early education professionals, and school personnel. Front-line human service staff today often lack the skills needed to mobilize diverse resources and work collaboratively with other systems and disciplines, be comfortable addressing a complex interplay of problems and exercising front-line discretion; build respectful, trusting relationships; work with both children and families, and see children in the context of families and families in the context of communities; and work comfortably in settings that are in continual evolution.

Both in-service and preservice training must begin to include health and social service and education professionals together, if these varied disciplines are to work collegially.

The process of training professionals for more effective,

responsive, outcome-oriented, family-centered front-line practice
will involve clarifying professionals' roles. As schools work more
closely with human service agencies, there is a tendency, on the
one hand, to believe that teachers can now "hand off" children
with problems to social service agencies. On the other hand,
some educators fear that teachers will be forced to be social
workers, becoming deeply involved in solving family problems.
When staff from all professions train together, they can develop
a common approach and create mutual understanding of how
each profession can work effectively with families and children
in their own domain, still carrying out their special professional
roles, while pushing the boundaries of their job description to
create a seamless fabric of services, supports, and responsive institutions. Existing training institutions may not all be up to equip-
ping human service professionals with the necessary skills and
mindsets and flexibility.

I have told the story about a Homebuilders worker who en-
ters the home of a family in crisis, to be greeted by a mother's
declaration that the one thing she does not need in her life is
one more social worker telling her what to do. What she needs,
she says, is to get her house cleaned up. The Homebuilders thera-
pist responds by pitching in, starting with the kitchen. After they
worked together for an hour, the two women were able to talk.
It may have been an unorthodox way of forging a therapeutic
alliance, but it worked.

I told this story at a meeting some months ago, and a distin-
guished professor of psychology interrupted to say *that* was going too far. Cleaning a client's home, she claimed, was
unprofessional. There is a sense, of course, in which she is quite
right. In most professions, highest status is conferred on those
who deal with issues from which all human complexity has been
removed. Narrowly drawn boundaries that limit what is expected
of a professional are the essence of professionalism for many.
New kinds of training programs must help professionals to expand not only their tools but also their vision.

Institutions of higher education must be persuaded, if they
have not already accepted the challenge, to enlist in this cause.
It is true that "explaining, not changing, is the university's expertise," as Patricia Graham, former dean of the Harvard Graduate School of Education and now president of the Spencer
Foundation, points out in her wonderful book *S.O.S.: Sustain Our
Schools* (1992). Nevertheless, she maintains, universities must more

vigorously support their schools of education and social service, and the university as a whole must enlist in efforts to improve schools and help children and to meet the distinctive needs of urban school systems.

Third, *we must apply all the ingenuity we can muster to making bureaucracies operate less bureaucratically.*

Whether it is possible to gentle the heavy hand of bureaucracy is surely central to the question of whether it is possible to scale up from past successes within the public sector. In *Winning the Brain Race* (1988), David Kearns and Denis Doyle have written that the very purpose of bureaucracies is to institutionalize the suspension of individual judgment. If that is so, and if in order to succeed we need *more* flexibility, *more* informed, trained, individual judgment, rather than less, we must learn how to modify the functioning of bureaucracies to establish the climate in which competent professionals can flourish. We should not be in the position of having to continue to rely on mavericks who will buck the system until they burn out.

Current antibureaucratic trends in business, with managers struggling to find alternatives to top-down, centralized decision making, provide some encouragement to all those working in large institutions, public and private. So does the urgency of the need in virtually every sector of society to find ways to "reinvent" large institutions so that they will become more responsive.

I believe that over the last twenty-five years, many of us have overestimated the extent to which equity and quality could be safeguarded by regulation, and underestimated how much detailed mandating and strict rules could undermine the exercise of responsiveness, flexibility, and discretion in the provision of human services.

The alternative is neither to privatize nor to give up on accountability. The alternative is to buy some freedom from the constraints of centralized micromanagement by a new willingness to be held accountable for the results achieved. This brings me to the matter of shifting to outcome-based accountability as one way of moving institutions to a less bureaucratic mode of functioning.

*Fourth, the strategy of shifting to outcome-based, results-based accountability should be seen as one of the most promising trends now under way.*

The use of outcome indicators that reflect common sense and common understanding may be the most powerful force to (1) focus attention on the mission rather than the rules,

(2) permit flexibility and autonomy at the front end, (3) encourage cross-system collaboration, (4) promote a communitywide "culture of responsibility" for children and families, and (5) provide evidence to funders and the public that programs are indeed meeting their intended purposes.

Outcome accountability has, of course, become a significant part of the education reform conversation. The next leap is for whole communities to adopt common outcome goals, whose realization requires the participation of all elements of the community, including both the education and human service sectors.

But the move to outcome accountability is hard. There is fear that it will be used as a cover for further cutbacks in funding and will lead to the abandonment of efforts that are difficult to measure. Demands for documented outcomes can drive programs to "creaming," to duck hard cases, and to distort their activities by emphasizing those that will show measurable and rapid results. Early-childhood people fear that efforts to assess whether children are ready for school will label five-year-olds and will ignore the fact that the schools have to be ready for the children.

All of these and many other legitimate concerns suggest that the shift to outcome accountability must be made carefully and thoughtfully. It must be made by those who care about both the process and the results, and not left to those who find it easy only because they do not understand the issues.

I believe that a focus on outcomes can help to put service integration efforts into proper perspective. Because fragmentation is such a big problem in existing services, a great deal of energy is currently going into efforts to link services together. But while collaboration is a necessary condition for providing effective services, it is not sufficient. Alone, it will not improve outcomes. It is futile to put together services that are of mediocre quality, that are rendered grudgingly, and that are rendered by professionals who do not work respectfully with families and are unable to respond to the unique characteristics of the community they serve. The shared commitment to improve outcomes for children is what can make efforts at collaboration fall into place—not as an end, but as an *essential means* of working together toward improved outcomes.

The most difficult issue raised by a new emphasis on outcomes accountability is also, in my view, the one with the most exciting potential: *A focus on outcomes clarifies what funders and the public can expect in relation to investments made.* The new conversation about outcomes is promising (or threatening) to end a conspiracy of silence between funders and program people, exposing the fact that human service providers, educators, and community organizations are consistently expected to accomplish massive tasks with trivial resources and completely inadequate tools. An outcomes focus forces the question of whether expectations about outcomes must be scaled down, or interventions must be scaled up.

In the past, when a significant discrepancy has occurred between aspirations and documentable accomplishments, the response has typically been to retreat from a commitment to outcomes. The retreat occurs as program managers and funders of promising programs and reforms face up to the difficulties of actually changing real-world outcomes, and recognize the relative weakness of single, underfunded interventions compared to powerful social, economic, and demographic forces that push outcomes in a negative direction.

If a parent education program is expected to reduce the incidence of child abuse (although it consists only of a few didactic classes) or if an outreach program to get pregnant women into prenatal care is expected to reduce the incidence of low birth weight (although the sources of prenatal care are overcrowded, impersonal, and have no capacity to deal with homelessness, drug abuse, or lack of social support), providers have typically asked evaluators just to measure how many people were reached or how attitudes and knowledge have changed, contending that it isn't *fair* to hold the program accountable for outcomes when the staff is doing the best they can.

If it takes comprehensive, intensive interventions to change outcomes, if—to be effective—interventions must be able to impact even widespread despair and hopelessness, we cannot get there from here by hiding from ourselves the limitations of most current efforts. People who caution against outcome accountability argue that even if we had evidence of efficacy from model programs, no one knows whether it would hold under conditions of large-scale, mainstream implementation. These same people should be arguing instead for creating the scaled-up conditions in which we can realistically expect that outcomes will improve.

The Princeton philosopher Cornel West wrote recently that neither liberals nor conservatives dare to face up to "the monumental eclipse of hope, the unprecedented collapse of meaning, the incredible disregard for human life" on the streets of the inner city, which obviously undermine most traditional attempts to help. Recognition that services alone may not be sufficient to change outcomes in the absence of changes in employment, economic security, physical safety, and housing is not an argument against outcome accountability. It is an argument for forging partnerships with the people working to create jobs, to improve housing and public safety, and to organize communities.

*Fifth, we must seize new opportunities to turn around the persistent poverty and social dislocation in inner-city neighborhoods.*

The destructive effects of hostile environments on the development of children and on the functioning of parents, which have long been apparent to teachers and others at the front lines, are now beginning to attract the attention of policymakers and funders. If we are committed to strengthening the family, we must give more attention to rebuilding local institutions— schools, churches, neighborhood centers, and recreational services—that support families.

To turn things around in areas of concentrated social dislocation, a critical mass of high-quality services and supports has to be made available not just to individually identified children or families in trouble, but to entire neighborhoods, entire populations at risk. Targeted, neighborhood-based efforts could make eligibility dependent on residence, and allow services to be designed to reflect the enormous impact of neighborhood life on family functioning and child development. The changes that the Commission on Chapter I has recommended are of course highly consistent with this approach. They are based on the now well-established premise that the factors implicated in persistent poverty and concentrated social dislocation will simply not respond to narrow, one-shot interventions, and that what is needed is a broad attack on many fronts at once, combining comprehensive, responsive services and restructured schools with reforms to improve housing and public safety, to re-create a community infrastructure, and to expand job opportunities and training, so that all of these will interact in an entire threatened community to reverse both family and neighborhood disintegration. The Clinton Administration's new neighborhood initiative is built on this same set of premises.

A broad range of reforms in a given community may indeed be easier to bring about than a narrow range, because multiple simultaneous change may create greater credibility for the effort than would narrow, piecemeal reform. Public policy would get away from making eligibility for services contingent on individual proof of failure, but would recognize that whole communities may be so depleted that a critical mass of new sources of opportunity and support are required if ordinary youngsters are to succeed in climbing out of poverty and despair.

When we break out of the rigidities that well-intentioned efforts of the past imposed not just on the organization and financing of services but also on our categorical ways of thinking, many new possibilities emerge. William Julius Wilson, a professor of sociology at the University of Chicago, spoke at the Clinton Economic Conference in December 1992 about the lack of high-quality, up-to-date career counseling that could ease the transition between school and work in inner-city schools. His proposal for specialized career counselors with reasonable case loads who could effectively help high school students to prepare for future career and educational opportunities could become part of a comprehensive strategy to change outcomes for these high-risk youth.

Previous attempts to target resources on neighborhoods of persistent poverty and social dislocation have never been sufficiently comprehensive and intensive. Even before they were launched, Model Cities, Community Action, and the Area Redevelopment Act of the 1960s were fatally diluted—each was to cover ten to thirty times the number of sites initially proposed, but with the original resources.

Today, the common interest in targeting adequate resources on the most devastated inner-city areas, and the long-term benefits of such investments, can no longer be denied. But a bolder stance toward the serious problems of children and families in the United States today requires a commitment to one more strategy.

*Sixth, new kinds of partnerships among schools and parents and communities must be forged.*

It is widely accepted that successful schools enlist parents in collaborative efforts to give children reasons to learn and offer support to parents who need help with their own lives as adults in order to be able to help their children. Sara Lawrence Lightfoot, a professor at the Harvard Graduate School of Education, points out that all children learn best when parents and teachers share similar visions, when there is a "sense of constancy" between home and school. A generation ago, schools did not have to work as deliberately and self-consciously at developing that relationship as they do today. A sense of constancy is harder to come by than it used to be, and it is harder to come by in the inner city than in places where informal connections are easier to maintain. When parents whose own school experience was one of failure face schools whose social network and style are totally dissonant and alienating, they communicate that to the children. The perception that school is the enemy can effectively destroy the chances that a child will learn.

Schools increasingly recognize the need for deeper parent involvement, but are discouraged because it often seems that there's no one out there to work with. Enlisting the overwhelmed and overstressed parents of today as collaborators requires more skill and ingenuity than ever before. Partnerships with community organizations can provide at least part of the solution, when schools join forces with others in the community to help strengthen families through family support services, school-based health or social services, the child welfare system, the churches, or Head Start programs. All of these can help to strengthen the bonds between parents and the schools, as schools become outposts of civility and concern, as well as centers of lifelong learning. But more than anything else, what is needed is a re-creation of community.

John Gardner, Secretary of Health, Education, and Welfare under President Lyndon Johnson, said recently that the soil in which shared values are rooted and nurtured—the family and the community—is being blown away in the dust storm of contemporary life, leaving our children with no sense of belonging, no sense that life extends beyond selfish interests and has meaning beyond the acquisition of material goods.

In her book *The Measure of Our Success: A Letter to My Children and Yours* (1992), Marian Wright Edelman describes her own growing up in Bennettsville, South Carolina:

> Child-rearing and parental work were inseparable. I went everywhere with my parents and was under the watchful eye of members of the congregation and community who were my extended parents. They kept me when my parents went out of town, they reported on and chided me when I strayed from the straight and narrow of community expectations, and they basked in and supported my achievements when I did well. Doing well, they made clear, meant high academic achievement, playing piano in Sunday school, participating in other church activities, being helpful, displaying good manners, and reading. The adults in our churches and community made children feel valued and important. They took time and paid attention to us. They struggled to find ways to keep us busy. They valued family life, family rituals, and tried to be and to expose us to good role models. . . . We always knew who we were and that the measure of

our worth was inside our heads and hearts and not in our possessions or on our backs.

Edelman's book makes clear that while our life chances are affected by individual endowment and family circumstances, they are also powerfully determined by how well the community and the society support families in their child rearing and in the other tasks of daily life. Everyone agrees that it takes a village to raise a child. But in the inner city, the village has disintegrated. That is why we need bold and comprehensive strategies. Incrementalism will not do it. There are chasms you cannot cross one small step at a time.

It became hard, in the last decade, to think boldly. We learned to think small and to content ourselves with fiddling at the margins. But it is rapidly becoming clear that some of our most urgent problems will not be solved unless we dare to adopt a bolder vision—a vision that is built on a shared understanding that we cannot allow the richest country in the world to declare bankruptcy in our civic life. I believe we are indeed on the verge of new opportunities that could transform the widespread yearning to do better among so many Americans into effective and lasting action, into action that would make all community institutions work more effectively on behalf of all America's children and families. We know we have the elements of past success to build on, and we know that we cannot do it at bargain basement prices, and that we cannot do it overnight. But we can be certain that if it is done well, it will make a difference in the life of this nation.

As Marian Wright Edelman sometimes says, we are at a point in this country today when doing what is right coincides with what we have to do to save our national skins! The people who are committed to social justice can join with those whose highest priority is a work force that can win the international economic competition. This means that the critical mass of support for needed change is now at hand—especially when you figure in that there is now an administration in Washington that sees children and families and education as central, not only in its rhetoric, but also in its investment of resources, and in its commitment to eliminating the barriers that have made it so hard to put things together at the local level.

I think we can now act together—schools and universities, local, state, and federal governments, educators and human service professionals, philanthropists, families, and communities. Across generation, class, and race we can build on what brings us together, recognizing that we are caught, in the words of Martin Luther King, "in an inescapable network of mutuality." Together we can take the needed action that would dramatically raise the chances that the children growing up without hope today will become full participants in the thriving American communities of tomorrow as well as the chances that we will *have* a thriving America tomorrow.

## REFERENCES

Edelman, Marian Wright. *The Measure of Our Success: A Letter to My Children and Yours.* Boston: Beacon Press, 1992.

Graham, Patricia. *S. O. S.: Sustain Our Schools.* New York: Hill and Wang, 1992.

Kearns, David T., and Doyle, Denis P. *Winning the Brain Race.* San Francisco: ICS Press, 1988.